CW00542597

THE PRISONER OF KATHMANDU

The Prisoner of Kathmandu

CHARLES ALLEN

First published in Great Britiain in 2015 by
Haus Publishing Ltd
70 Cadogan Place
London SW1X 9AH
www.hauspublishing.com

Copyright © Charles Allen, 2015

The moral right of the author has been asserted.

A CIP catalogue record for this book is available from the British Library

ISBN 978-1-910376-11-9
eISBN: 978-1-910376-30-0

Typeset by MacGuru Ltd
info@macguru.org.uk

Printed in Spain.

All rights reserved.

Contents

The prisoner

I imagine him striding north along Jalapahar Ridge towards Darjeeling's Observatory Hill. He is fifty-seven – which is old by British Indian standards. He would look then pretty much as he does in a photograph taken soon after his final return to England, now part of a collection of his papers and drawings in the Natural History Museum in London. There is something of the peppery Indian Army colonel on half-pay about him: trim and dapper, moustachioed and bewhiskered, his right hand thrust into his coat a la Bonaparte. He has the air of someone who does not suffer fools gladly, a little uneasy, on the defensive.

Let us imagine that we find him at that glimmering hour before dawn in the summer of 1858. Though we cannot see them yet, the lower foothills of the Himalayas and the Indian plains beyond are blanketed in mist. The birds are completing their dawn chorus – and Brian Houghton Hodgson knows every one of their calls.

Brian Hodgson is on his way to meet an old friend, Dr Archie Campbell. They have known each other ever since Campbell came to join Hodgson at the British Residency in Kathmandu in 1832, initially as Residency Surgeon and then as his Political Assistant. Five years later Campbell was promoted to become the first superintendent of the new sanatorium of Darjeeling. And now the tables are turned. Now it is Dr Campbell who is the *burra sahib*, whereas Brian Hodgson is a man with no official status. And it is Campbell who now lives in the big house, Beechwood, complete with neo-classical pediment and columns that he has patently modelled on Hodgson's British Residency in Kathmandu. Hodgson, by contrast, lives in a small bungalow that could almost be described as a shack. He has named it Brianstone, after himself.

These two have arranged to meet on the cart-road that runs north and south above Darjeeling's military sanatorium – and there, indeed, is Dr Campbell waiting for him. There are no known images of the man who, thanks to his encouragement of settlers and his planting of the first tea-bushes in his own garden, will later be described (in the *Darjeeling District Gazeteer*) as the 'real founder of the prosperity of the district'. So we must continue to exercise our imaginations as we observe these two stepping out briskly along the ridge towards Darjeeling Hill.

Just below St Andrews Church they pause by the roadside. Hodgson unlatches the gate that opens onto the small cemetery cut out of the hillside. Below it, descending in elegantly curved tiers down into Happy Valley, are the tea gardens.

Now Hodgson leads the way to a headstone that marks the remains of one of the graveyard's earliest occupants. The inscription is clearly legible:

H. J.
ALEXANDER CSOMA DE KOROSI
Who, to follow out Philological Researches,
Resorted to the East;
And after years passed under privations,
Such as have been seldom endured,
And patient labour in the cause of Science,
Compiled a Dictionary and Grammar
Of the Tibetan Language,
His best and real Monument.

On his road to H'Lassa,
To resume his labours,
He died at this place,
On the 11th April 1842,
Aged 44 years.

His Fellow-Labourers,
The Asiatic Society of Bengal,
Inscribed this tablet to his memory.

It was Archie Campbell who nursed Alexander Csoma de Körös on his deathbed and who buried him. But it was Brian Hodgson who had known him best, even though the two of them never met. Each working in isolation in their respective Himalayan eyries – the one in Ladakh and the other in Nepal – these two together had helped lay the foundations of modern Buddhist studies through their individual researches and their donations of Tibetan and Sanskrit scriptures.

But it is not Csoma's grave that Hodgson has come to see. This is where two years earlier Hodgson laid to rest his only son. Let us imagine Dr Campbell hanging back a pace or two to give his old friend space as he reads the words that he himself wrote:

Sacred
To the memory of
HENRY HODGSON, Esq.,
born in Kathmandu October 18th 1835
and died at Darjilling, April 18th 1856,
aged 21 years.
This monument is erected by his father
Brian Houghton Hodgson, B.C.S.,
to commemorate the many amiable qualities
and high promise of his beloved son.

Brian Hodgson has come to say goodbye. He first came to Darjeeling, at Dr Campbell's suggestion, in 1846 and now, twelve years on, it is time for him to go home. But that is 'Home' only in the Anglo-Indian sense of the word, with a capital H. The fact is that Brian Houghton Hodgson has no home, neither in England nor in Darjeeling.

They have timed their visit well. As Brian Hodgson turns away from his son's grave, the sun crests the flank of Observatory Hill behind them. Let us allow them a clear morning on a cloudless day, so that they can watch the vast, snowy, glittering flanks of Kanchenjanga to their north turn from grey to flamingo pink. To their south, too, they can see how the land falls away into the vastness of the Gangetic Plain, stretching endlessly into the distance, dark purple and murky green.

But Brian Houghton Hodgson looks neither north nor south. He has eyes only for the western horizon.

Now the sun's rays light up the summits of the highest peaks on earth, more than a hundred miles away, with the still unnamed Mount Everest tucked in somewhere among them. However, Brian Hodgson seeks to look further still – even though he knows that the combination of intervening mountain massifs and the curvature of the earth makes that impossible.

But what the eyes cannot see his imagination and his memory can: the fecund bowl with its flat plain of padi-fields rimmed by the mountains of the Nepal Valley. If Hodgson has a home anywhere it is surely here: more specifically, on the northern outskirts of the city of the wooden pagodas, Kathmandu. For twenty-two years he was confined here. Not a prisoner in the literal sense, but a prisoner all the same, a hostage to fortune, forced by a combination of health and politics to live a restricted life – even though it was that same restriction that gave his life meaning, made his achievements possible.

One last look then, because this is as near as he can ever get, and will ever get, to his old home, his prison. What an irony! Brian Hodgson the free man, but a prisoner still, now locked out rather than locked in, forbidden to return to the one place where he came to feel most comfortable. He is now the classic exile who must endure the ache of knowing that he can never go back, never finish what he started.

It is just as well he does not know that he has another thirty-three years to live.

Brian Houghton Hodgson was born a Georgian in 1801 and died a late Victorian in 1894. By profession he was a member of the Bengal Civil Service and a servant of the Honourable East India Company (HEICo), by inclination a devotee of Orientalism – but Orientalism in the true meaning of that word, which is the study of Oriental languages, literature and culture. Hodgson has been called 'the father of Himalayan studies' and 'the hermit of the Himalayas', although neither title is strictly accurate. But then neither is this book's title, *The Prisoner of Kathmandu*, even though Hodgson passed his best years constrained by the orders of the governments of Nepal and British India. Yet those same constraints helped make Hodgson a man ahead of his time, and when banished from Kathmandu he remained trapped in his own past.

Hodgson came to India as a clever, mollycoddled seventeen-year-old. Thanks to a combination of influential connections and his own vulnerable health, he was found comfortable, but isolated, political postings in the foothills of the Himalayas that lasted for well over two decades, most of it spent in what was then the Nepal Valley, better known today as the Kathmandu Valley. How he lived there, initially as Assistant to the British Resident, then as Acting Resident and finally as Resident, and what he achieved there over the course of twenty-three years, is the chief concern of this biography. These were Hodgson's glory years, when he came into his own: firstly, as a diplomat who turned a deeply hostile nation into an ally; and secondly, as a collector who by degrees transformed himself into a scholar committed to exploring and understanding the culture of the Himalayas in almost every aspect, from its languages and religions to its zoology and ethnography.

In December 1843 Hodgson was to all intents sacked by the new Governor-General and forced to quit the British Residency in Kathmandu that he had made his home and where he was raising a family. He left behind a local wife and, very probably, a new-born daughter. He returned to England with his two older children but failed to settle, so went back to India in a private capacity intent on resuming his studies. Forbidden to re-enter Nepal, he made a new home for himself in the hill station of Darjeeling, abutting Nepal's eastern border. Here he gathered about him some of his former staff from Nepal and settled down to further research, becoming increasingly reclusive in the process. Yet he kept abreast of events in Nepal and in 1857, the year of the Sepoy Mutiny in India, he played a crucial role in bringing Nepal into that bitter conflict on Britain's side. After twelve years in Darjeeling his English wife became ill and the Hodgsons returned to England. Again, Hodgson sought to resume his studies but found himself outpaced by younger and better qualified scholars.

Hodgson died in many respects a forgotten man, with little honour in his own country, his early achievements largely a matter of history. His sole biographer tells the story of how Hodgson, in his

eighties, was introduced to the Italian philologist Angelo de Guber-
natis, who was unable to believe his eyes, exclaiming 'Surely not the
veritable Hodgson, the founder of our Buddhist studies! He, alas, is
dead these many years!'

That biography appeared soon after Hodgson's death. It was
written with his full approval by a long-time admirer, who was
understandably uncritical and fulsome in his praise. Just over a
century later the Indian scholar Dr K. L. Pradhan published a slim
but useful study of Hodgson's years in Nepal as *Brian Hodgson at the
Kathmandu Residency*. More recently still, David Waterhouse edited
a series of scholarly essays on Hodgson that was published under the
aegis of the Royal Asiatic Society under the title *The Origins of Himalayan Studies: Brian Houghton Hodgson in Nepal and Darjeeling
1820–1858* (2004).

I have taken full advantage of all these published sources as well
as more recent and current scholarship, to say nothing of the many
scholars and specialists whose advice I sought, as well as the librarians, archivists, curators and keepers of collections at the British
Library, the British Museum, the Bodleian Library, the Royal Asiatic
Society, the Linnean Society, the Zoological Society of London,
the Natural History Museum, Kew Gardens, the Royal Edinburgh
Botanic Garden, the Calcutta Botanic Garden and other institutions with historic links to my subject. My debts to them are, I hope,
acknowledged in full at the back of this book.

One characteristic common to Hodgson's biography and more
recent Hodgsonian material is the compartmentalisation of his work
into the various disciplines that his studies took. Here I have tried
to avoid that by putting his work in its fullest context. However, my
main purpose is not to enumerate or spell out Hodgson's achievements but to focus on the man himself and his times in India and
Nepal.

One of Hodgson's most important contributions to our understanding of the Himalayan environment was his patronage of local
artists, scholars, collectors and, alas, hunters. Tucked away in many
of the institutions listed above are some magnificent collections
of manuscripts, artefacts, drawings, paintings and specimens, all
sourced and donated by Hodgson. I have drawn heavily on those

collections to integrate into my text of a number of black and white illustrations. I hope that by giving you, the reader, just a hint of this wonderful illustrative material I can whet your appetite, leading you seek out the originals for yourself online or, better still, in the British Library, the Royal Asiatic Society, the Natural History Museum or the Zoological Society of London.

Where there are significant gaps I have also drawn on a few of the watercolours of Dr Henry Oldfield, even though that worthy doctor only arrived in Nepal a decade after Hodgson's forced departure. Oldfield was second only to Hodgson in the number of years he lived in Nepal and in his paintings he created a unique record of the Nepal Valley as it was just after Brian Hodgson's time – a colourful medieval kingdom that is now a lost world. Again, I can only give the reader a glimpse of Dr Oldfield's work, but his family left two magnificent collections of his paintings to the British Library and to the Royal Geographical Society and many of these images, too, are accessible online.

This book is also in part a personal tribute to a country I came to love as a teacher with Voluntary Service Overseas in Kathmandu back in 1966–67 and in the course of many visits since. For all the tribulations Nepal has suffered in the last quarter of a century, there still exists a genuine bond between that country and my own. But it was not always so. This book's publication more or less coincides with the bicentenary of the Treaty of Sugauli, signed on 2 December 1815 on Indian soil in the wake of a hard-fought war between Britain and Nepal, although the treaty was only ratified on 4 March 1816 on Nepali soil as British troops closed in on the Nepal Valley. That bicentenary marks two centuries of alliance between Britain and Nepal – but an alliance that was forged in bitter enmity on the part of Nepal. It was, in large part, thanks to Brian Hodgson that this enmity was diffused and transformed into a lasting friendship.

Hodgson found his mantra in the famous declaration of Sir William 'Oriental' Jones, jurist, linguist and pioneer Sanskritist who stepped ashore at Calcutta in 1783 with the declared intent to study Asia 'in all its aspects'. The chief means to this end was the Asiatic Society of Bengal, co-founded by Jones in 1783 and modelled on the Royal Society in London. Where this second body differed markedly from the first was that its members were drawn largely from the two higher castes of British society in India, the 'Civil and Military' – that is to say, the HEICo's civilian administrators and its military officers – together with a rich leavening of surgeons. These amateur savants were a tiny minority of the British in India, never amounting to more than two to three hundred men, but they were arguably the best of them, in that they thought differently from their peers, were genuinely fascinated by the alien cultures in which they found themselves and sought to explain that culture to the wider world. They were, in a word, Orientalists.

That word Orientalist has acquired highly pejorative connotations ever since the publication in 1978 of Edward Said's *Orientalism,* which sought to demonstrate that the interpretation of the Orient by Occidental scholars was deeply flawed by virtue of their imperialist bias. Said's *Orientalism* had a huge impact on Middle Eastern, Near Eastern and Asian studies. It raised genuinely valid questions about negative stereotyping of the colonised 'other'. Even so, Said's scholarship has since been shown to be deeply flawed and highly selective. That should have given pause for thought but it did not, so that in many academic circles Said's text continues to be read uncritically as a blanket condemnation of all Occidental scholarship involving the Orient. The chief victims of this reverse stereotyping have been the Orientalist scholars themselves, their pioneering work traduced by lazy and even mendacious scholarship with more than a tinge of racism about it.

I have previously described the role played by British Orientalists in the rediscovery of India's pre-Muslim history and the recovery of its Sanskrit literature, and I have continued that process of rehabilitation here. Professor Deshpande of Jawaharlal Nehru University once described the College of Fort William in Calcutta as 'the single most important intervention that colonialism made in the cultural life of India over the last two centuries'. Along with the Asiatic Society of Bengal, that institution played a hugely significant role in the revival of Bengali culture and what has been called the Bengal Renaissance. As did those supposedly wicked Orientalists who fought side by side with the Bengali intelligentsia in trying to hold back the Anglicist and Evangelical tide that swept through Bengal from 1813 through to the fatal year of 1857. So I make no apologies for devoting an entire chapter to that ideological struggle, in which Brian Hodgson played a relatively minor but ultimately significant part.

Charles Allen, Camden, England
December 2014

This work was all set for printing when the news came through of the Nepal earthquake of 25 April 2015, followed by a series of aftershocks that are still being felt. Many of the historic temples and buildings described and illustrated in this book have been destroyed or badly damaged, among them the Madam Puraskar Pustakalaya Archive, Kathmandu's principal language library and conservation resource. A proportion of royalties from the sale of this book will go towards the restoration of that archive and other such institutions that have suffered damage. For more information see: www.britainnepal.org

Brian Houghton Hodgson. NHM Hodgson Collection
037022. © The Trustees of the Natural History Museum.

'Perpetual peace and friendship': Makwanpur, 4 March 1816

Not so long ago the Ranas were the rulers of Nepal – not as kings but as prime ministers. Although governing in the name of the kings of Nepal, the senior members of their clan held absolute power for over a century from 1846 to 1951. Today they no longer have any political clout, and the powers they once exercised are now celebrated only in the grandiose family portraits that line the walls of the last of the Rana family mansions still standing in Kathmandu Valley. However, in one particular Rana home, belonging to the most senior branch of the family, a more modest painting catches the eye: a watercolour by an English artist that portrays a most curious scene.

Two squads of soldiers face each other across a valley floor with their muskets at the 'present'. They are dressed in the red jackets, white cross-belts and pantaloons worn by infantrymen at the time of the Napoleonic War. The only irregularity is that that the soldiers on the left wear black shakoes and those on the right wear white. That difference identifies the former as belonging to a British regiment of foot and the latter as local sepoys – infantrymen of the kingdom of Nepal. Between them are a cluster of civilians, some in local and some in European dress. Two raise their hats to acknowledge the salute paid to them.

The subject of the painting is the ratification of the Treaty of Sugauli on 4 March 1816 – or, rather, an idealised representation of the event painted thirty-three years later (*see Plate 1*). That ratification marked an end to a hard-fought war between the HEICo and the mountain kingdom of Nepal that had dragged on for fifteen months before concluding with one final battle fought out on the heights above Makwanpur.

So this is where this scene is set: the Makwanpur Valley, in the foothills just south of the great bowl that should properly be called the Nepal Valley rather than the Kathmandu Valley. The ridge above the trees on the right is where the Nepali army made its last stand on 29 February.

Outnumbered, outgunned and outmanoeuvred, the Parbatiya or 'men of the hills' who made up Nepal's fighting elite proved no match for General Sir David Ochterlony and his seventeen-thousand-strong army from the plains of India. But they stood their ground and died in a manner that astonished their opponents. That redoubtable old soldier John Shipp, author of *Memoirs of the extraordinary military career of John Shipp, late a lieutenant in His Majesty's 78th Regiment, written by himself,* was present at Makwanpur as a junior officer and left a vivid account of the way the enemy they called the Gorkhas fought and died:

> I never saw more steadiness or more bravery exhibited by any set of men in my life. Run they would not; and of death they seemed to have no fear, though their comrades were falling thick around them, for we were so near that every shot told ... Two six-pounders now began to play with grape on the poor and brave fellows ... The havoc was dreadful, for they still scorned to fly ... I do repeat again, I never saw such soldiers ... Reader, believe me when I assure you that these results of war were no sights of exultation or triumph to the soldiers who witnessed them.

Appalled by this slaughter, General Ochterlony had at last given the order to cease firing. Those of the enemy who were left alive were allowed to walk away and their wounded attended to. Ensign Shipp's company was then given the task of collecting and burying the Nepali dead: 'In two days eleven hundred were committed to the grave, having almost one general tomb; and it would have much edified those babblers who rail so much against soldiers' cruelties and vices to have seen the tears of compassion trickling down the cheeks of both Natives and Europeans on the occasion.'

News of the disaster was carried by runners to the royal court in Kathmandu, the Durbar. Its implications were inescapable. Nothing could now prevent the foreign-born, without caste *Firingis* from marching down into the Nepal Valley and occupying Kathmandu – nothing except peace.

Before Makwanpur the clan leaders, generals and priests who surrounded the eighteen-year-old king of Nepal had been divided into hawks and doves – or, more accurately, what passed in Nepal for doves. Both camps were dominated by members of the same warrior tribe, the Khas, whose grandfathers had helped the present king's grandfather and founder of the Shah ruling dynasty to unite the Parbatiya hill-tribes of the central Himalayas into a nation and whose fathers had then gone on to conquer their neighbours to east, west and south. It had been a heady half-century, of victory piled on victory that had only reinforced the Parbatiyas' belief that they were invincible, superior in every respect to those contemptible plains-dwellers, the Madheshis – and that included the red-faced *Firingis*, whose supposedly invincible armies they had twice beaten back from their borders.

Leading the doves was the old battle-scarred general Amar Singh Thapa. He had been against the war from the start, having recognised that the HEICo – which its familiars liked to call 'John Company' or 'the Honorable Company', and which Thapa and his compatriots knew as *Jan Kampani Bahadur* – was a power like no other. Its troops had on occasion proved vulnerable but the *Jan Kampani* had brought an entirely new concept of warfare to the Indian sub-continent. Its soldiers fought not as individuals but as one disciplined body, it had far superior weaponry and seemingly unlimited assets, and it would keep on advancing until it had achieved its aims. 'We have hitherto but hunted deer,' Amar Singh Thapa had warned the young king. 'If we engage in this war, we must prepare to fight tigers'.

But the king had sought counsel elsewhere – and, in particular, in the person of forty-one year-old Bhimsen Thapa, a ruthless political operator who had been the dominant figure in the king's life for much of his childhood. Bhimsen not only had the king's ear, he also had him by the vitals. And sixteen months earlier he had given the king the worst possible advice:

Through the influence of your good fortune, and that of your ancestors, no one has yet been able to cope with the state of Nipal. The Chinese once made war upon us, but were reduced to seek peace. How then will the English be able to penetrate into the hills? Under your auspices, we shall by our own exertions be able to oppose them with a force of forty-five *lakhs* [four and a half million] of men, with which we shall expel them.

Bhimsen Thapa had gone on to draw a parallel with the failure of the *Jan Kampani Bahadur*'s forces to take the Maratha fort of Bharatpur in 1805, being four times repulsed with a loss of over three thousand men dead or wounded: 'The small fort of Bharatpur was the work of man, yet the English, being worsted before it, desisted from the attempt to conquer it. Our hills and fastnesses are formed by the hand of God, and are impregnable. I therefore recommend the prosecution of hostilities. We can make peace afterwards on such terms as may suit our convenience.'[1]

But Bhimsen Thapa had been proved wrong on every count. When the British invaded Nepal the Khas had been unable to muster even half a *lakh* of fighting men – and Nepal's mountains and fortresses had proved far from impregnable.

The Parbatiyas had indeed fought like lions, shocking their opponents into acknowledging that they were the most dangerous foe yet encountered on the Indian sub-continent. 'We have met with an enemy who has decidedly greater bravery and greater steadiness than our troops,' wrote the British political officer Charles Metcalfe soon after the start of the war. 'None ever displayed so much bravery in action, so much system, skill and so much well-tuned confidence.'[2]

And yet the first round of the war had ended with the loss of all the land west of the River Rapti that the Parbatiyas had conquered and ruled over for the last thirty years: the hill-country of Kumaon and Garhwal. Desperate to regroup and knowing that the *Jan Kampani* had other enemies besides themselves on the sub-continent, they had played for time. Bhimsen Thapa had sent representatives to the Sikh ruler of the Punjab, to the Chinese, to the Bhutanese, even to the Marathas, calling on them to form an alliance against the British. And at the same time he had sent other representatives down to the plains to meet the British at Sugauli, eighty miles due south of Kathmandu, with orders to talk only of peace.

But the treaty that the British offered them at Sugauli had been little short of a surrender demand. True, the first clause had promised 'perpetual peace and friendship between the East India Company and the king of Nepal'. But the remaining eight clauses were of a very different tenor. Not only were Kumaon and Garhwal to be lost to them for ever but also other lands to the east and the south; in particular, the narrow strip of forest, swamp and grassland that ran all the way along the edge of the plains bordering Nepal's foothills. This was the Tarai, and without the Tarai Nepal was nothing, for only here in the plains was it easy to cultivate rice, graze cattle and cut timber. 'Never will we consent to give up to you the Terai,' a Khas officer had warned Edward Gardner, another of the political officers accompanying Ochterlony's army in its occupation of Kumaon. 'Take the Terai, and you leave us without the means of subsistence, for without it the hills are worth nothing ... Keep it, and in wresting it from your hands, we will devastate your provinces down to the Ganges.'[3]

What that same Nepali officer had not told Gardner was that the Tarai also contained Nepal's secret weapon: an exceptionally virulent form of fever caused by an invisible miasma that they knew of as the *ayul* and the British came to call 'Tarai fever'. Only a few scattered jungle tribes could live within this lethal belt, having over centuries acquired a degree of immunity to the *ayul*. To everyone else, including the Parbatiyas themselves, the *ayul*'s supposed poisonous miasma was close to fatal – except during the winter months from late October to mid-March. It was therefore part of the Nepalis' military strategy to make HEICo's armies fight on into the summer months. The result was that in the first round of the war it was the Tarai fever rather than Nepali shot and *kukris* that had inflicted the most damage.

The Treaty of Sugauli had also stipulated that Nepal and Britain, as represented by *Jan Kampani Bahadur*, were to exchange ministers to reside at one another's courts. That meant a British representative in Kathmandu as a Resident – a deeply insulting demand. *Firingis* had no place in the system of *Varna* that ordered Hindu society into four levels of caste, with the Kshatriyas and Brahmans who made up the Khas tribe occupying the top two tiers. *Firingis* were literally outcasts, and their mere proximity to a Khas polluted him. The king of Nepal was the earthly manifestation of the god Vishnu and by simply coming into his presence a *Firingi*, such as a British Resident, polluted both him and all his court.

But much more than caste pollution was at stake, and no one at the king's Durbar knew this better than Bhimsen Thapa. He had spent four years in exile in Varanasi (Benares), and there he had seen how the *Jan Kampani Bahadur* worked. He had heard accounts of the Company's violent overthrow of the powerful ruler of Mysore, Tipu Sahib, and he had seen at first hand how nearby rajas and maharajas were swallowed up or their kingdoms reduced to power-less protectorates – and always accompanied by protestations of per-petual peace and friendship. Varanasi, the city sacred to every Hindu as the seat of salvation, was itself now part of the *Kampani Raj*, its revered maharaja reduced to the status of a puppet.

And yet even Bhimsen Thapa had been forced to acknowledge that the terms of the Sugauli treaty must be accepted – if only to buy time. And so on 2 December 1815 the king's representatives had bowed before the British and accepted a copy of the treaty with its nine clauses. They had agreed that within fifteen days it would be ratified by their king by the affixing of his red seal, the *Lal Mohur*.

Fifteen days passed and then a month and still not one of Nepal's potential allies – whether Marathas, Sikhs or Bhutanese – had responded to Nepal's appeals for help. General Sir David Ochterlony was no fool. He knew precisely what the Nepali leadership was up to because his agents had intercepted their letters. He was also fully aware that Bhimsen Thapa and his friends were again banking on his military columns moving at their usual cumbersome pace, so again making them vulnerable to the Tarai fever.

Ochterlony had anticipated the Nepalis' gamble and had prepared for it. By the third week of December four military columns were on the march, his own advancing with such astonishing speed that it was behind the Parbatiyas' main defensive line before they could react. In January and February every hill-top fort and redoubt that the Nepalis had reinforced was either battered down or bypassed.

One final day of hard fighting back and forth along the ridge at Makwanpur on 27 February and it was all over.

Now even Bhimsen Thapa and the most bellicose of his colleagues had to taste the bitterness of defeat. Accordingly, at the king's Durbar in Kathmandu the *Lal Mohur* was affixed to the Sugauli treaty and brought to Makwanpur by the king's emissary, a Brahman named Chandra Shekher Upadhya.

When Upadhya arrived at the British camp on the afternoon of 3 March General Ochterlony turned him away. 'I represented to him ... in plain and strong language,' boasted Ochterlony in his despatch to the Governor-General in Calcutta, 'the duplicity, folly, and perfidy which had marked every stage of their conduct ... He entreated me in the most submissive manner to accept the treaty and display the forbearance and moderation of the British Government, and said that the penitent always found mercy before the throne of heaven; that mercy became the powerful, and that in the name of the Rajah and of the state, he implored it.'[4]

Ochterlony ordered the king of Nepal's emissary to return in the morning and to present the treaty with the king's seal to him on his knees and in the presence of representatives of the hill-rajas of Kumaon and Garhwal and the adjoining Tarai plains whose lands they had overrun. And that was how Ochterlony reported it done.

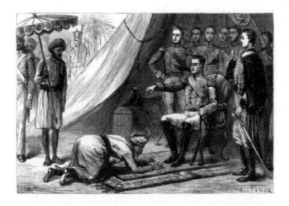

This supposed submission is portrayed in an engraving by a Victorian artist who did his best to re-imagine the scene as played out at Makwanpur on 4 March 1816 (*see above*). The unfortunate emissary Chandra Shekher Upadhya throws himself at the feet of the conqueror, who is youthful, glamorous and implacable – not quite as Ochterlony was in real life, which was short, thick-set and bulbous-nosed, and by 1816 a grizzled old warrior with white hair and lacking one eye.

But there is official history and what is so often the untold reality. The soldier John Shipp was present at this supposed submission and he set down a very different account. As Shipp remembered it, the Raja of Nepal's emissary Chandra Shekher Upadhya was received with full honours and shown the respect due to him as representative of the ruler of a foreign power – even though Shipp was wrong in supposing that Upadhya was the king's uncle:

> To do honour to the reception of such a personage the two flank companies of the 87th Regiment, and two flank companies of the 25th Native Infantry formed a street to the general's tent ... Shortly afterwards we saw him descending the hill in a superb palanquin, attended by about twenty armed men on foot. At the end of the street he was met by the adjutant general, quarter-master-general, and several other staff-officers; and after a little hugging, they led him on, taking his hands in theirs in token of friendship. Thus they proceeded to the general's tent, the street presenting arms, which he perfectly understood, and to which he bowed in a most majestic manner.

So here was the scene portrayed in the painting: the reception of the king of Nepal's representative as seen from the tent of General Sir David Ochterlony, given some artistic licence (*see Plate 1*).

Ensign Shipp also witnessed Ochterlony receive Upadhya with every sign of affability: 'Our brave general met him at the door of our tent, where the greeting was most laughable ... The manners of our visitor were those of a perfect courtier; but he was free, affable and jocular. In two hours after the customary sprinkling of scents, the treaty of peace was ratified, and he returned home with pleasure in his eye.'

As far as Ensign Shipp was concerned, the king of Nepal's emissary left Makwanpur all smiles. But that was nothing more than a brave front. The Treaty of Sugauli, as it was finally ratified, now carried an additional sub-clause by which yet more Tarai country was lost to the HEICo: 'The whole of low lands between Gandaki and Koshi in which the authority of the East India Company has been established'. This was the Nepali territory captured by Ochterlony's four columns in the course of the last phase of the war.

And, to cap it all, when Chandra Shekher Upadhya and his delegation began the return journey to Kathmandu their party were joined by a very unwelcome fellow-traveller: Lieutenant John Peter Boileau of the 10th Bengal Native Infantry, selected by his commander to proceed to Kathmandu until such time as a proper British Resident could be appointed. And Lieutenant Boileau did not travel alone. With him went two companies of light infantry drawn from the 18th, 21st and 23rd Bengal Native Infantry and the Champaran Light Infantry, a total of two hundred and eight sepoys, together with their *bhisties* (water-carriers), *lascars* (baggage and tent handlers), *beldars* (navvies), *dhobis* (washermen), *mehtars* (sweepers and cleaners) and all the other camp followers that were part and parcel of any Bengal Army contingent on the move.[5]

As soon as Boileau's party had been safely despatched Ochterlony's army withdrew at speed, every man eager to get through the Tarai before the fatal *ayul* could strike him down.

Today the circumstances of the signing of that one-sided treaty at Sugauli and its ratification at Makwanpur tend to be brushed over. Both countries involved are united in agreeing that it marked the beginnings of an alliance between their two nations that evolved in time into a very genuine friendship, with mutual respect and admiration on both sides.

But that was not how Sugauli was seen at the time.

General Ochterlony returned to Calcutta to the sound of gun-salutes and the ringing of church bells. He received the congratulations of the Court of Directors of the HEICo in London and the thanks of both Houses of Parliament. A grateful sovereign conferred upon him the Grand Cross of the Order of the Bath. On every side there was the warmest praise for the brisk and relatively casualty-free

manner in which Ochterlony had disarmed an aggressive and poten-
tially dangerous neighbour.

On every side, that is, except Nepal.

The scribes who maintained the state chronicle of Nepal, known
as the Parbatiya, put the best gloss they could on these disastrous
events:

> Raja Girban-juddha Vikram Shah reigned twenty years ... In his
> reign a war broke out with the British in the *Tarayani* [Tarai],
> but depriving them of wisdom, the Raja saved his country. Then
> calling the British gentlemen, he made peace with them, and
> allowed them to live near Thambahil [Thamel Bahal].[6]

But everyone knew what that intrusion really meant. Very soon
after the news of General Ochterlony's acceptance of the *Lal Mohur*
had reached Kathmandu a violent storm struck the hill of Swayambhu. This was the Valley's most ancient monument and its very
essence, self-created in the form of a lotus floating on a lake. The
Bodhisattva Manjusri had himself come to worship this lotus and, to
make it accessible to humanity, had cut a gorge through the southern
side of the valley. The waters had drained away and the lotus became
a hill crowned by a great stupa. The storm of March 1816 struck that
stupa so hard that it brought the great beam at the heart of the dome,
the *harmika*, crashing down on the shrines below. This was immediately understood to be an omen, foretelling disaster for the country
and the loss of Nepal's sovereignty.

Throughout Nepal the Treaty of Sugauli was seen at the time, and
for years afterwards, as a catastrophe; a national humiliation without
parallel. It left the Durbar – meaning the king and court together
in government – even more bitterly divided than before, with each
party blaming the other. But whatever their caste and whatever their
differences, what all sides were agreed upon was that a British presence in their capital city was not to be tolerated, that the British
would do all in their power to absorb Nepal into their ever-growing
Raj. The only acceptable response was to regroup, rearm and go to
war as soon as possible, to reclaim what they had lost and to drive the
British back into the sea.

'A European Gentleman and his *Moonshee* or Native Professor of Languages'. A coloured lithograph from a drawing by Sir Charles D'Oyly, one of Brian Hodgson's first patrons in India. From *The Costume and Customs of Modern India*, published in London in 1813.

2

'Qualified to discharge the duties of the public service': Haileybury, Fort William College and Kumaon, 1816–20

England in the summer of 1816 was at peace for the first time in years. Waterloo had been won and Napoleon Bonaparte safely tucked away in far-off St Helena. The news of General Ochterlony's military and political triumphs in the Himalayas was received with indifference. Compared with the high price of corn and a second bitterly cold summer in succession the HEICo's little wars in the Orient were of little concern – except to its shareholders and those families who saw India as a place of employment for their younger sons; in the cynical words of the leading historian of the day, 'A vast system of outdoor relief for Britain's upper classes.'[1] India was no longer the land of nabobery, where ten years' exile might purchase an estate, a knighthood and a seat in Parliament, but it was still a land of opportunity.

Indeed, these were good times to be a Briton in India. During Lord Hastings's five years in office as Governor-General he went to war against five separate enemies. No sooner had the Gorkhas of Nepal been driven back into their mountain heartlands than he launched the largest British army yet seen in India against the Pindari hordes that were ravaging central India, himself taking the field as the last Governor-General to lead an army into battle. A fast-moving campaign fought on several fronts developed into a very serious affair, as first one and then another and then a third grouping of John Company's most dangerous enemies took them on in what became known as the Third Maratha War.

By June 1818, when all the fighting was done and the last treaties signed, the HEICo would find itself in effective control of every patch of Hindustan south and east of the River Sutlej. Vast swathes of territory would be absorbed into the Bombay Presidency or packaged into a new administrative region to be known as the Central or Upper Provinces. The three defeated Maratha overlords would each be allowed to retain their own states, which they, along with the Mughal emperor in Delhi and a number of Rajput rajas, might govern so long as they behaved themselves and acknowledged Britain as the sovereign power.

This combination of conquest, treaty and forfeiture meant that every year more military officers were needed to lead an ever-growing Indian Army, and more civil servants to govern John Company's new subjects, and to keep its new allies in order – Nepal among them.

At this same time the HEICo was working hard to clean up its act. In 1813 the British parliament put John Company's rule in India on a legal footing by declaring it to be, in essence, a sub-contractor governing on behalf of the British crown. Its civil representatives in India were no longer to consider themselves factors of a commercial concern but as 'ministers and officers of a powerful sovereign ... required to discharge the functions of magistrates, judges, ambassadors and governors of provinces'.[2]

These were the words of the ambitious Governor-General Lord Wellesley, who had initiated the professionalisation of the HEIC's civil administration by founding in 1800 the College of Fort William in Calcutta. This was to be the 'Oxford of the East', where young probationers fresh from England would spend two or even three years immersing themselves in the languages and culture of the people they were to govern.

This emphasis on Orientalisation, with Indians brought in as teaching assistants, was to play a major role in the revitalisation of Bengali culture. But it also alarmed the HEICo's Court of Directors, always fearful of the corrupting influence of Indian ideas. Won over by the impassioned arguments of Charles Grant, a much admired senior director who had become a zealous Christian reformer after losing his children to smallpox in India, the Court voted to set up a second college in England – not as an adjunct to Fort William College but as an overtly Christian counterbalance.

Established initially in the medieval Hertford Castle in Hereford and then in 1809 at a grandiose purpose-built mansion at Haileybury in Hertford Heath, the East India College's overt purpose was to provide the young gentlemen nominated by the HEICo's directors for its civil service with the best possible vocational training, while at the same time inculcating in them the Christian principles required of future rulers of men: 'Overarching the whole curriculum was to be a concern for religion and morality, for without a full attachment to the Christian faith ... the young civil servants would not be able to fulfil their trust either to Great Britain or to the people of India'.[3] This was to be crammed into four terms spread over two years.

One of the early beneficiaries of the Haileybury hot-house was a teenager named Brian Houghton Hodgson. On the day the Treaty of Sugauli was ratified at Makwanpur Hodgson was a month into his first term at the college and had just turned fifteen.

Brian Hodgson was born on 1 February 1801[4] in the parish of Prestbury in Cheshire, the second of seven children who survived into adulthood and the eldest of three brothers. He was also the fourth in a line of 'Brian Hodgsons' who between them totted up 346 years. His family, he used to say, was distinguished for only two things: longevity and field-sports. Yet despite his being an enthusiastic sportsman as a boy it must have appeared unlikely to his family that he would maintain the family tradition. Two portraits of him at seventeen show a pretty, pink-cheeked boy with delicate features that border on the effeminate. One is a watercolour, too faint to bear reproduction. The other was done in oils, painted by order of his doting mother to mark his graduation from the East India College, Haileybury. It shows an introverted youngster seemingly more suited to the library than the playing field (*see Plate 4*).

Brian Hodgson's father had tried and failed to live in the manner of a country squire, a ruined man thanks to his investing his all in a cousin's failed bank. The huge debts incurred had set the family on a downward spiral only kept within the bounds of respectability by the kindness of relatives and friends. The constant threat of penury darkened young Brian Hodgson's childhood and helped determine his future as the family bread-winner. But until that time came, a matriarch held the family together: the strong-minded Mrs

Catherine Hodgson, known in her youth as the toast of Lancashire and in her later years as a formidable woman of letters.

Mrs Hodgson had a talent for making friends in high places and when circumstances forced the family to move downmarket to a smaller house in Congleton in East Cheshire she sought out the wealthiest man in the county: Mr James Pattison, local mill owner and City of London merchant, who in time rose to be a Member of Parliament and Governor of the Bank of England. More importantly, Pattison was a senior director on the Court of Directors of the HEICo and shortly to become its Deputy-Chairman and then Chairman – posts he subsequently filled for three terms.

Mrs Hodgson could hardly have found a more powerful friend. This was still an age of patronage and one of Pattison's perks was the right to nominate for Company service each year one military cadet and one civil service trainee or 'Writer' – an already archaic term harking back to the days when John Company's merchants began their eastern careers as clerks. To join the Company as a Writer at this time was to become a member of the best paid organisation in the world, in which some four hundred and sixty Civilians shared out between themselves according to rank a vast purse that averaged out at 20,000 rupees per man per year or £2500 – the modern equivalent being something in excess of fifty times that sum, so more than £125,000.[5] The idea was to discourage corruption but it meant that these nominations were greatly sought-after, and in 1816 it was Pattison's nomination that secured young Brian his Writership, even though he was still officially under age.

Haileybury was to be the making of Brian Hodgson, as it was for some of the brightest young men in England and Scotland. For all the opprobrium that had been heaped upon it, the HEICo was still a major force in British politics, so that when the college was set up in 1806 it attracted some of the brightest and most ambitious academics in the country, mainly from Cambridge. The undoubted star of its teaching staff was the Professor of Political Economy, the already famous Dr Thomas Malthus, author of *The Principles of Population* and much else besides. Some of the most influential intellectuals and Whig politicians of the day met regularly in Dr Malthus's house at Haileybury and – thanks to another of his mother's influential friends – it was in this same house that young Brian was lodged as a boarder for his first term. He would afterward relate how he passed his evenings sat in a corner listening to the talk of great men hitherto known to him only as names in the newspaper. They included George Canning, President of the Board of Control, who once came to Hodgson's room together with his patron James Pattison and proceeded to give 'a most masterly resume of Indian history', as well as advising him to read Orme's *History of the Military Transactions of the British Nation in India*.

But influential as Malthus and Orme were, by far and away the most important lessons learned at Haileybury came from James Mill, whose long-awaited *History of India* was finally published in three heavy volumes in 1817. Mill prided himself on never having left the country, which in no way prevented him from building his theories around his own prejudices. This might not have mattered but for the fact that his *History* set the tone for British policy in India for the next forty years with, some would say, disastrous consequences.

It was James Mill who came up with the quip about Britain's empire being 'a vast system of outdoor relief for Britain's upper classes'. He was highly critical of the way in which the HEICo had gone about winning and governing its Indian territories. And yet, imperfect as it was, Mill still saw a reformed Company as a force for good. It had, in his view, a crucial role to play in civilising India, given that the country was populated by 'a rude and credulous people' notable only for their superstition, ignorance and maltreatment of women.

This was a direct challenge to the Orientalist view of India that had first been enunciated just a quarter of a century earlier when the pioneer Sanskritist, Sir William Jones, had shown the world with chapter and verse of rediscovered literature just how rich and diverse India's ancient culture was. Jones and a handful of like-minded Orientalists had set up the Asiatic Society of Bengal in Calcutta to study India in all its aspects – which Mill condemned as a waste of time: 'Everything we know of the ancient state of civilisation among the Hindus conspires to prove it was rude.'

What could be described as the mission statement for future Indian civil servants like Brian Hodgson had been set down by Mill in 1810:

The stage of civilisation, and the moral and political situation in which the people of India are placed, render the establishment of legislative assemblies impracticable. A form of arbitrary government by European honour and European intelligence is the only form which is now fit for Hindustan. But that government should be one, the interests of which are identified with the interests of the country ... mild and paternal in its existence.[6]

In sum, Britain knew what was best for India, which was benevolent despotism.

Besides political education, Haileybury required every future Civilian to go to India with at least two native languages under his belt. A surviving East India College certificate dating from his graduation in December 1817 shows Brian Hodgson to have been a very diligent scholar – as might be expected of a student whose parents had already had to find £200 to pay for his two years at Haileybury. Distinctions in Bengali, Persian, Hindustani, Classics and Political Economy at the end of his final year placed Hodgson at the head of his intake: 'The College Council, in consideration of his distinguished Industry, Proficiency and Conduct, place him in the First Class of merit, and assign him the Rank of First on the List of Students now leaving the College for the Presidency of Fort William'.[7]

That top placing gave Brian Hodgson the right to choose which of the Company's three Indian Presidencies he wished to serve in: Madras, Bombay or Bengal. The last was where the action lay and the seat of government and Hodgson plumped for it. In early March 1818 he received formal notification of his appointment as a Writer on probation from HEICo's Court of Directors and put his signature to a Deed of Covenant, by which he agreed to be a covenanted servant of the Company and to abide by its rules. Very soon after he boarded the 600-ton East Indiaman *Sovereign*, anchored off the Downs outside Portsmouth, and paid over to its captain the sum of £105 allotted to him to cover passage, accommodation and table. On 30 April 1818 the *Sovereign* and three other Company ships set sail for the Cape of Good Hope, Madras and Bengal. On that same day Hodgson was officially listed as a Writer.

Shipping to and from India was largely dependant on the winds. To catch the full force of the South-West Monsoon the spring fleet should have rounded the Cape of Good Hope by mid-summer. It had then to reach India's western seaboard before the onset of the North-East Monsoon in November, when the wind patterns reversed. The *Sovereign* and the rest of the fleet made a speedy passage round the Cape to drop anchor off Calcutta's Fort William on 29 August 1818.

Brian Hodgson was not yet eighteen when he stepped ashore at the landing place of Chandpal Ghat. The *barasaat* or 'welcome rains' – usually referred to by the Europeans as the Rains (with an implied or written capital R, along with the Hot Weather and the Cold Weather) – was then in full spate. Even in our own era of five-star hotels, air-conditioning and bottled water, Calcutta in the Rains comes as a shock to the uninitiated: a suffocating combination of heat and humidity that, even after the brief respite of the first drops of rain, builds and goes on building like a pressure-cooker without a release valve – two months of torrential deluge and all-pervading damp in which disease and distemper flourish.

Hodgson was required to report to the HEICo's Fort William College to complete his civil service training. He duly did so on 30 August and thereby qualified to begin drawing his first salary of 300 sicca rupees a month and to be ranked 466th in the Company's order of precedence for its civil servants. However, he failed to attend the college for the next two and a half months.

The explanation for this absence lies in some brief notes Hodgson made for his biographer almost seventy years later: 'Could not work owing to the effects of the climate. Lost rather than gained knowledge ... My medical adviser recommended me to throw up the service and go home. "Here," said he, "is your choice – six feet underground, resign the service, or get a hill-appointment."'[8]

Hodgson's frail constitution was no match for the climate of Bengal. He collapsed with what was diagnosed as 'liver disease'. But returning home was out of the question. He was now the family breadwinner and back home they were depending on him not just to repay the costs of his education and outfitting for India but also to help support his parents and his younger brothers and sisters.

Fortunately, Hodgson had friends in high places – and two friends in particular: British Calcutta's most glamorous couple – the aristocratic Sir Charles D'Oyly, Bart., and his young wife Eliza.[9] Sir Charles's easy-going patrician charm and wit, coupled with a talent for drawing, had secured him a large circle of friends in Calcutta – including the Governor-General, the Hon. Francis Rawdon-Hastings (first ennobled as Lord Moira for his distinguished military services in the American and French wars, and afterwards as Lord Hastings) and his wife, Lady Hastings, a young lady less than half his age with a title in her own right who, in the words of a contemporary historian, 'lived with him in India in the full blaze of viceregal splendour'.[10]

Lady Hastings was a flirt and a schemer who with her doting husband's blessing gathered about her in Calcutta a smart set of aristocratic friends, Sir Charles D'Oyly among them. It was through her that Sir Charles met and married in 1815 the pretty and musical Miss Elizabeth Ross, who happened to be Lady Hastings's second cousin newly arrived in India.[11] A portrait drawn by her husband shows an attractive and self-confident brunette with a determined chin and a fondness for ringlets.

The D'Oylys were a glamorous and outgoing couple and by the time of Brian Hodgson's arrival in Bengal their drawing room on Chowringhee vied with Government House to become the most exclusive salon in Calcutta. Here Eliza D'Oyly presided over musical soirees and her husband over a more informal drawing circle. European Calcutta was no longer the hard-drinking, two bottles of claret per man per meal community it had been in the days of William Hickey[12], but those in the upper tiers of this small community still enjoyed an extravagant life-style of balls, fetes, theatricals, evening carriage drives, and, for the men, a regular diet of riding and hunting with shotgun and hogspear.

Sir Charles's generation belonged to the old mercantile school that Lord Wellesley had condemned as unfit to rule an empire, he and his immediate contemporaries being the last to have come through the mill of learning on the ground rather than in the classroom. A distinct cultural gap was now beginning to widen between such men and the new breed of civil servants such as Brian Hodgson, serious young men who talked of duty and ideals and took a dim view of the

Eliza D'Oyly. A vignette drawn in pencil by her husband Sir
Charles D'Oyly at the time of their marriage in Cawnpore in 1815.
BL Macnabb Collection WD 4057. © The British Library Board.

frivolous lives of their elders. Indeed, Hodgson was nicknamed the
'young philosopher' by his fellow Writers in Calcutta, which suggests that he was not the liveliest of companions.

And yet it was the D'Oylys who shaped young Hodgson's future.
A letter of introduction from his aunt secured their attention, and
within weeks he had been adopted by Lady D'Oyly as her particular
pet. It might have been his youth or his vulnerability, but in any event
the D'Oyly's opened their doors to him. Despite differences in age,
rank and outlook, they became friends – and Eliza D'Oyly as close a
friend as propriety allowed. Thanks to Hodgson's continuing isolation, what began as a teenager's crush became over the years something altogether more pathetic. 'So long as I lived in the world,' we find
him writing to his sister twelve years after he first met Eliza D'Oyly,
'I was, by all men's voices, a "lady's man," and truly I feel not that I

am altered, albeit I have not seen the fringe of a petticoat for eight years ... I have ever worshipped woman, and have ever held her to be worthy of the worship of the highest and greatest of our sex.' Another four years on and he was still as lonely as ever, so little wonder that he should have declared Eliza D'Oyly to be 'all that I desire to honour and love'.[13] Only with the ending of Hodgson's enforced celibacy did that worship finally mellow into a platonic friendship that lasted up to the widowed Elizabeth D'Oyly's death in 1875.

By December 1818 Brian Hodgson was well enough to begin his studies at Fort William College, where the emphasis was very much on reaching a high level of proficiency in at least two languages. The preferred options were Bengali and Persian – inherited by the British as the language of diplomacy on the sub-continent – which required hours of one-to-one tutoring from the college's native *munshis*.

Surprisingly, the dominant figure at Fort William College at this time was a Baptist missionary: William Carey, head of the Hindu Languages Department.[14] 'The Colloquial Hindoostanee, the classic Persian, the commercial Bengalee, the learned Arabic, and the primeval Shanscrit are spoken fluently, after having been studied grammatically by English youths,' Carey had famously declared in 1804, in a speech delivered in Sanskrit. 'Did ever any University in Europe, or any other literary institution in any other age or country exhibit a scene so interesting as this?' He went on to prophesy that the college's influence would be felt for years to come: 'Good has been done which cannot be undone. Sources of useful knowledge, moral instruction, and political utility, have been opened to the Natives of India which can never be closed; and their civil improvement, like the gradual civilisation of our own country, will advance in progression, for ages to come.'[15]

By the time of Brian Hodgson's arrival Carey's prediction was well on the way to being realised. Fort William College had indeed become the chief catalyst in the revival of Indian culture, with scholars from as far afield as Benares and Delhi flocking to Calcutta in search of meaningful employment.

Brian Hodgson's graduation from Fort William College in August 1818 was celebrated with a 'public disputation'; the college's equivalent of a graduation ceremony, staged at the Court House building before a gathering of distinguished guests that included the Governor-General, the Lord Chief Justice, the Bishop of Calcutta – and, of course, Lady Hastings and her cousin Lady D'Oyly. For the many Bengali intellectuals associated with Fort William College as much as for Calcutta's white community, this it was the most important social occasion of the year, and was described in detail in that month's *Calcutta Journal*:

> In a state chair covered with crimson velvet and richly gilt, with a group of aides-de-camp and secretaries standing behind him, sat the Governor-General. Two servants with state *punkahs* of crimson silk were fanning him, and behind them again were several Native servants bearing silver staffs. Next to him, on either side, were seated the examiners, and below them again, the most distinguished ladies of the Presidency. Next, in an open space, were two small rostrums for the disputants, and chairs for the professors ... and in the rear of all, the bodyguard were drawn up in full uniforms of scarlet with naked sabres.[16]

After what sounds like an interminable series of public debates, during which Brian Hodgson was required to oppose two motions in Bengali and in Persian, the college's Visitor rose to announce that of the twenty-six Writers under examination eighteen had been found qualified to discharge the duties of the public service, among whom Brian Hodgson stood first: 'After being attached to the institution for the short time of nine months he has obtained a degree of honour of a high proficiency in the Bengalee and a medal of merit for rapid and considerable progress in Persian.'[17] Under a scheme of monetary rewards initiated by Lord Wellesley these marks earned Hodgson 1500 rupees, a very useful sum but which he had to set against his debts, for like every other college student Hodgson had borrowed heavily from the Calcutta *banias*, always happy to lend large sums at high rates of interest to youngsters with good prospects – that being the means by which the foundations of some of Calcutta's most distinguished Indian families were laid.

The Visitor in question was none other than the Governor-General himself, Lord Hastings. Despite being a military man, Hastings

The Anglo-Irish general Francis Edward Rawdon-Hastings,
1st Marquess of Hastings, who served as Governor-General of
India from 1813 to 1823. Detail from an engraving of a portrait by
Martin Shee painted shortly before Hastings left for India.

took his civil duties very seriously. He was at his desk at four in the
morning every day, never decamped to the hills in the Hot Weather
as his successors did and expected his civil officers to follow his lead.
He now closed the proceedings with a speech of almost Messianic
fervour, reminding the eighteen successful graduands that they were
now administrators of 'an immense empire ... altogether unprec-
edented in its nature', armed with exceptional powers that carried
exceptional responsibilities:

> You will have a large population looking up to you for justice
> and protection ... You will have to exercise temper, judgment
> and perfect impartiality, together with zeal and devotion to
> public business. You are called on to love and cherish the people
> under you and to enter into their feelings, pay attention to their

peculiarities, and view with gentle charity their prejudices and weaknesses ... Go forth with parental dispositions towards the natives. Be their protectors, their consolers, the cheerers of those around you. Instil the universal principles of morality, open the minds of the rising generation, enable them to exert their reason, and obnoxious customs will silently die before the light diffused.[18]

Nowhere in Lord Hastings's speech was there any mention of Christian duty. This was Orientalist paternalism from start to finish – and a heavy burden to place on the shoulders of eighteen- and nineteen-year-olds. It may well have left them inspired, perhaps, but also quaking in their buckled shoes at the thought of what lay before them.

To be so directly under the Governor-General's gaze did Hodgson's prospects no harm at all. On the very next day, 20 August 1819, the first postings for the Company's newly qualified Writers were published in the Civil Appointments List, wherein it was stated that Mr B. H. Hodgson had been made Assistant to the Commissioner of Kumaon. The appointment came with a princely salary of 750 sicca rupees per mensem, amounting to an annual salary of £1125 (about £60,000 today).

Kumaon was a lifesaver for Hodgson because it was in the Himalayas. Today it forms the eastern half of the Indian state of Uttarakhand, a roughly rectangular tract of mountain country approximately one hundred miles in length and width that rises from the Gangetic plains in a series of ever-higher mountain ridges to culminate in the Central Himalayan Range. It divides north and south down the middle into two political divisions: Garhwal in the west and Kumaon in the east, abutting Nepal. It was a country, in the words of one of Hodgson's contemporaries, 'blessed with a delicious climate, the rigours of the winter solstice being moderated by great solar radiation, while the summer heats are moderated by the contiguous eternal snow-topped Himalaya'.[19] Exactly the same could be said for Kumaon's eastern neighbour, Nepal. Chance and patronage could not have combined more happily to Brian Hodgson's advantage.

In Hodgson's day, and for long after, the most sought after postings in the Bengal Civil Service were those that came under the control of the Foreign and Political Department, answerable directly to the Governor-General and staffed by a cadre of strong-minded individuals with good diplomatic skills who acted as Agents to the Governor-General. They and their assistants were generally known as Politicals as distinct from Civilians. As representatives of the Governor-General, they served as Residents at the courts of the so-called native princes – the maharajas, rajas and nawabs with whom the HEICo had entered into various forms of alliance. Also coming under the direct control of the Governor-General was a smaller group of Politicals known as Commissioners whose job it was to govern newly-acquired borderlands not yet in a fit state to be administered by a Civilian cadre.

These Politicals were all picked men. They acted as the Governor-General's eyes and ears and, if necessary, his diplomatic gloved fist. They had to know when to stand up to the local ruler and when to defer, when to enforce the Governor-General's will and when to advise him that to do so would be counter-productive. Above all, they had to be confident enough to be able to make decisions on the spot, since Calcutta was in most cases weeks rather than days away. Isolation was part and parcel of the job – and enough Politicals had been cut down on duty in remote corners of the sub-continent for it to be thought of as a risky calling. The salaries were commensurate with the risks.

Of all these political postings only two were sited in the Himalayas – Nepal and Kumaon – and both were sought after. For all his academic distinctions, the likelihood of someone of Hodgson's age and inexperience being given such a plum as Kumaon should have been out of the question. But the right to make these appointments rested with the Governor-General, Lord Hastings, and at his side stood Lady Hastings. There can be no doubt but that it was she and her cousin Eliza D'Oyly who together pulled the strings that drew eighteen-year-old Brian Hodgson to his destiny in the Himalayas.

Appointments and salaries were with immediate effect, but the Rains were still in full spate and the rivers in full flood, so Hodgson could not have left Calcutta before mid-September. In the meantime we may imagine the newly-appointed Assistant Commissioner using an advance against his salary to equip himself for his new post and to begin sending regular drafts home to help support his family.

Hodgson had also to learn what he could about Kumaon, and his first action would have been to seek advice from Lord Hastings's Private Secretary, Sir Charles Metcalfe, a baronet like Sir Charles D'Oyly but made of sterner stuff. Metcalfe had just completed eight years as British Resident and Agent to the Governor-General in Delhi, the key post on what was now British India's northern frontier. Although still in his early thirties, he was regarded as the most brilliant member of Hastings's circle of advisers and bound for the highest office. He had been the first student to be enrolled at Lord Wellesley's Fort William College, where he had caught the Governor-General's eye, resulting in his early selection for political service. As a junior assistant to the then Resident in Delhi, he had made his mark by concluding a treaty with the Sikh ruler of the Punjab, Ranjit Singh – and had returned to his post with a Sikh *bibi*, a mistress with whom he lived in unostentatious amity.

Said to be 'uncommonly plain' both in face and in manners, Metcalfe was austere, taciturn, never happier than when poring over papers at his desk, and more admired than liked – but he was a good man to have on your side.

Another Civilian who was to play an important role in young Hodgson's life was a more genial character: Henry Thoby Prinsep, the son of a well-known old Indian hand and eldest of six brothers all seeking positions for themselves in India. He claimed that he had only secured his position as Lord Hastings's Private Secretary 'in consequence of my having been a fellow-passenger of his wife',[20] but H. T. Prinsep was in fact admirably qualified. He had been at Lord Hastings's side throughout the entire course of the Nepal, Pindari and Maratha wars and was now writing an account of these campaigns in between drafting new land ownership laws for Bengal.[21] At the time of Hodgson's appointment he had just returned to Calcutta after taking leave to meet up with the youngest of his brothers in Cape Town. This was twenty-year-old James Prinsep, a shy young man of no obvious talents for whom he had secured a junior position at the Calcutta Mint. Neither brother could have imagined how closely their fates and Hodgson's were to be bound together a decade later.

The Bengal Civil Servant Henry Thoby Prinsep, eldest of the
Prinsep brothers in India and a committed Orientalist. A
portrait by Colesworthy Grant published in his *Lithographic
Sketches of the Public Characters of Calcutta* in 1840.

Travelling across the Gangetic plains in the month of September
was no joke in Hodgon's day. The one escape from the heat lay in the
river. For those heading into Upper Bengal it was customary to hire a
large river boat known as a *budgerow* and proceed against the current
by a combination of sail, oar and pole, tying up each night beside the
river bank. This was the most likely mode by which Brian Hodgson
covered the first leg of his journey up the River Ganges, probably as
far as Allahabad, a distance of approximately eight hundred miles,
covered at a rate of about twenty miles a day. It was slow going but
it was comfortable. The river breezes kept the temperature at a toler-
able level and the flies and mosquitoes away.

By the time Hodgson reached Allahabad the Rains had given way to the Cold Weather, which in Northern India brings with it as near perfect a climate as any Englishman could wish for. It allowed him to continue the rest of his journey by road, following the ancient highway that afterwards became known as the Grand Trunk Road (today the GTR). It was unfit for any wheeled vehicle other than the bullock-cart so Hodgson had to choose between riding or being carried by a team of men in a box-like litter: the *palki* or palanquin, the preferred mode of travel for persons of status. Bumpy and uncomfortable though it was, the *palki*'s relay of bearers made it possible to travel through the night, so that as many as eighty miles could be covered in twenty-four hours.

Hodgson's next objective was Delhi, where Emperor Akbar II presided over an entirely nominal Mughal empire from his palace in the Red Fort. For all his grand titles, the emperor was now little more than a pensioner of the HEICo, still the owner of vast estates but without any authority beyond the walls of his fort. The formal powers that his forefathers had once enjoyed were now vested in the Governor-General and his representative in Delhi in the person of the Resident: General Sir David Ochterlony, victor of the Nepal War.

Ochterlony was at that time enjoying his second tenure as British Resident in Delhi. He was now sixty years of age, which was ancient for a European in India. He was white-haired, florid-faced and entering his dotage, but still living life to the full in his own idiosyncratic style, having turned his back on his native America and declared India to be his only home.

When Ochterlony had first come to Delhi back in 1803 a Residency had been provided for him just outside the city walls in the form of an abandoned library that had once belonged to a Mughal prince.[22] But as Ochterlony's career flourished so too did his ambitions and by the time of his return he had built himself a palatial garden house two miles outside the city on Delhi Ridge: the Mubarak Bagh, or 'Garden of Happiness', which combined Western and Eastern architectural features to match his own divided life-style. On official duty he presented himself as the very model of a British Political, but at all other times he dressed and behaved in the manner of a Muslim nawab.

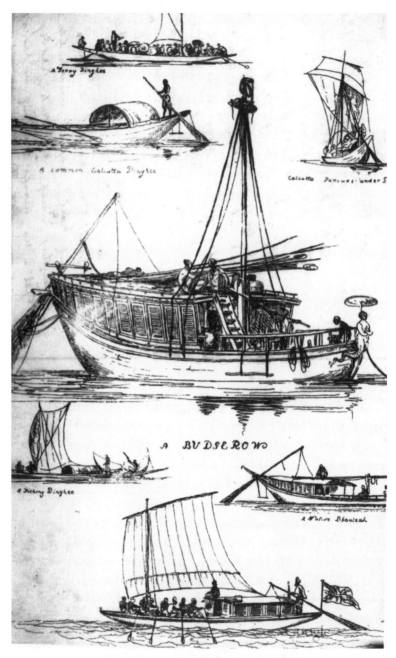

A *budgerow* (centre) proceeding up the Ganges, together with other lesser forms of rivercraft. Lithograph of drawings by either James or William Prinsep to illustrate George Prinsep's article in river transport published in the second volume of *Gleanings in Science*, 1830.

A Civilian being conveyed up country in a *palki*. Detail from one of a series of engravings from Sir Charles D'Oyly's 'burlesque' poem *Tom Raw, the Griffin*, in which he satirised the travails of a newcomer to India, published in 1828 with engravings based on his own drawings.

Hodgson had encountered such Indianised characters in Calcutta – in particular, the elderly general Charles 'Hindoo' Stuart, who made no secret of his admiration for Hindu culture, took morning dips in the River Ganges accompanied by his Hindu *bibi*, and advocated that European women in Calcutta should abandon their corsets and stays in favour of the 'simple, sensible, and sensual' Indian sari. But unlike Stuart, Sir David Ochterlony had chosen to go Mughal. At the Mubarak Bagh he kept a *zenana*, or women's quarters, occupied by a harem of wives, concubines and their children. He was at this late stage of his life in thrall to the mother of his youngest child, a Brahman dancing girl from Poona who had converted to Islam and now exercised such a hold over him that she was known throughout Delhi as 'Generallee Begum'.

Despite their differences in age, rank and culture Ochterlony and Hodgson were both members of the new aristocracy. They were Politicals and they looked after one another. So it would have been quite natural for Hodgson to have been put up by the Resident in Delhi. Hodgson may well have joined the general for his regular late afternoon constitutional known as the *hawa khana* or 'eating the air', when Ochterlony led his Generallee Begum and his lesser wives in a promenade down to the River Jumna and back, each wife seated behind curtains on her own elephant.

Everything Brian Hodgson had been taught at Haileybury must have led him to raise his eyebrows at the old general's life-style. A short note in Hodgson's handwriting about 'the costly and pompous style then inseparable from our Indian embassies' suggests that he was not entirely happy about the manners of senior officials such as Ochterlony. Keeping *bibis* was still the norm rather than the exception for Ochterlony's generation. But from the journal kept by Lady Nugent, a visitor to Delhi a few years earlier, we know that at least two of General Ochterlony's junior assistants, William Fraser and the Hon. Edward Gardner, followed his example. 'They both wear immense whiskers,' she wrote, 'and neither will eat beef or pork, being as much Hindoos as Christians; they are both of them clever and intelligent, but eccentric; and, having come to this country early, they have formed opinions and prejudices, that make them almost natives.'[23]

Despite their supposed eccentricities, both Fraser and Gardner went on to acquit themselves well. When the first British victories forced the Gorkhas out of Kumaon and Garhwal, each was placed in charge as local Commissioners: Gardner in Kumaon and Fraser next door in Garhwal.

The term 'White Mughals' suits such men.[24] They had no fixed notions about British cultural superiority and their generous salaries and allowances enabled them to live in a manner that in many ways mirrored the courts of the Indian rulers to which they were attached. That exotic lifestyle was already seriously under threat when Brian Hodgson arrived to India. His generation had been trained to look askance at such behaviour – and yet the example was there and it was not forgotten.

For Brian Hodgson all thoughts of pomp and extravagance ended when he and his small retinue crossed the bridge of boats laid across the River Jumna beyond the walls of Delhi. His destination lay approximately 190 miles due west of Delhi at the point where the great Gangetic plain ended and the Himalayan foothills began. Overlooking the plains was the hill town of Almora, the regional headquarters of the two regions of Kumaon and Garhwal, united under the jurisdiction of one man: George Traill, Commissioner for the Affairs of Kumaon and Garhwal.

Traill was no White Mughal. He followed hard on the heels of Sir Charles Metcalfe and, like Metcalfe, had no time for fine living. But whereas Metcalfe eschewed the great outdoors, Traill revelled in it, being a backwoodsman to the hilt. He was only nine years older than Hodgson and more a Civilian than a Political, having learned his trade over the course of five years as an assistant commissioner and town magistrate in the plains. He had then been promoted to take up the same assistant commissionership that Hodgson was now about to fill, arriving in Kumaon in the summer of 1815 to serve as assistant to Edward Gardner. After the ratification of the Treaty of Sugauli in March 1816 Gardner was appointed to be the first British Resident in Kathmandu and Traill moved up the ladder to fill his boots. Sixteen months later his authority was extended to cover both Kumaon and Garhwal under the single umbrella title of Kumaon.

By the time of Hodgson's arrival in the hills some time in late October or early November 1819 George Traill was well into his stride, a tough-minded, no-nonsense individual who worked himself and others hard and brooked no opposition. Apart from a brief period of 'acting' in the plains during another civil officer's leave, Traill was to remain in the hills for twenty-one years, earning for himself the title of 'the king of Kumaon'.

Traill's 'kingdom' was made up of some eleven thousand square miles of the Central Himalaya Range, beginning at the edge of the plains below the first range of foothills and then rising northwards, range by range, to the snow peaks bordering the Tibetan plateau.

There is no flat country to speak of, only a jumble of more or less parallel river valleys separated by steep ridges cut in here and there by deep gorges where the monsoon rains and melting snows have worn channels through the folded rock and earth. In Traill's time the only townships were to be found among the lowest range of foothills adjacent to the plains, with Almora occupying a hilltop where a once important Gorkha fort had stood. Elsewhere there were only tiny settlements clinging to the hillsides wherever an acre or two of flat ground could be carved out, linked to each other by mountain trails barely wide enough to allow one traveller to pass another. According to Traill's 'Statistical Sketch of Kumaon', his province contained 9,034 villages made up of a total of 44,569 houses, 'giving an average of five houses to every village'.[25]

This was a hard country, made harder still by the brutal way in which the Nepalis had imposed themselves on the populace during their brief occupation. British accounts of their rule of India tend to exaggerate the misgovernment and neglect suffered prior to the advent of British rule with all its blessings. But in the case of Kumaon there was no need for exaggeration. All accounts agree that in seeking to wring every rupee out of the people the Gorkha soldiery had so devastated the country that entire villages had been left deserted, their inhabitants either enslaved, fled or starved to death.

Traill's first action had been to lift all but the mildest of the many taxes imposed on the inhabitants. He and his staff then set about the process known in British India as settlement, which meant visiting every inhabited area to establish exactly how many persons lived there, how they lived, who owned what and what resources there were in the area, after which a new and more equitable revenue system was drawn up that took account of such factors as existing hereditary rights, forest rights, grazing rights, water rights and even individual human rights, since bonded serfdom and domestic slavery continued to survive in much of India in various forms.

This was the task to which Brian Hodgson was put in the winter of 1819–1820, the outcome of which was to form a small part of George Traill's remarkable 'Report for Kumaon', submitted by him to Government in 1824 (and afterwards published as 'Statistical Sketch of Kumaon'), which became a template for administrators in other parts of India. It was a hugely valuable apprenticeship. It taught Hodgson the discipline of systematic inquiry and how to go about it. It showed him the need for accuracy in the gathering of facts and how much that depended on good human relations, on getting to know the local inhabitants and respecting their customs and habits.

Although they welcomed the British as liberators, the Kumaonis and Garhwalis were still highly suspicious of their motives. They were badly bruised by what they had gone through and their trust had first to be won. It meant dealing with people face to face, diplomatically and openly and showing great patience all the while – and it meant a lot of what we now call trekking, even if in Hodgson's day that meant travelling with a military escort, a long line of porters and a large retinue of servants to pitch his tent, cook his meals, wash his clothes and provide him with hot water to wash and shave with.

In the process Hodgson discovered what countless visitors to these hill regions have since learned for themselves, which is that Kumaonis and Garhwalis are free of many of the prejudices found in the plains and easier to get along with, ready to share a joke and hospitable to a fault – indeed, in so many respects similar to their neighbours to the east, the much-hated Nepali Parbatiyas – which is hardly surprising, since the two peoples have very similar cultures and live very similar lives.

George Traill was Hodgson's first real role model. He took his orders from him for no more than eight months at the most but at a formative stage at the start of his career. He saw how Traill went about things, how he was his own master, how certain he was that he and he alone knew what was best for the people he governed, irrespective of what his superiors might think in far off Delhi and even more distant Calcutta. This was how a frontiersman acted, decisively and promptly. Years later Hodgson would jot down his impressions of Traill and what he meant to him:

> The Commissioner, who spoke and wrote the local language, dispensed with all formalities, settled cases in court like the father of the family, and encouraged every one who had a complaint to put it in writing and drop it into a slit in the court door, of which he kept the key. Answered *viva voce*, in court or out. He was of active habits and went everywhere throughout the province, hearing and seeing all for himself. His cheerful, simple manners and liking for the people made him justly popular. Took a hint from him when myself in authority in Nepal.[26]

But as admirable as Traill's methods were for administering Kumaon, it was not the best example for a future diplomat.

At the time of Brian Hodgson's appointment as Assistant to the Commissioner for Kumaon a new Assistant to the Resident at the Court of Nepal had also been named: Robert Stuart, who was a year younger than George Traill and had previously served as Third Assistant to the Resident at Ambon in the Moluccas spice islands.

On 14 March 1820, after some eighteen months in Kathmandu, Stuart succumbed to what was described as 'an inflammation of the lungs occasioned by a sudden attack of violent cold'. He was not the first fatality among the Residency staff; eight months earlier the commander of the Resident's military escort, Lieutenant Alexander Ayton, had died of malaria in Calcutta, leaving as his legacy the manuscript of the first grammar of the Nepali and Newari languages, afterwards published by Fort William College.

However, Stuart was the first Briton to die in Kathmandu. A plot was found for him a short distance to the north-west of the Residency, where he became the first occupant of what is now the British Cemetery in Kathmandu.

Stuart's untimely death in Kathmandu settled Hodgson's fate.

It took almost a month for the news to reach Calcutta, so it was not until 6 May that Stuart's replacement was named. It then took another three weeks for the news to reach Almora, so that it was not until June 1820 that Brian Hodgson learned that he had been appointed Assistant and Secretary to the British Resident in Kathmandu. He was nineteen years and four months old.

The last leaf of the *Lalitavistara Sutra* carries a miniature showing
Pandit Amritananda presenting the manuscript to Captain Knox
under the moon. BL IO San 688f.253v. © The British Library Board.

3

'Spying on the nakedness of the land': Assistant to the Resident, Kathmandu, 1820–24

When, in February 1793, the first British envoy entered the Nepal Valley he was accompanied by a large number of local porters, a remarkable number of whom lacked noses and lips. Having read a recently published account of Nepal written by a Capuchin missionary, the envoy, Captain William Kirkpatrick, knew why.

Father Giuseppe di San Martello had come to Kathmandu just as Prithvi Narayan Shah of Gorkha was completing his conquest of the Valley. 'When I arrived in that country at the beginning of 1769 [actually 1768],' he afterwards wrote, 'it was a most horrid spectacle to behold so many people hanging on the trees in the road.' Having failed to take the Valley by force, Prithvi Narayan Shah had resorted to a blockade, executing anyone suspected of trading with its Newar inhabitants.

Within months of Father Giuseppe's arrival, the Gorkhas had taken the town of Kathmandu in a surprise night assault without a shot being fired. Only the strongly defended town of Kirtipur held out, twice beating back the Gorkhas before its famished inhabitants surrendered on promise of an amnesty. Angered by their resistance, the new king of Nepal had exacted a dreadful punishment:

Prithwinarayan ... issued an order to Suruparatna, his brother, to put to death some of the principal inhabitants of the town, and to cut off the noses and lips of every one, even the infants, who were not found in the arms of their mothers; ordering at the same time all the noses and lips which had been cut off, to be preserved, that he might ascertain how many souls there were, and to change the name of the town to Naskatapur, which signifies 'the town of cut-noses'. The order was carried into execution with every mark of horror and cruelty, none escaping but those who could play on wind instruments ... Many of them put an end to their lives in despair; others came in great bodies to us, in search of medicines; and it was most shocking to see so many living people with their teeth and noses resembling the skulls of the deceased. [1]

Raja Prithvi Narayan Shah's cruelty stood him and his immediate successors in good stead. The Gorkhas gained a reputation for ruthlessness that hastened their conquest of Nepal and its immediate neighbours. Only China was unimpressed, which was why in 1792 the Nepal Durbar turned to the HEICo as a possible ally.

Eager to gain trade concessions that would allow it to trade with Tibet and China through Nepal, John Company sent Captain Kirkpatrick to Kathmandu in the following year. But his delegation arrived too late – the Nepalis had come to an accommodation with the Chinese and were now desperate to get rid of their unwelcome guests. Kirkpatrick's party was permitted to camp for a week at the foot of Swayambhunath Hill – that wooded knoll just west of Kathmandu that serves as the platform for the most spectacular of Nepal's many spectacular religious monuments. Kirkpatrick was politely received by the young king, Rana Bahadur Shah, but it was his uncle, the regent, who did all the talking. Kirkpatrick and his party were then sent packing, having gained little more than some second-hand information about the country and its people, but in the knowledge that they had at least 'removed the veil which had so long interposed between the two countries'. [2]

Raja Rana Bahadur Shah was aged eighteen at the time of Kirkpatrick's visit but a ruler in name only. A consultative body known as the *Bharadari Sabha*, or Assembly of Lords, composed of the heads of the leading Khas families – the bharadaris – had been set up by Rana Bahadur Shah's father to advise the ruler but had since split into factions, leaving the regent in unchallenged authority. However, the raja had one particularly devoted ally who had known him since the age of eleven when they had together undergone the *bratabandha* sacred thread ceremony that initiated them into their

Kshatriya warrior caste. The friend's name was Bhimsen Thapa and in 1797 he became the king's personal bodyguard.

With Bhimsen's help Rana Bahadur Shah was finally able to throw aside his uncle and have him imprisoned. But years of indulgence as a child king of quasi godlike status had undermined his character. Disinheriting his eldest son, he declared his heir apparent to be an infant son born to him by his third queen, a Brahman widow from the plains of India. What made this union a particularly heinous crime in Hindu law as then applied in Nepal was not that the king had taken the woman by force but that he had broken two caste taboos: widow remarriage and marriage between a Brahman and a Kshatriya. This unfortunate third queen then contracted tuberculosis – smallpox by another account, poisoned herself by a third – and died, whereupon Rana Bahadur Shah went mad with grief and guilt. 'By the advice of evil councillors Rana Bahadur Shah seized a Brahman's daughter by force as a concubine,' is how a Nepali chronicle described these events:

> By reason of his cohabitation with a female of a sacred caste his senses left him and he became mad. He became very fond of bull fighting and killed innumerable monkeys and vultures ... He fell into open dissension with his bharadaris and destroyed and polluted the temples as well as the images of the deities and murdered the *Vaidyas* [physicians] because they could not cure his concubine against the will of providence.[3]

His madness led to the king's enforced abdication and exile in favour of his two-year-old son, who was proclaimed Raja Girvan Yuddha Bikram Shah. In 1800, escorted by Bhimsen Thapa and clad in the saffron robes of the ascetic, ex-king Rana Bahadur retired to Benares in 1800, supposedly to take up the life of an ascetic. With him went his first wife, Rani Rajareshwari, the Senior Queen.

Meanwhile in Nepal a courtier named Damodar Pande, whose father had been the late Raja Prithvi Narayan Shah's close friend and counsellor, formed a political alliance with the Second Queen and took over the reins of government as *Mukhtiyar*, or Chief Minister. Fearing that the mad king would attempt to reclaim his throne, Damodar based his foreign policy on keeping Rana Bahadur at arms length in Benares under British protection – which meant being obliging to the *Jan Kampani Bahadur*. The outcome was a commercial treaty with the HEICo in 1801 that included an exchange of representatives.

This led to the arrival in April 1802 of the first British Resident in Kathmandu in the person of Captain William Knox, who had served as escort commander on the earlier Kirkpatrick embassy. He was accompanied by a number of Europeans that included Captain Charles Crawford, military engineer and map-maker, a geologist named Blake and Dr Francis Buchanan, a surgeon turned surveyor.[4] Buchanan deserves special mention, not least because he changed his name to Hamilton to receive an inheritance and thereby caused enormous confusion to future students of natural history and Buddhist studies.

More significantly, Buchanan-Hamilton (as we shall now call him) was one of small group of men, all doctors of medicine by profession, who advanced the cause of scientific progress in India out of all proportion to their numbers. The majority came from modest backgrounds, very different from the sons of the gentry who made up the bulk of the Company's Civil and Military. But where they had the edge was in their education. Many were products of Scotland's public education system and, like Francis Buchanan-Hamilton, had come through the medical schools of Edinburgh and Glasgow, the most advanced in the Western world. They were trained to be curious, methodical, and suspicious of authority – classic products of the Scottish Enlightenment – and they served both John Company and the cause of science extraordinarily well.

Captain Knox and his party were received kindly by Damodar Pande and provided with a large house in the grounds of an extensive royal garden known as the *Ranikabagh* or Queen's Garden, laid out just to the north of Kathmandu. According to local legend, this was an area of ill-omen, haunted by spirits of the dead known as *bhoots*. Whatever the truth of such a story, part of this considerable plot of land afterwards became the grounds of the British Residency – today known as Lainchour and divided between the British and Indian Embassies.

But Damodar's treaty backfired on him. The exiled king's Senior Queen, Rani Rajareshwari, raised a party of courtiers against him,

A detail from the first map of the Nepal valley, drawn by Captain
Charles Crawford in 1803, showing Kathmandu and the adjacent
towns of Patan (bottom centre) and Kirtipur (bottom left). The
British Residency was established to the north-east of Kathmandu
in an area known as Rani Bagh, here marked as 'Ranny Bhaug'.
Courtesy of Dr Mark Watson and the Linnean Society.

and Captain Knox and his party found themselves virtual prison-
ers within the grounds of the Residency, prevented from having
any contact with the local people unless sanctioned by the Nepal
Durbar. They remained there for eleven months, becoming increasingly isolated, their mail being subjected to ever stricter censorship,
until Knox had no option but to withdraw to India.

In political terms the mission achieved very little, but it did not
return empty handed. Both Buchanan-Hamilton and Crawford

succeeded in gathering a mass of new intelligence about the country. Captain Crawford was able to compile the first detailed map of the Valley, as well as two less accurate maps of Nepal and its trade routes to Tibet. But it was Buchanan-Hamilton, with the experience of an earlier mission to Burma behind him, who made the most of a unique opportunity. Being an experienced botanist, he soon realised how rich the country was in hitherto unknown plants. He at once asked for a fellow botanist from Calcutta to be allowed to join him, only to be told that 'the strongest objection would be made to the coming of any person who had no evident employment but that of spying on the nakedness of the land'.[5]

Fortunately, Buchanan-Hamilton had with him a number of Indian assistants, who were put to work to 'obtain information, so far as I prudently could, without alarming a jealous government, or giving offence to the Resident'. He was also able to hire some local men to collect plant specimens for him, including some Newars drawn from the gardener caste and 'a slave of the raja of Gorkha, who entered into my service in order to bring plants from the Alpine regions'.

Thanks to these men Buchanan-Hamilton was able to record over eight hundred new species of plants and collect a large number of plant specimens, besides despatching quantities of seeds, fruits and bulbs to the HEICo's botanic garden outside Calcutta. And thanks to the Indian artist he had brought with him, he returned to Calcutta with over a hundred coloured drawings of orchids and other plants.

This was the first scientific collection to come out of Nepal and had Buchanan been allowed to write up his material he would have been recognised by his peers as the founder of Himalayan botanical studies. But circumstances went against him and, as far as Nepal is concerned, Buchanan-Hamilton is best remembered for his *Account of the kingdom of Nepal and of the territories annexed to this dominion by the house of Gorkha*, published in 1819 some years after his visit.

Sketchy as it now appears, Buchanan-Hamilton's *Account* opened a window into the hitherto hidden lives of the people of Nepal. Its author was the first Westerner to understand that the name 'Nepal', which for centuries had referred only to its central valley, had since Prithvi Narayan Shah's invasion been applied to all areas he had conquered: 'Nepal, a name celebrated in Hindu legend, in a strict sense, ought to be applied to that country only which is in the vicinity of Kathmandu, the capital; but at present it is usually given to the whole territory of the Gorkha Rajas.'

Buchanan-Hamilton can also be credited with the discovery that what his predecessors had taken to be an orthodox Hindu kingdom was also populated by followers of a far older established religion in the form of Buddhism, which had survived and flourished in the Nepal Valley long after it had been extinguished down in the Indian plains. He was also the first outsider to realise that the Newar inhabitants of Nepal Valley – 'a race addicted to agriculture and commerce, and far more advanced in the arts than any other of the mountain tribes' – practiced a form of Buddhism very different from that found in Ceylon, Burma or China (*see Plate 15*). Perhaps because his chief informant in these matters was a Calcutta Brahman and not a Buddhist, Buchanan-Hamilton misunderstood as much as he learned, but his unique qualification as an observer of two forms of Buddhism was subsequently to give him an inimitable insight as a pioneer contributor of what we would now term Buddhist studies.

When William Knox led his party out of the Nepal Valley in December 1803 he, too, took with him part of its Buddhist culture: a souvenir in the form a handwritten manuscript set down on a series of narrow folios placed one on top of another, and decorated with images from Buddhist iconography.

What was particularly gratifying to Knox was that this bundle carried on the inside of its wooden cover a beautifully drawn miniature portrait of himself, dressed in full military fig, seated on a chair and holding a Buddhist prayer-wheel, while opposite him a pandit knelt at prayer before his deities (*see Plate 2*). There was even a second portrait of himself drawn on a separate leaf at the end, not quite so well executed, but showing him graciously receiving the manuscript from the same pandit (*see Plate 3*).

Today the focus is very much on that second kneeling figure: Pandit Amritananda, his face and details drawn with such care that we can make him out to be a man in his prime, with large eyes, a sweeping moustache and a small goatee beard.

The circumstances in which Knox acquired this manuscript remain a mystery. Quite unknown to Knox, it was a copy of an important Buddhist text known as the *Lalitavistara Sutra*, which tells the story in Sanskrit of the Buddha Sakyamuni from the time of his descent from the Tushita heaven up to his first sermon delivered at the Deer Park outside Benares – a key event in Buddhist history known as the First Turning of the Wheel of the Dharma. Knox afterwards presented his manuscript to the library of Fort William College, where it remained all but unnoticed for two decades. More years passed before a translation revealed its subject – as well as the name of the donor of this particular copy, as explained in a colophon on the last folio:

> By order of William Douglas Knox, whose liberality and other virtues surpass the divinities and prove him to be an *avatara* of Buddha and who is adorned with the title of *Iftikara-ud-Dow-lah* [Glory to Greatness], *Ihtishamu-ul-Mulk* [Magnificence of Kings], and *Shahamat-i-Jang* [Bravery in War], the copying of the manuscript was undertaken by Buddhist Pandit Amritananda of Patan in Nepal.

The retreat of Captain Knox's party from Nepal was followed by the return from his self-imposed exile of ex-king Rana Bahadur Shah, although not before the grounds for his rehabilitation had been laid by Bhimsen Thapa, working in alliance with Bhimsen's father and six brothers and the ex-king's Senior Queen Rajareshwari. Damodar Pande came out to oppose them but as soon as his men saw their ex-king's banner they laid down their arms, allowing Rana Bahadur Shah to make a triumphal return to Kathmandu.

Damodar Pande and his son were beheaded, Bhimsen Thapa was appointed Chief Minister and, for her pains, the Rani Rajareshwari was sent into enforced retirement. To further consolidate his position, Bhimsen Thapa ordered a second round of beheadings in the name of the king and blinded four possible contenders to succession in the Shah royal family.

The future security of ex-king Rana Bahadur Shah and his illegitimate son, still ruling as the official king, now seemed guaranteed. But then in April 1806 Rana Bahadur Shah was persuaded by Bhimsen Thapa to marry his niece, sixteen-year-old Tripura Sundari Devi Thapa. This was not well received by the ex-king's half-brother Sher Bahadur. The one accused the other of plotting against him, they quarrelled, Sher Bahadur drew his sword and killed the ex-king, and was then himself cut down by the ex-king's bodyguard, Bal Narsingh Kunwar. Bal Narsingh and Bhimsen Thapa immediately set about a general massacre of all courtiers suspected of having links with the regicide.

As many as ninety-three men are said to have died in a welter of blood, their places in the Durbar being filled by other members of the Thapa clan. Queen Rajareshwari and the late ex-king's remaining wives, along with all his concubines – fifteen in total – were then taken, not to the royal cremation ground at Pashupati where the remains of the ex-king had been cremated, but to an out of the way rivulet some twelve miles away. There they were forced to commit a mass *sati* or self-immolation to the accompaniment of mass drumming to drown their screams.

The newly-married-and-widowed Rani Tripura Sundari Devi was appointed regent to her step-son, nine-year-old Raja Girvan Yuddha Bikram Shah. But, of course, it was Bhimsen Thapa who called the shots, secure in the knowledge that he had no obvious rivals – or, at least, not until the king came of age. A precedent was set: that of a bloody coup within the confines of the Durbar, leading to the rule of a strongman in the name of the king.

From Bhimsen Thapa's point of view, the one remaining threat both to Nepal and to his own authority came from the *Jan Kampani Bahadur*, whose machination he had got to know all too well from his four years in exile in Benares. The HEICo was 'a power that crushed thrones like potsherds,' he is said to have declared.[6] It had to be resisted at all costs. So Bhimsen Thapa played his military hand as best he could. He confiscated Brahman lands to raise funds to enlarge his army and employed French military advisers to modernise it. But he misjudged the limits of *Jan Kampani*'s patience. Having conquered all the hill country to west and east the still restless Parbatiya warriors had no further outlet for their predatory instincts except southwards into the Indian plains, which they continued to raid and occupy at will. In 1813 the British magistrate at Tirhoot reported that 'between 1787 and 1813 upwards of two hundred villages had been seized by the Nepalese on one or other unjustifiable pretext'.[7]

It had to end in tears and it did – in the humiliation of Sugauli with its intolerable conditions that included the imposition of a British Resident.

But in one respect fortune continued to smile on Bhimsen Thapa. In the very wake of the ratification of the Treaty of Sugauli, the Goddess Sitala Devi entered the Nepal Valley in the form of small-pox. 'The rivers, tanks and canals were crowded with dead and dying,' records a Nepali chronicle. 'In the streets a man had scarcely room to walk, the dogs dragged away the neglected and putrefied corpses and vultures died with surfeit of human flesh.'[8] Among those carried off by the goddess was the king himself, Raja Girvan Yuddha Bikram Shah, who died on 20 November 1816, one month after turning nineteen. His three-year-old son and heir Raja Rajendra Bikram Shah was placed on the throne and his mother, Rani Tripura Sundaru, declared queen regent for a second time.

Once again, Bhimsen Thapa found himself holding what consti-tuted almost a full hand. The only remaining obstacle was the acting British Resident, who had now to be kept in strict *purdah*, as far as the treaty allowed.

That acting Resident was Lieutenant John Peter Boileau, who had presented his credentials to the late king in formal Durbar on 17 April 1816 and within days had written to Calcutta to complain that he was effectively under house arrest:

A company of *Sipahees* [sepoys] have been ordered by Bhimsen Thapa to be dispersed between my house and the city during all hours, and to apprehend any person who may be thought to hold communication with me; and it has been given out in the city that any one so offending shall be punished.[9]

Boileau was told to keep his head down and be guided by 'a spirit of conciliation and prudence' so as to 'remove the characteristic jeal-ousy of the Nepalese Government'.

The same orders were given to the Hon. Edward Gardner when he took over from Boileau in June 1816. Governor-General Lord

Hastings was then engaged in directing all his forces against the Pindari hordes that had arisen 'like masses of putrefaction in animal matter, out of the corruption of weak and expiring states'[10] and were now ravaging Central India. The last thing he wanted was another round of hostilities with Nepal. So Gardner was given the strictest instructions to keep out of internal Nepali politics and to stay on good terms with Bhimsen Thapa. To this end he brought with him an olive branch: the return of all the precious Tarai country that had been added to Lord Ochterlony's list at Makwanpur; that is to say, the plains country lying between the Kosi and Rapti Rivers.

This act of magnanimity only bolstered Bhimsen Thapa's position by appearing to vindicate his hard line. He saw to it that Gardner met only his designated officials and restricted his visits to the infant king to the two major public festivals of the year: the spring festival of *Holi* and the autumn festival of *Dashami*. The king's return visits to the British Residency Bhimsen carried out himself in the king's name.

Edward Gardner found Bhimsen Thapa an awkward man to deal with. 'His eyes revealed a quick intelligence,' he noted in one of his early reports. 'At thirty-seven he was tall, his figure spare, his countenance animated'. Gardner was in no doubt that it was Bhimsen Thapa himself who was behind all the hostility directed at him as Resident, a man 'from whom, it may be safely said, we have since experienced the utmost intensity of Gorkha hate, and from whose hands we have seen vividly displayed the workings of a system grounded on fraud and deeply tinged with unchangeable and bitter jealousy'.[11]

Gardner had every cause to be so suspicious. On two separate occasions Bhimsen's emissaries had been intercepted carrying letters to one or other of the Maratha powers calling for secret alliances against the British. And year by year Nepal's standing army of regular soldiers was growing in numbers, bolstered by a unique system of rotating enlistment known as the *Pajani*, by which after one year of paid service a soldier was taken off the roll to become an unpaid auxiliary for two years before enlisting again for another year. What this meant in effect was that a standing army of 10,000 soldiers in 1816 was actually an army of 30,000 fighting men. Three years later those numbers had grown to 12,000 and 36,000 – far in excess of what was needed to keep the country in order.

The Bengal civil servant and diplomat the Hon. Edward Gardner. Detail
of an aquatint by Sir Charles D'Oyly, probably drawn in 1819 when
Gardner was aged 38. BL WD 4061. © The British Library Board.

This steady enlargement of Nepal's army coupled with Bhimsen
Thapa's intrigues with hostile principalities led Gardner to believe
that Bhimsen Thapa intended to break the peace treaty at the first
opportunity. And yet, for all these provocations, relations between
the Durbar and the Residency began to thaw, to such a degree that
in 1820 Gardner was allowed to invite a guest to Nepal in the person
of Dr Nathaniel Wallich, superintendent of the Calcutta Botanic
Garden.

Dr Wallich was another member of that band of medical men
whose scientific skills were highly prized by the HEICo – this
despite his Danish nationality and his official status as an enemy.
Born Nathan ben Wulff, the son of a wealthy Jewish merchant of
Copenhagen, Wallich had come out to Bengal in 1807 as surgeon
to the little Danish trading settlement of Serampore, upriver of

Calcutta, only to discover that Denmark's alliance with France had made him a prisoner of war. Impressed by his learning, his jailors had released him into the care of Dr William Roxburgh, superintendent of the Company's botanic garden outside Calcutta. But Wallich's interests extended far beyond botany and medicine. One of his first known actions after his release from captivity had been to join the Asiatic Society of Bengal.

This learned body owed its existence to the genius and energy of Sir William 'Oriental' Jones. With the support of Warren Hastings, the then Governor-General, Jones had founded and then guided the Society through its first decade before his death in harness in 1794. The Society had subsequently lost some of its momentum but the two hundred or so enthusiasts who made up its membership were all followers of Jones's Orientalist creed, with the more serious-minded among them writing up and presenting papers at the Asiatic Society's bi-monthly evening meetings prior to their publication in its august journal, *Asiatic Researches*.

No sooner had Wallich joined the Asiatic Society of Bengal than he was proposing that the Society should form its own museum, to be stocked with 'all articles that may tend to illustrate Oriental manners and history or to elucidate the peculiarities of Art and Nature in the East'. He himself would prime the pump by donating plants and other items from his own collection and other members of the Society would be asked to donate not only 'historical reliques' but also 'animals, minerals and metals'.

Wallich's proposal was received with enthusiasm and on 1 June 1814 he became the superintendent of the Asiatic Society's Oriental Museum – the first such museum in Asia, today known as the Indian Museum. Under Wallich's enthusiastic guidance donations poured in from almost every corner of the sub-continent. Three years later Wallich took over from Roxburgh as superintendent at the Calcutta Botanic Garden, and it was in this capacity that he first wrote to Edward Gardner in Nepal, initiating a correspondence that eventually led to both Gardner and his assistant Robert Stuart themselves taking up botany and plant-collecting. Initially, Wallich sent two of his Indian assistants to help with the collecting process but then in 1820 he received permission from the Durbar to join Gardner in Kathmandu.

Dr Wallich's visit got off to a dreadful start. Robert Stuart had been sent down to the Indian border to escort Wallich up from the plains but returned to Kathmandu in a state of collapse. Within a week he was dead. 'His disorder,' wrote Gardner in the letter that carried news of his death to Calcutta, 'which has been supposed to have fallen upon his lungs, terminated suddenly and fatally on the evening of yesterday, the 14th instant.'

Stuart's untimely death hit the other three other British occupants of the Residency hard: Lieutenant Charles Rogers, commander of the escort, Dr C. E. Everest, the Residency surgeon, and Gardner himself. Gardner and Stuart came from much the same background, the one the fifth son of Baron Admiral Lord Gardner, the other the eldest son of a Scottish baronet. They had also shared a common pursuit in gardening and plant-collecting and despite a difference of nine years in their ages had grown close during their eighteen months together.

Gardner felt Stuart's loss keenly. The formal phraseology he employed in writing to Charles Metcalfe in Calcutta with the news could not entirely mask his own grief:

> By those who had the advantage of knowing his private character and worth, which stood in the highest standard for honour, integrity, and principle, and every amiable quality that could do credit to, and render a man estimable, his death must in a peculiar manner be deplored; and in making this painful report to you, I have some consolation in expressing the sentiments which I have ever felt towards him, and which I am persuaded all who had any concern with him must fully participate with me on this melancholy occasion.

What was of considerable comfort to Gardner in the wake of Stuart's death was Nathaniel Wallich's presence in the Residency. By some accounts, Wallich was a difficult man to get along with. He was said to be ill-tempered, egotistical and jealous. But to those who shared his interests he was 'a man of warm affection, or ready wit, a most amusing companion'.[12] He and Gardner enjoyed each other's company and it was during the Dane's prolonged stay in Nepal that the British

TO,
The Memory, of
ROBERT STUART, ESQ.ᴿ
Third Son of
SIR JOHN STUART, Bᵀ.
Of ALLANBANK in NORTH BRITAIN
And Afsistant to the first British Resident
At the Court of the RAJA of NIPAUL
Who died at this Capital
On the 14ᵗʰ. of March,1820.
A few of his Friends
Have recorded on this Monument
A slight and sincere
Though melancholy Testimony
Of the Ability, Excellence, and worth,
Which, while he lived
Commanded their Esteem, Love, and Respect.
And, now that he has been taken from them
Connect the remembrance of him
With their warmest feelings.

Simpson & Llewelyn Sct.

The inscription on Robert Stuart's headstone in the British
cemetery, Kathmandu, bearing the tribute written by
Edward Gardner. Photo by Dr Mark Watson.

Residency's garden was first laid out – no doubt to include specimens of the *Gardneria* genus of flowering plants, the orchid *Neogyne gardneriana* and the evergreen Himalayan shrub *Edgeworthia gardneri*, known as the paper-tree and still used today for making hand-made paper, all plants named by Wallich after his fellow enthusiast.[13]

Wallich had the Nepal Durbar's permission to stay for a year, but just as his time was drawing to a close he went down with a bout of a recurring and debilitating illness that sounds very like malaria. This meant that he missed the narrow window of safety for crossing the Tarai and so had to stay on in Nepal for a second summer.

That same danger of crossing the Tarai in the wrong season also prevented Brian Hodgson from entering Nepal before the onset of the Cold Weather in October 1820. When at last he arrived in Kathmandu he found himself – still not yet twenty years of age – very much the junior among four older men who had had plenty of time to get to know each other. Even the youngest, Lieut. Charles Rogers, was a decade older. And yet, on the evidence of a number of surviving letters written by Hodgson to Dr Nathaniel Wallich after the latter's return to Calcutta, it is clear that a close bond developed between them, even though Wallich was twice Hodgson's age. In the earliest of these, written in May 1824, Hodgson signs off, 'I hope thou art well & fit & busy. Gardner joins me in Love. Ever thine, BH Hodgson'. Perhaps the youngster saw Wallich as something of a father figure, since there is little evidence that Hodgson took a serious interest in Wallich's botanical pursuits.

Beyond those few letters we know next to nothing about Hodgson's first years as assistant to Edward Gardner. Decades later the elderly Hodgson jotted down some bland words about his superior in one of his notes intended for his biographer: 'Found in Kathmandu in the head of the embassy another man to form myself upon, a man with all the simplicity and more than the courtesy of Traill – a man who was the perfection of good sense and good temper; who, liking the Nepalese and understanding them, was doing wonders in reconciling a Court of Chinese proclivities to the offensive novelty of responsible international dealing through a permanent diplomatic establishment in their midst.'

The surgeon-cum-botanist Dr Nathaniel Wallich lecturing to students
at Fort William College, drawn by Colesworthy Grant and reproduced
in his *Lithographic Sketches of the Public Characters of Calcutta*, 1838.

Part of Brian Hodgson's job description as Gardner's assistant was
to act as his Private Secretary and handle all correspondence coming
in and out of the Residency, so he must have spent hours closeted
with Gardner in the main Residency building. Yet nothing survives
other than those careful words about 'another man to form myself
upon' and 'the perfection of good sense and good temper'. If Gardner
kept a *bibi*, Hodgson was too polite to mention it in any of his correspondence, though it must be remembered that those few letters of
his that have survived – in particular, those written to his parents
and his sister Fanny – were afterwards subjected to the censorship of
Hodgson's second wife and his biographer.

As for Edward Gardner, his official letters show a cautious, con-
scientious political officer who stuck to the official line as dictated
by Government House, Calcutta. His letters to Nathaniel Wallich
reveal him in a slightly more relaxed mood, but even here the correspondence is almost entirely taken up with chat about plants and
plant species.

Gardner's orders required that he remain passive in the face of
every provocation. It meant that there was very little to do except to

file reports, answer the official mail, pay the occasional formal visit and attend the odd festival. This was in marked contrast to what Hodgson had previously experienced in Kumaon, where he had woken every morning knowing he had a full day of vigorous activity ahead of him. We can be sure that a great deal of time and effort was initially devoted to his learning the two principal languages of Nepal: Parbatiya, as spoken by the Gorkha conquerors and their followers (today called Nepali); and the unrelated *Nepal Bhasa*, also known as Newari, as spoken by the Newars of the Nepal Valley. Both these languages were set down in the script already familiar to Hodgson as Indian Devanagri with only minor differences.

These new languages were learned with the aid of *munshis*, most probably one for each of the tongues. With so much time on his hands and, given that Hodgson had already demonstrated his proficiency in learning in Bengali and Persian, we can be assured that Hodgson came to speak and write both Nepali and Newari with fluency.

But there are limits to how much time even the most academically inclined can devote to learning two new languages before it becomes a chore. So it is hardly surprising that after some eighteen months in Kathmandu Brian Hodgson began to wish he were somewhere else.

However, Hodgson's closest allies were no longer in a position to help. Lady Hastings's husband had tarnished an otherwise outstanding record as Governor-General by allowing himself to be drawn into a Calcutta banking scandal and was now clearing his desk prior to his departure.[14] And Lady Hastings's cousin, Hodgson's adored Eliza D'Oyly, was herself no longer placed to pull strings in Government House, having been forced to move up-river to Patna when her husband Sir Charles was appointed Opium Agent for Bihar. Patna was the cultivation and manufacturing base for the Company's fast–expanding opium trade with China – a highly lucrative business, worth several million pounds sterling to the HEICo. But important and well paid as this new post was, it placed the D'Oylys far outside Calcutta's social orbit.

But there was always Henry Thoby Prinsep, who was now Persian Secretary to Government and very much the rising man. An appeal for his support seems to have done the trick, leading to Brian

Hodgson's return to Calcutta in November 1822 to become acting Deputy Secretary under Prinsep in the Persian Section of the Foreign and Political Department. This was not a position to be sniffed at because it put Hodgson at the centre of all things political. He had only to keep his head and promotion to another political agency or a higher post in the secretariat was bound to follow in due course.

The problem, just as before, was the Bengal climate.

The Hot Weather and Rains of 1823 very nearly did for Hodgson. Once again he found himself with no option but to find a refuge in the hills – or go home with his tail between his legs. But this second time around he was out of luck. His place as assistant to Edward Gardner in Kathmandu was now filled by his replacement, and George Traill in Kumaon likewise had no vacancy. It was a desperate situation, which could only be resolved by another death or the further intervention of one or other of his friends in high places.

The D'Oyly's were still marooned up-river at Patna and Henry Thoby Prinsep had just left Calcutta on extended furlough and was not expected to return to India before another two years. However, at this point a new saviour appeared on the scene: William Butterworth Bayley, another member of that coterie of brilliant, ambitious young men hand-picked by Lord Wellesley to carry forward his vision of empire. Unlike Sir Charles Metcalfe, Bayley was a secretariat man to his very fingertips, much more suited to running things behind the scenes than making a name for himself in the field. In 1823 those fingers were to be found in virtually every government pie, Bayley being a member of the Governor-General's Supreme Council, President of the Council of Fort William College, Secretary of the General Committee for Public Instruction and Vice-President of the Asiatic Society.

Bayley was, by every account, a decent man with a reputation for 'unfailing kindness of heart', his only weakness his modest disposition. Hodgson went to him cap in hand and was given unequivocal advice. 'Go back to Nepal and master the subject in all its phases,' he was told. He should learn all he could about Nepal and be patient. 'In the present times you can learn little there. But we have had one fierce struggle with Nepal and we shall have yet another. When that event occurs there will be very special need for local experience.'[15]

This was bitter but sound advice, and the outcome was that Brian Hodgson returned to Nepal – but not as the Assistant to the Resident. A purely nominal post had been invented for him, together with a nominal salary. He was to be the Residency Postmaster, with responsibility for the Residency's mail – to all intents, assistant to the Assistant to the Resident, a job usually filled by a Indian clerk. It must have been a very chastened young man who in the early months of 1824 found himself back at the British Residency in Kathmandu.

Hodgson's one-horned Indian rhinoceros. According to Hodgson's handwriting on the drawing, this painting was done when the animal was nine years old, so in 1833. NHM Hodgson Collection 069562. © The Trustees of the Natural History Museum.

4

'The strenuous idleness of woodcock shooting': Postmaster and Assistant to the Resident, Kathmandu, 1824–25

William Pitt Amherst, 1st Earl of Amherst, is best remembered as the British envoy who refused to kow-tow to the Emperor of China and was sent packing, along with his embassy. However, in 1823 he succeeded Lord Hastings as Governor-General of India. Raised as a courtier and more used to following orders than giving them, the amiable Lord Amherst arrived in Calcutta hoping to pursue a more pacific course than that taken by his predecessor.

Henry Thoby Prinsep saw Lord Amherst at first hand as one of his under-secretaries and was not impressed. 'He wanted altogether that confidence in his own judgement and power of correct and prompt decision which is required to govern men and command their respect and obedience,' he wrote of his chief in a memoir. Nor was he impressed by His Lordship's sense of his own prestige: 'Lord Amherst had extraordinary notions of the importance of a very punctilious ceremonial. He never moved from one room to another without a long train of *chobdars* (that is, servants with silver maces) preceding him. When he rode out with Lady Amherst, it was a rule that she should never advance beyond his horse's quarter; and in all things he required similar formal observances.'[1]

Despite Lord Amherst's good intentions he was almost immediately dragged into a two-year war that proved hugely costly, both in terms of lives and sicca rupees, and left his reputation in tatters. The aggressors in this instance were the rulers of Ava, in what is now Burma, who had enjoyed much the same rise and expansion by conquest as the Gorkhas of Nepal up to the point when they spilled over into the HEICo's eastern borders. Their belligerence raised the spirits of Bhimsen Thapa in Nepal who sent messengers to Ava in hopes of forming a new anti-British alliance. But those hopes were soon dashed. Despite losing almost half their numbers to malaria and dysentery, the HEICo's armies duly triumphed and in February 1826 a peace treaty was signed that won John Company two more coastal provinces and the future security of its Assam borders.

In the course of the war with Ava large numbers of British soldiers encountered for the first time a flourishing Buddhist culture. Calcutta's *Quarterly Oriental Magazine* and the *Bengal Almanac* were filled with accounts of such exotic sites as the vast gilded edifice outside Rangoon known as the *Shwe-dagon* or 'Golden Temple', which struck one British officer as 'stupendous proof of the labour to which religious superstition can prompt a nation'.[2]

Buddhist studies was then in its earliest infancy, dominated by the German Orientalist Julius Heinrich Klaproth and the French savant Jean-Pierre Abel-Rémusat, both drawing largely on the reports of Jesuit missionaries in China. But increasing contact with the Buddhist cultures of Ceylon, Burma and Nepal now began to shift the focus southwards, with Britons leading the enquiries. As one country's Buddhist practices were compared with another, disparities and contradictions began to emerge. It became known that Buddhism's origins were as much historical as mythical and that it roots lay within India itself. Buddhism had spread north as far as Mongolia and as far east as Java and Japan, and yet within India itself it had disappeared so completely as to leave virtually no trace.

A great many wrong conclusions were being drawn, not least by Calcutta's great Sanskritist, Dr Horace Hayman Wilson, whose views on Buddhism continued to be shaped by his readings of orthodox Brahmanical texts, which was rather like trying to understand Martin Luther's Protestantism by consulting the Vatican library. Wilson's problem was one that he shared with every other Orientalist at the time, which was that their information was coming to them at second hand through biased sources. What was lacking was direct access to original material. And it was here that Brian Houghton

Hodgson unknowingly had the edge, along with his fellow hermit in the Himalayas, Alexander Csoma de Körös.

Brian Hodgson's return to Kathmandu as Residency Postmaster was the lowest point in his career until the disaster of his enforced departure from Kathmandu two decades later. If he was to remain in the Bengal Civil Service and continue to provide for his family then he had to find some means of distinguishing himself. That was the classic means of advancement in British India, often achieved through the active prosecution of what was known in Anglo-Indian argot as a *shoke*, from the Arabic *shauq*, meaning an all-consuming hobby or quest.

A *shoke* was a great antidote to loneliness. Edward Gardner's *shoke* was his gardening and plant-collecting, and it could be said that Hodgson already had a *shoke* of sorts in his reading. 'I have drawn the chief joys of my life from this fount,' Hodgson would later write of his love of books. He had always been a voracious reader and ever since his first appointment to Kumaon had indulged in the luxury of ordering books by the box-load from Calcutta. But all such extravagances had had to end with his new posting and the greatly diminished salary attached to it. A new and less expensive *shoke* was now required – and urgently, with time running out on him.

There is some evidence that Hodgson flirted with the idea of following his superior and his ill-fated predecessor Robert Stuart by taking up botany. In a letter to Dr Nathaniel Wallich, written in 1824, he asks him to identify four plants he has sent him, including one with a strong but not unpleasant odour. Nothing came of it, perhaps because botany was very much Edward Gardner's *shoke*.

So Brian Hodgson turned his attention to the animal kingdom, kicking off with woodcock and snipe – or possibly a wild dog – or even an Indian rhinoceros. Unicorns and antelopes were also involved, although probably a little after. Whatever beast or bird it was that started it, zoology was certainly involved.

It was a given that in the Cold Weather months every British *sahib* on the Indian sub-continent worth his salt should spend his early mornings galloping about on a horse and his late afternoons loosing off with a shotgun at any available form of wild fowl other than peacocks – viewed by Hindus as the vehicle of the god Vishnu and thus sacred. Hodgson was as keen as the next *sahib* on riding and on shooting for sport, known throughout the sub-continent as *shikar* – one of the many Persian words that had crept into the vernacular of Hindustan and enthusiastically adopted by the British.

Despite the restrictions imposed on their movements Hodgson and his colleagues at the Residency were permitted to take specified rides and to go out into the surrounding fields after lesser game, or what Hodgson described as 'the strenuous idleness of woodcock shooting'. Hodgson would in due course write to his sister Fanny that: 'In the six colder months I follow the woodcock and pheasant with all the energy of a Nimrod, and I always relish the sweet air and noble scenery of this fine region.'[3] And like so many young hunters before and since, a passion for *shikar* evolved by degrees into a keen interest in wildlife for its own sake.

The Nepal Valley in the 1820s was utterly different from the overcrowded, desperately polluted conurbation that is the Kathmandu Valley today. What had once been a primeval lake had dried into a more or less flat plain filled with soft alluvial silt ideal for farming, blessed with enough rainfall to produce two harvests a year: rice in the spring and wheat and pulses, along with a second rice harvest, in the autumn. This fecundity had enabled the Valley's Newars to develop a unique mountain valley civilisation rich in religious art and architecture and concentrated on four main towns, leaving the rest of the valley to the cultivators known as *Jyapu*. Most of the valley floor was thus under the *Jyapu* hand plough, broken here and there by small copses and winding streams, making it ideal country for the genus *Scolopacidae* in the form of snipe and woodcock.

'In Nepal, as in England, the snipe is not entirely migratory,' Hodgson was to write of the former, 'They are most abundant at the close of the rains, when the whole country is covered with rice then ready for the sickle; every field presenting a swamp, just freed from water. In the spring they are found in the corn and mustard fields, near the permanent swamps; of which there are many in Nepal. In the winter they are scarce, for want of cover.' The best months for *shikar* were in the autumn, when the Rains had cleared: 'In October, in a single rice-field, twenty and thirty birds will be found, huddled together: and every Indian Sportsman knows that in a snipe country his two guns are never suffered to grow cold.'[4]

The woodcock followed much the same pattern, although these were entirely migratory:

The woodcock makes his appearance here, probably about a month after the close of the rains, and remains with us until the accession of the Hot Weather ... From the multitude of small-sized birds killed in November, I conjecture that the woodcock breeds near to us in the north, just beyond the influence of the Rains; that he remains on the Indian side of the Himalaya, except during the rainy and hottest months of the year; and that during the other eight months, by descending and ascending the various steps of the ladder of the Himachal, he preserves (as he may, almost with out an effort), that moderate temperature which he loves. The central region, equidistant from the snows, on one hand, and the plains on the other, seems to be his favourite abode.

Here was Hodgson the hunter learning by methodical and accurate observation, although it would be another six years before this particular essay on the common and rare species of snipe and woodcock found in Nepal was fit to publish.

As to his first appearance in print, it was the rhinoceros that won the honours – specifically, *Rhinoceros unicornis*, the one-horned Indian rhinoceros that had once roamed the entire Gangetic and Indus plains but was now confined to the riverine grasslands of Assam and the Nepal Tarai.

A number of these one-horned rhinoceri were housed in a menagerie belonging to the king of Nepal, Raja Rajendra Bikram Shah. When Hodgson first came to Kathmandu the boy-king was nine years old and very much under the respective thumbs of his stepmother the Queen Regent and the Chief Minister Bhimsen Thapa. Edward Gardner was only allowed to speak directly to the boy during the two annual state festivals but he and his junior officers were, it seems, permitted to visit the royal menagerie, located within the grounds of the Rani Bagh gardens – today the modern royal palace grounds vacated by the last king of Nepal in 1990.

Hodgson was a regular visitor to the menagerie even before his first withdrawal from Kathmandu, and there in about December

1822 he witnessed a pair of rhinos mating – decorously described by him as 'voluntarily associated'. Then some seventeen or eighteen months later, in early May 1824 – that is to say, after his return to Kathmandu – Hodgson saw the product of that same union: a three-day-old rhino calf, which he described as 'distinguished in its exterior character from its mother, by a bright pink suffusion, which pervaded its hide, and by the absence of the nasal horn'.[5]

Hodgson took measurements of the creature – the length of the head along the crown was one foot and half an inch; the circumference of same was two feet; circumference of body two feet, two and a half inches; length from tip of the snout to tip of the tail four and a half feet – and returned to the Residency to write an excited account of what he had seen for Dr Nathaniel Wallich at the Calcutta Botanic Garden:

> As the whole mystery of procreation, gestation etc among the rhinoceros is, I fancy, utterly unknown, I proceed to tell you what I have learned & seen on the present occasion. The female is one of a herd which has been several years in the possession of the Court; the males & females of which, however, had never previously had any carnal connexion with each other; she lent herself voluntarily to the male about 18 months ago – and the fruit of the intercourse was a fine young animal.[6]

How Dr Wallich responded is not known but Hodgson returned to the royal menagerie many times thereafter to study the rhinoceros calf and to repeat his measurements. He had read that the French scientists Buffon and Desmarets had stated that the gestation of the rhinoceros did not exceed nine months, and here was proof that this was not so. Hodgson's correction of their error formed the basis of what was to become his first scientific paper: 'Remarks on the procreation of the Rhinoceros'.

In that same excited letter written to Wallich in early May 1824 Hodgson also speculated on the existence of the supposed Tibetan unicorn, perhaps unaware that the one-horned *qilin* had been a fixture in Chinese mythology for millennia. 'Is it not singular,' he declared, 'that the Bhotias continue most steadfastly & universally to maintain the existence of the Unicorn; draw its figure without a moment's hesitation; & fluently describe it in terms, which turned literally into fiction, would be closely those used by Pliny to characterise the *"fera monaceros"*? I shall however doubt & shall do so till mine eyes behold the beast.'

'Bhotia', which Hodgson variously spelled 'Bhotea', 'Bhootea' or 'Bhoteah', was the Nepali term for the people of the land of Bhot, the proper name for Tibet – the last being an alien word of Persian origin quite unknown to Tibetans and Nepalis alike.

What had sparked Hodgson's interest in the Tibetan unicorn was the acquisition of the horn of just such a supposed creature by the commander of the Residency escort, Lieutenant George Robinson, who had sent it to Dr Wallich for presentation to the Asiatic Society of Bengal's new museum. Wallich had done as asked, informing those present at a meeting of the Society that the horn had been brought to Nepal 'by a Bhootea from the neighbourhood of Lassa, together with a rude drawing of the animal, which was represented in the form of a unicorn' – adding that, in his opinion, 'it will be found to be a species of Antelope'.[7]

Quite by chance, within days of writing to Wallich about his disbelief in Tibetan unicorns, Hodgson's eyes did indeed behold just such a unicorn's horn – or rather, a second horn of the supposed creature. This he found suspended from the ceiling of the temple on the summit of the nearby hill known to him as 'Sumb'hoo Nath' – an edifice that he would come to know extremely well over the next few years. This horn had only recently arrived from Tibet – more specifically, from a 'tract of country situated a few days to the north-west of Digurche [Shigatse], known to the natives by the name of *Chaugdung* [*Chang-tang*, the great Tibetan plateau]'.

This second unicorn horn was also despatched to the Asiatic Society's museum by way of Nathaniel Wallich, together with further drawings of the supposed unicorn made by a Tibetan peasant:

The drawings are stated to convey the true image of a living animal of the deer kind, out of the centre of whose forehead grows a horn of the description transmitted. The animal is described as gregarious, gramnivorous, and its flesh is good to eat. Its name is *Chiroo*, its colour bright bay ... The testimony of the poor *B'hoteas,* whom trade and religion bring down annually to Nepaul, appears to be uniform respecting the existence of this animal; but they hesitate about procuring it, though urged by the promise of a liberal reward. They declare that the *Chiroo* is too large and fierce to be taken alive, or to fall under their simple weapons, but they sometimes find the horns, naturally shed by the living, or remaining after the decay of the dead animal. These horns they dedicate to their divinities.[8]

Hodgson's promise of a 'liberal reward' had the desired effect, because more examples of supposed unicorn horns began turning up – but now in pairs, and in one instance, still affixed to a skull, allowing Hodgson to write his second zoological paper: 'On the supposed unicorn of the Himalayas'.[9] As Hodgson explained in his accompanying letter to Dr Wallich, he now had clear proof that the supposed unicorn of Tibet was just as he and the doctor had surmised, being nothing more than a 'bicornate Antelope', known to the Tibetans and Nepalis as the *Chiru*.

The Wallich correspondence preserved at the Calcutta Botanic Garden shows that at this same time Hodgson sent Wallich a second package, with instructions to forward it to the Museum of Natural History in Paris. This second packet contained a pair of horns and the pelt of the *Chiru* together with a copy of Hodgson's paper refuting the claims of the two French savants Buffon and Desmarets.

Thanks to Wallich, Brian Hodgson's first two papers came before the members of the Asiatic Society of Bengal at the first meeting of the year of 1825, held at its new premises at the corner of Chowringhee and Park Street on 5 January. Under the Society's rules these meetings were bi-monthly, and held at eight o' clock in the evening on the first Sunday of the month. In the Chair on that occasion was its Secretary, Dr Horace Hayman Wilson, who showed no interest either in the single-horned rhinoceros or the bicornate antelope.

Although Dr Nathaniel Wallich was by now one of the Asiatic Society of Bengal's leading lights, he remained always in the shadow of the genial but formidable Dr Horace Wilson, who was to dominate the Asiatic Society of Bengal for over two decades as its Secretary and as the editor of its journal *Asiatic Researches*. Dr Wilson's

(Left) The omniscient Orientalist and Sanskritist Dr Horace
Hayman Wilson, who dominated the Asiatic Society of Bengal as
its Secretary from 1811 to 1832. A watercolour painted in 1821 by his
deputy at the Calcutta Mint, James Atkinson. National Portrait
Gallery. (Right) The unfortunate Dr Clarke Abel, whose support
for Brian Hodgson's first excursions into zoology ended with his
death in November 1826. From a contemporary engraving.

day job was running the Calcutta Mint but with his finger in a great
many other enterprises. As a translator of Sanskrit texts and champion of Hindu culture Wilson was peerless. But while he shared Sir
William Jones's passion for Sanskrit he lacked his breadth of vision
and his spirit of enquiry. He showed little interest in natural philosophy, which was now in the process of rebranding itself as science and
natural history.

It was partly to bypass this intellectual logjam that in 1824 Dr
Wallich proposed the formation of the Asiatic Society's Physical Committee, which was duly set up with Dr Clarke Abel as its Secretary.

Dr Abel was yet another of those versatile doctors of medicine
who, like Drs Buchanan-Hamilton, Wallich and Wilson, had turned
their medical training to wider use.[10] As Secretary of the Asiatic Society's Physical Committee, Dr Abel saw to it that Hodgson's letter on
the Indian rhinoceros was read at that committee's second meeting,
held on 9 February 1825, with Dr Abel in the chair. There was only
an audience of five, but it was Brian Hodgson's first brush with fame
as a budding zoologist. It also led Dr Abel to write enthusiastically
to Hodgson suggesting that they collaborate in gathering zoological

material from Nepal – to which Hodgson replied with equal enthusiasm, inviting him to 'send up a native or two to cure & kill beasts'. He also sent Dr Abel more information about the supposed Tibetan unicorn together with a complete skin with horns attached. This became Brian Hodgson's second paper, 'On the supposed unicorn of the Himalayas', which Dr Abel presented at the third meeting of the Physical Society, albeit in summary form.

As with the rhinoceros, it was the king of Nepal's menagerie that had delivered this complete specimen into Hodgson's lap. The creature had been captured alive on the Tibetan plateau, where the *Chiru* grazed in great herds. It was a young specimen and had been given to the Tashi Lama, the seventh in a line of reincarnate lamas (better known today as the Panchen Lamas) and second in religious authority only to Tibet's Dalai Lama. It had then grown to maturity at the Tashi Lama's monastic seat of Tashi Lhunpo and had then been presented by him to the king of Nepal. At this point Bhimsen Thapa had got to hear of Hodgson's quest for the Tibetan unicorn and had offered the British Residency this newest occupant of the royal menagerie.

So Bhimsen Thapa's gift had joined the Residency's own menagerie, only to die within a month of apparent heatstroke, having failed to adjust to the lower altitude and greater heat: 'His panting showed that even the climate of Nepaul was oppressive to him; he at length sank under a temperature which rarely exceeded 80°.' Part of the antelope's difficulties, Hodgson had discovered, lay in his two layers of fur: an outer layer 'so thick as to present to the hand a sense of solidity; and beneath lay a spare fleece of the softest wool'. That same fine wool is why Hodgson's Tibetan antelope has in recent years been hunted to the edge of extinction.

With this paper Hodgson finally disproved the widespread belief in a unicorn-like creature in Tibet: 'The zeal of Hr. Hodgson ... has at length settled the question respecting the *chiru*, or antelope of the Bhoteahs.' In recognition of Brian Hodgson's discovery, Dr Abel proposed that the Tibetan *Chiru* be given the scientific name of *Antelope hodgsonii* – a generous act that delighted Hodgson. 'This is a pretty compliment & pleases me,' he remarked in a letter to Dr Walllich, 'Not so much because of the fame of the thing but because it shows

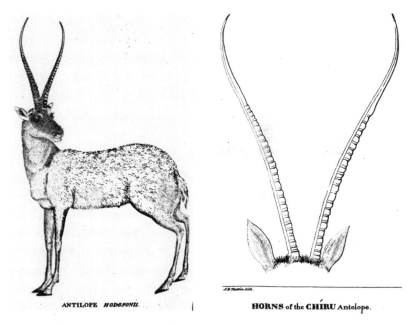

ANTILOPE *HODGSONII.* | HORNS of the CHÍRU Antelope.

The *Chiru* or Tibetan antelope, *Parthelops hodgonii*, and its horns, as reproduced in *Gleanings of Science* in November 1830. These engravings were the first of Brian Hodgson's zoological illustrations to be reproduced, based on drawings by his premier artist, the *chitrakar* Raj Man Singh.

in Dr A. a liberal & gentlemanlike spirit.'[11] In later years Dr Abel's classification was revised to *Panthelops* but *hodgsonii* it still is.[12]

By coincidence, among other papers read at that same third meeting of the Asiatic Society of Bengal's Scientific Committee was one by Horace Wilson's junior assistant at the Bengal Mint, James Prinsep, youngest brother of Henry Thoby Prinsep. Young James was at this time based in Benares and had made a year's worth of meteorological observations the subject of his paper. For him, too, this was to be the first of scores of papers to be read at the Society and subsequently published in the *Asiatic Researches*. Even more remarkably, that same meeting also heard for the first time the name of a third figure who would also be inextricably linked with Hodgson, Prinsep and Buddhist studies: 'An enterprising individual by the name of Mr Alexander Csoma de Körös, a native of Austrian Transylvania and a Hungarian by origin, has succeeded in effecting a journey from

Europe to Tibet, and has been engaged for some time past ... in prosecuting his studies in Ladakh.' Having settled in a Tibetan monastery in Ladakh, this humble and eccentric Hungarian traveller had been taught Tibetan by a Lama and was now engaged in studying 'a large collection of Tibetan Books, three hundred and twenty volumes, which form the basis of the whole system of Tibetan Literature, and Religion'.

Hard on the heels of the unicornate rhinoceros and the bicornate antelope came the wild dogs.

During his first tour in Nepal, Hodgson had tried to tame a number of wild dogs – not the domestic kind gone feral but what was known in India as the *Dhole* (*Canis alpinus*), a species distinct from the main dog family which lived in the jungle and hunted in packs. These *Dhole* were among the earliest denizens of a menagerie started in Edward Gardner's time within the grounds of the British Residency that at various stages held wild sheep, wild goats, at least one yak, various species of deer, several civets, at least six wild cats, one tiger, an unknown number of bears, and an aviary filled with Himalayan pheasants, hornbills, parrots and other birds.

To what extent Hodgson contributed to the enlargement of this zoo is uncertain but he certainly spent a great many hours observing its occupants. For a period of ten months he tried to make pets out of the wild dogs and failed – with the exception of one animal. This was a young specimen which grew tame enough to allow itself to be stroked and was evidently sufficiently docile to accompany him when he first quit Kathmandu for Calcutta in December 1822. For reasons which can only be guessed at, this semi-domesticated pet failed to settle in wherever it was Hodgson was living and was presented by him to the Calcutta menagerie at Barrackpore, where it promptly died.

Again, it was Dr Abel who helped Hodgson make his research more widely known. This was after Hodgson had sent him the pelt of one such animal together with an accompanying note stating that the specimen had been procured 'from the northern side of Himalaya and that its Bhoteah name is Wah'.[13] Although never published, this first note constituted yet another small milestone in his progress towards scientific credibility.

The *Buansu* or wild dog of Nepal, known in India as the *Dhole*,
shown together with the Indian jackal (top left) and Indian fox (top
right). An engraving based on drawings by an unnamed Nepali
artist published to illustrate Hodgson's much improved account
of wild dogs. Published in *Asiatic Researches*, Vol 18, 1831.

Hodgson's rhinoceros, his wild dogs and the Tibetan antelope all
went on to have extended lives in later papers that became increasingly erudite. The rhinoceros, for example, reappeared in an article
on 'On the Growth and Habits of a Young Rhinoceros', published in
the *Edinburgh Journal of Science*, Volume 7, in 1827, allowing Brian
Hodgson – here mistaken for his more senior but unrelated namesake,
John Hodgson, Surveyor-General of India – to correct the animal's
gestation period from eighteen to seventeen months, and to give an
update on its rate of growth: 'From three days to one month it gained
five inches in height, five inches and three quarters in length, and three
inches and three quarters in circumference; while, from the age of one
to fourteen months, it increased one foot seven inches in height, two
feet in length, and two feet seven inches in circumference ...'

The creature's growth continued to be measured and reported on up to December 1825, leading the correspondent to declare that 'the diminished ratio of increase of height remarkable in the later period of development, renders it probable that the animal will yet be a long time in arriving at its adult state, a supposition which is also rendered probable by its seventeen months' gestation, and the slow growth of its horn'.

Hodgson's invitation to Dr Abel to send a hunter up to Nepal came to nothing, in part because the latter had failed to take into account the delicate political situation in Nepal and proposed despatching a Portuguese-Indian named Periera. This threw Hodgson into a panic because he had failed to inform Edward Gardner of his invitation. He hastily wrote back to Dr Abel to explain that he was only permitted to invite 'native' Indians and that they would have to come under the guise of his servants. When Dr Abel failed to reply Hodgson became increasingly alarmed, thinking that he had upset his most valuable ally at the Asiatic Society of Bengal. He then wrote in some distress to Dr Wallich asking him to intercede on his behalf.

The misunderstanding was soon cleared up. However, a surviving letter from Hodgson to Wallich, sent in September 1825, exemplifies a flaw in Brian Hodgson's character that was to dog him throughout his professional life: a tendency in times of stress to lose all sense of proportion, or, as we might put it today, to lose the plot. It led him to write interminable, meandering, increasingly incoherent letters in which he went over the same ground time and time again – and which must have sorely tried the patience of their recipients. In one such letter, Hodgson tries to explain to Wallich that he wants him to find out if Dr Abel had been offended – but without letting him know that he is making this enquiry on Hodgson's behalf. He makes the point with variations over five closely-packed pages, as in the following excerpt:

If you can <u>indirectly</u> hear as much from Dr Abel, you might, in a light & careless way, and <u>as coming from yourself</u>, tell him that this too is a mere bugbear.... If you are on easy terms with Dr A you can perhaps – without mentioning this letter – draw out from him the simple facts – what his past silence means &

what his future intentions be? Like enough, however, his silence has merely proceeded from business, or amusements of another sort – & so means nothing – in which case you should not let him have an inkling of this letter, on any account, but you might say, as from yourself, that (in regard to his future intention to prosecute the plan of sending folks up here) you had heard he meant to send up a native or two, to cure & kill beasts, & if he was still bent on that plan, he should send a word to him [that] the time was now come [sic]. I don't however propose to indulge the gentleman in his caprices – if he be subject to such, & would not have you broach that proposition unless you find room for belief that his past apparent sins of omission were the unintentional result of his vocations of pleasures at the City of Palaces [Calcutta]. And lastly, my dear Wallich, do the thing (if you have time to do it all) without letting him see that I am your prompter ... etc[14]

In Kathmandu Edward Gardner and his staff had followed the progress of the war in Burma with keen interest, knowing that an adverse outcome was bound to have a knock-on effect in Nepal. But once Arakan had been occupied in April 1825 Bhimsen Thapa became markedly more relaxed in his relations with *Jan Kampani Bahadur*. A wary friendship of sorts began to develop between Nepal's Chief Minister and the two official representatives of the British Government in India. 'I persevered,' Hodgson afterwards wrote of his own efforts to get on better terms with Bhimsen Thapa. 'Time, patience, and dextrous applications to the superior intelligence of the Chief Minister, at length rewarded my toils.'[15]

Although still confined to the Nepal Valley and still watched, Hodgson and his colleagues were now permitted to wander without hindrance through the market squares and backstreets of Kathmandu and Patan.

In our age of mass tourism it is easy to forget how isolated Nepal was at the start of the nineteenth century and how astonishing the four towns of the Valley and their outlying temples and shrines must have appeared to Hodgson and his fellow Britons. It was all new to them, even to those who had known the temple city of Benares. Nowhere on the Indian sub-continent was there anything to match

the sheer diversity and colour of the religious architecture packed
into those few square miles. Even to this day, after all the moderni-
sation and the destruction of so many old buildings that has taken
place in recent times, no first-time visitor can walk through the
central *chowks* of Kathmandu, Patan, Bhatgaon or Kirtipur without
being blown away by what is on display (*see Plate 10*).

Nowadays we come prepared. In Hodgson's day there was no
such forewarning. Some of the stone structures and their attendant
deities he and his friends recognised as Hindu temples and Hindu
gods – but not the multi-tiered towers on their pyramidal stone
plinths, with their brazen roofs and their intricately carved wooden
underpinnings, structures that seemed to have more in common
with the pagodas on Chinese porcelain than anything in India – nor
the hundreds of semi-hemispherical structures of stone with their
curious spires that were to be found in abundance in every shape and
size and were unlike anything they had ever seen – and certainly not
the statues and bronzes attached to them, which were of a totally different order to the Hindu pantheon.

All these structures and their attendant deities Dr Francis
Buchanan-Hamilton had correctly identified as Buddhist in his
Account of the Kingdom of Nepal, published in 1819, but without
being able to explain how or why.

In his old age Brian Hodgson would claim that it was soon after
his first arrival in Nepal in 1821 – when he was barely twenty years
old – that he first began to 'devise means of procuring some accurate
information relative to Buddhism: for, though the popular investigations of such a subject was foreign to my pursuits, my respect for
science led me cheerfully to avail myself of the opportunity afforded,
by my residence in a Bauddha country, for collecting and transmit-
ting to Calcutta the materials for such investigation'.[16]

But this was Brian Hodgson indulging in a little tidying of his own
history. Even after his return to Kathmandu in the spring of 1824 he
showed no particular interest in the religious pursuits of the inhabitants of the Valley – and when he did it was focused not on Nepal and
its people but on their neighbours to the north: Bhot and the Bhotias.

The one surviving piece of evidence to support Hodgson's claim
is an inscription written in ink at the base of a crudely painted

An undated drawing in pencil captioned in Brian Hodgson's
handwriting 'The Vihar of Kathya Swayambhu in the City of
Kathmandu with its various Chaityas & Mandala', better known
today as the Kathesimbhu Bahal or Dharmakirti Vihara (Monastery).
It is also signed by Hodgson's premier *chitrakar* Raj Man Singh.
RAS Hodgson Collection 022.032. © Royal Asiatic Society.

watercolour of the Amitabh Buddha that now forms part of the
Hodgson Collection at the Royal Asiatic Society in London, to
which it was presented in 1826. This inscription reads 'Mythological
picture from Naypaul. Brought by Mr Hodgson in 1823'. The numeral
'3' is probably a slip of the pen or an error, with 1825 the intended date.

The Royal Asiatic Society of Great Britain and Ireland (to give
it its full name, but hereafter shortened to Royal Asiatic Society)
had been set up in London in March 1823 by Henry Colebrooke
and other retired members of the Asiatic Society of Bengal as a
sort of mirror image of that society, and with very much the same
aims. Among those who answered its appeal for books, manuscripts
and other objects of interest was Colonel William Franklin, a well-
known Orientalist and antiquarian, who is recorded on 4 November 1826 as the donor of a number of sculptures, manuscripts and
drawings, including Hodgson's Amitabh Buddha painting. On that
same day of 4 November 1826 the Royal Asiatic Society archivist also

recorded the receipt of donations from Brian Hodgson himself, but brought to England on Hodgson's behalf by Colonel Franklin.

This was, in fact, Hodgson's third unsolicited gift of Buddhist material to a learned body, the first having been made to Fort William College Library in 1824 following an appeal for original manuscripts from the college's longstanding Professor of Bengali, the Baptist missionary William Carey. The only evidence for that first donation of manuscripts is in a letter partially quoted by Hodgson's biographer, W. W. Hunter. It was dated 5 December 1824 and addressed to William Butterfield Bayley, who at this time was a member of the Governor-General Supreme Council and a member of the Council of Fort William College.

In his letter Hodgson somewhat pointedly states: 'What I have already sent have cost me sundry rupees too numerous to be mentioned – yet cheerfully given'. He then goes on to express his astonishment at how many Tibetan manuscripts are available in Nepal: 'I saw the other day a house full of manuscripts, hardly one legible, and the instance I am told is not a solitary one in this valley. Do look at the first five numbers on my list. That is, look at the great work so indicated, and tell me if in so large a body some soul of Tibetan literature must not needs be found ... Nepal has many old valuables going fast to oblivion, and Tibet probably has many more. But these things are expensive'.[17]

So here is evidence that Hodgson was collecting religious manuscripts of Tibetan origin and sending them down to Calcutta in 1824 – and at his own cost. Bayley evidently took the hint because it was soon afterwards agreed by the Fort William College Council that Hodgson's costs should be met. Subsequently, on 9 March 1825 the fruits of Brian Hodgson's second collection of Tibetan Buddhist material were laid before the members of the Asiatic Society of Bengal.

And what a bizarre array of articles they were – ranging from ritual drums and religious utensils to wooden printing blocks and paintings on cloth. However, the bulk of the donation was indeed made up of manuscripts, nearly all in the distinctive bold lettering of the Tibetan form of the Sanskritic script.

This material had come from two sources. Some had been obtained, as Hodgson explained, 'from the Bhotea peasants and monks whom religion or trade bring down annually to Nipal'. That Hodgson was regularly mixing with such Bhotias at this time is confirmed by an aside in one of a handful of surviving letters written to his little sister Fanny. It dates from 1825 and in it Hodgson speaks of being 'busy among my bluff friends from Tibet, who are now here on their annual visit'.[18]

Those Bhotias were mostly traders and sheep- and goat-herders who crossed the Central Himalayan Range into Nepal in early summer when the snows on the mountain passes began to melt. They wore heavy, brightly-coloured robes made from yak hair, their hands and faces were blackened with dirt and they stank of the yak butter with which they smeared their extremities to give some protection from exposure (*see Plate 14*). Not surprisingly, the manuscripts and charms that Hodgson bought from them he described as 'somewhat decayed and soiled – but usually quite legible'.

The first point of call for these summer visitors to the Nepal Valley was invariably the awe-inspiring monument known to Hodgson as the Khesa Chit – but better known today as Bauddha or, more popularly, Bodhnath: a vast semi-hemispherical mound, set on a series of platforms and topped by a cube roofed with a spire, that rose out of the valley floor two miles north-east of Kathmandu. According to the Tibetans, it had been constructed in the eighth century by the first king to unite their people under one rule and had ever since been maintained by their lamas, drawn from the oldest school of Tibetan Buddhism, the *Nyingmapa*, sometimes referred to as the 'Red Hats'.

The Bodhnath stupa was barely half an hour's ride across the fields from the British Residency and in Hodgson's time it was surrounded by nothing more than a few thatched huts. Today this is the hub of a large and thriving community of Tibetans in exile, where a score of monastic institutions representing all the schools of Tibetan Buddhism compete for space with souvenir shops, rooftop restaurants and coffee bars.

The cleaner manuscripts in Hodgson's donation were also Tibetan in origin, but these had come from another source altogether: Hodgson's 'Swogoombhoo Nath' – more accurately, Swayambhunath, the hill temple of the 'Self-created Lord' – agreed by one and all to be the oldest religious structure in Nepal (*see Plate 11*).

A pencil drawing of the Bodhnath stupa done in Western style by an unnamed *chitrakar*, undated but (from the watermark) from 1841 or after. RAS Hodgson Collection 022.038. © Royal Asiatic Society.

As at Bodhnath, the most striking feature of this dome were the pairs of eyes painted onto the four sides of the cube at the base of its spire. Set into niches on the sides of the dome at the cardinal points were statues, representing what Brian Hodgson would come to recognise as the *Dhyani Buddhas,* or the Celestial Buddhas, enormously important figures in the Buddhism of Nepal and Tibet. Surrounding the dome were both Hindu and Buddhist temples, including the prayer-hall of a Tibetan monastery.

Hodgson was then unaware that the Tibetan presence at Swayambhu was of comparatively recent origin. A century earlier a king of Gorkha had been unable to produce a son and heir and had turned for help to a lama of Tibet. A son was duly born who rose to become Raja Prithvi Narayan Shah, the unifier of Nepal. The lama's reward was a grant of land at Swayambhunath upon which he built his monastery.

This picturesque hilltop temple and its Tibetan monastery evidently struck a chord with Hodgson and it became a favourite

Swayambhu hill viewed from the road to Kathmandu. Detail from an undated pencil drawing signed by Hodgson's premier artist Raj Man Singh. RAS Hodgson Collection 022.009. © Royal Asiatic Society.

destination on his early morning rides: 'The majestic size and severe simplicity of outline of this temple, with its burnished cone set off by the dark granite of woods, constitute the *chaitya* of Swayambhu Nath a very beauteous object.'

It must surely have been of this site that Hodgson was thinking when he wrote in a letter to his sister Fanny of how it was his custom to 'go alone, for my companions are no antiquaries, and explore some old Buddhist temple and muse and meditate, like the famous Roman amid the Ruins, upon the changes and chances of the world. Here are before me the traces of a creed which once divided with Brahmanism the minds of the Hindus, but of which no visible trace, nay, not even an intelligible legend, remains in all the vast continent of India!'[19]

With a little effort one can follow Hodgson's footsteps up the supposed 365 steps that take you past the squabbling families of monkeys to the summit itself, where a few more strides bring you to the two shrines that flank the top of the stairs. Turn right and you come almost at once to the curtained entrance of the Tibetan prayer hall, where morning and evening the monks in their yellow and red robes chant their prayers to the accompaniment of horns, trumpets and drums.

When Hodgson first climbed to the top of Swyambhu hill the scene would have been rather different from what we see today. The great dome at the centre together with its cube and spire had been wrecked by the great storm of 1816. Because this had occurred immediately after the defeat of Makwanpur and the foisting on Nepal of a British Resident, the event had been interpreted as a bad omen and no repairs had been attempted. However, in 1825, what we should from now on refer to as the *stupa* and *harmika* were opened up to allow a new central beam to be set in place and a new pinnacle – more properly, a *hasti* – erected and faced with gilt. At this same time the stupa was newly plastered, and the *harmika* repainted with four sets of eyes, representing the all-seeing compassion of the Buddha.

This restoration was witnessed by Hodgson and his colleagues. In the notes accompanying his donation Hodgson states that he got to know the monastery's 'principal officiating Lama, resident there', and 'an intelligent *Gelung*, or monk' – who may well have been one and the same. Either way, his contacts with the lamas at Swyambhu were so productive that he was able to secure from them a number of religious texts printed from hand-cut wood blocks as well as a range of items that included:

> Four large works – in print – whose reputation had gained them a place in the archives of Swogoombhoo Nath ... Another large work – manuscript – with an illuminated frontispiece ... A large collection of *Juntras* [charms] or *Taveezes* [charms, from the Arabic *taweedh*] – all printed, and in fine condition ... Some remarkable little pictures of *Muha Kalu* [Shiva as Destroyer] – in various forms – with, and without, a *Sukty* [*Shakti* or female principle] ... Emblems and prayers-addressed to the Angel of Death, in the event of sickness: obtained from the lama of Swogoombhoo, after he had used them himself in the case of his child's illness ... Curious little pictures, exhibiting the Lama, with a *Sukty*![20]

Also originating from this same source were ten large painted wall-hangings from Tibet known as *Thangkas*. These were said to

The prayer-hall of the Tibetan monastery at Swayambhu, with *thangkas* hanging from the central beam and cloth-wrapped sutras piled on the shelves. This was probably the scene of Hodgson's early discussions with the resident lamas, and it was here, too, that Hodgson found the horn of the Tibetan 'unicorn', which he correctly identified as coming from the *Chiru* or Tibetan antelope. Detail from a watercolour by Dr Henry Oldfield, dated October 1855. BL Oldfield Collection WD 3301. © The British Library Board.

show 'the chief Lama or *Budhs*; the "*Punj Budh*" or five celestial *Bhuds* of Bhote (and of Nipal); some subordinate Divinities, especially *Muha Kalu* – and other persons and things, full of meaning and interest, with reference to the Buddhism of Bhote'.

In Hodgson's accompanying letter he expressed his surprise that reading and writing should have been so widespread in Tibet 'as to reach persons covered with filth, and destitute of any of these luxuries which usually precede the luxury of books'. This, Hodgson presumed, was due to the extensive use of wood-block printing in that country, which was itself an equally striking phenomenon. He was also puzzled as to why the Tibetans' writing seemed to have such a close affinity to Indian Sanskrit even though their language did not. He had placed the Sanskrit Alphabet in front of his Tibetan lama, who had 'at once recognised in it the parent of his own language and, upon his proceeding to compare the two Alphabets with each other, the differences between them seemed to be extremely trifling'. As Csoma de Körös had already surmised, the Tibetan script was indeed derived from written Sanskrit.

The despatch of this donation to the Asiatic Society of Bengal, received in Calcutta in February 1825, probably took place at much the same time as Hodgson's donation to the Royal Asiatic Society, even if it was only handed over to the Society by Col. Franklin in November 1826. That, too, was largely made up of Tibetan articles, suggesting the same Tibetan sources.

Among the items listed in this latter donation was a 'Picture of *Wuh puh muh* [*Ö-pa-me*, the Tibetan name for the Buddha Amitabh], the fourth *Dhyani*, or Celestial Buddha – called *Umitabhu* in Sanscrit' – which we can probably link to Franklin's Amitabh Buddha donation mentioned earlier (*see Plate 12*). There was also 'a View of the *Goombu* [*gompa*, monastery], or Lama's Residence' – a painting in the Tibetan style showing in detail a hill covered with Tibetan houses with a monastery at the centre – almost certainly the great monastic complex of Tashi Lhunpo, home of the Tashi Lama, sited close to the regional capital of south central Tibet, Shigatse, which Hodgson knew as Digurche (*see Plate 13*).

The most bizarre item on the list – at least from Hodgson's point of view – was an amulet to be worn round the neck, listed by him as 'a Hollow Trinket for holding the Divine Lama's Excrement'. Other items included:

> The *Mooni*, or Praying Cylinder ... a Wooden Drinking Cup, constantly carried in the Bosom; Amulets, containing Deprecatory Prayers ... a Guard to protect the Eyes from the glare of Snow ... a Mould, for the casting of Earthen Idols ... Three Blocks of Birch, used in Printing ... a White Silk Scarf, to envelop Letters of Ceremony ... Models in Clay of the *Chaityee* or Pyramidal Temple, appropriated to the principal Gods of the Buddhists ... Several Printed and MS Tracts in the Bhotea Language ... a Buddhic Tract in the Newari, or Aboriginal Language of Nipal ... Religious Pictures of the *Siva Margi Newars*. [21]

These two collections of mostly Tibetan Buddhist bits and bobs sent down to India from Kathmandu early in 1825 show an inexperienced and undiscriminating collector at work. But they also tell us that Brian Hodgson at twenty-four had began to take a special interest in what had only recently been termed 'Buddhism' – a word that Hodgson particularly disliked, along with 'Buddhist'.

Yet Hodgson came away from his encounters with the Tibetan lamas of Bodhnath and Swayambhunath with few answers. Perhaps the lamas were ignorant or Hodgson asked the wrong questions, but the most likely explanation is the language barrier. Hodgson spoke Bengali, Urdu and Nepali but not Tibetan and it is highly unlikely that any of the interpreters attached to the British Residency did so either.

These interpreters were all Hindu Pandits, drawn from the Brahman priestly caste and recruited from the highly orthodox city of Benares, with a marked prejudice against Buddhists and what they regarded as the heresy of Buddhism. Hodgson would afterwards recall one example of such Brahmanical prejudice when he sought the assistance of one of the Residency Pandits in translating a Buddhist text: 'My pandit (a Brahman of Benares) soon declined co-operation with us, full of indignation at the author and his work!'[22]

There was also the element of local hostility, made up partly of Nepali xenophobia but also 'arising out of the jealousy of the people in regard to any profanation of their sacred things by an European'. Even in the 1960s the Newars continued to take pollution by those they considered outcastes very seriously. Western visitors had to avoid such seemingly innocent acts as allowing one's shadow to fall on a Newar, or touching his plate or drinking vessel. The Tibetans, on the other hand, had no such caste taboos, and it may be that Hodgson's first enquiries were directed towards the Tibetans visitors to the Valley simply because they were more open-minded.

But the decisive factor, surely, was the change of circumstances in Hodgson's own life.

In April 1825 Brian Hodgson received the news he must have prayed for throughout the previous fifteen months: official confirmation of his reappointment as assistant to Edward Gardner, together with the restoration of the generous salary that went with it. That reappointment changed everything. It was not just that Hodgson had a future once more. He now had a real incentive to continue. What had hitherto been nothing more than unfocused *shokes* now became serious studies.

THE CHAITYA OF DEVA PATANA.

'The stupa of Deva Patana', located between Kathmandu and Bodhnath, said to have been raised by Emperor Ashoka's daughter. A lithograph made 'from a drawing by a Nipalese Painter', *Transactions of the Royal Asiatic Society*, Vol. II, 1830.

5

'My old Bauddha': Assistant to the Resident, 1825–28

Even before his restoration as assistant to Edward Gardner in April 1825 Hodgson had begun to pay a hunter to bring him animal trophies from outside the Valley – a *shikari* who, from the evidence of the first specimens brought in, was a Bhotia or trans-Himalayan trader rather than a Valley dweller. Only the name of one of these hunters employed by Hodgson over the course of many years is known: Chebu Lama, which suggests a Sherpa, Tamang or Gurung origin.

However, the dramatic improvement in Hodgson's fortunes in April 1825 meant that he could now afford to employ more hunters and trappers as well as a local artist to draw some of these same specimens to his specifications. That first artist was initially put to work doing what he did best: drawing and painting miniatures for religious works such as illustrated manuscripts, wall hangings and temple decorations according to the set traditions of his ancestors.

A batch of such drawings, showing 'Buddha shrines and temples in Nepal', was presented by Hodgson to the Asiatic Society in Calcutta in December 1825. Their 'interesting character' was noted by Dr Horace Wilson but the only part of Hodgson's accompanying letter that Wilson found sufficiently interesting to publish was his account of the unnamed artist who had drawn them. He was a Newar and a Buddhist and he belonged to a hereditary caste of artists known as *chitrakars*, or 'image-makers', employed to paint wall-hangings, known as *paubhas,* with religious scenes:

The drawings are the work of a native artist, or *Chitrakár*, one of a numerous and respectable class. The artists of Nepal commence their education at ten years of age and hence acquire great manual dexterity, which is displayed in the minuteness and fidelity of their drawings. Their apparatus is of the simplest kind: for outlines slightly shaded, a piece of charcoal, and iron style, and one small brush made of goat's hair, are all the implements employed, with which the artists sits himself upon the ground, and without any support for his paper executes his drawings. The colours he uses are brilliant and durable, but as the study of natural tints is not part of the artist's training, it may be easily conceived that this is a branch of the art in which he does not particularly excel.[1]

Nothing more was said of the significance of these first donated drawings, and none of them appear to have survived.

'I kept constantly at work for years two native artists,' Hodgson would afterwards write of the thousands of drawings he accumulated over the next three decades, 'in copying whatever was forthcoming of architecture, of sculpture, or of picture[s] belonging to Buddhism, and as my artists were of that same creed, and were, moreover, superintended by a learned Pundit of the same faith, there was no danger of Brahmanical edifices or idols being taken for Saugata [Buddhist]'.[2]

'A learned Pundit of the same faith' – that was the key.

Almost by chance – or so it seemed – Hodgson had stumbled upon a quite exceptional informant: an elderly Buddhist scholar of whom he would afterwards speak in such warm terms as 'my old Bauddha', 'my old friend and preceptor' and 'my learned old friend Amritananda *Vajra Acharya*' – that term *vajra-acharya* being the title of a tantric master empowered to transmit the esoteric teachings of Vajrayana, the Diamond or Thunderbolt Path of Tantric Buddhism. In Amritananda's case that honorific was fully justified, for the Newar Pandit was to prove himself a veritable diamond of the highest quality.

'I privately instituted enquiries,' was how Hodgson explained the circumstances of their first encounter, in the course of which the reputation for knowledge of an old Bauddha residing in the city of Pátan, drew one of my people to his abode ... The Pátan Bauddha seemed very intelligent, and my curiosity was excited ... This old man assured me that Nepaul contained many large works relating to Buddhism; and of some of these he gave me a list ... His list gradually enlarged as his confidence increased; and, at length, chiefly through his kindness, and his influence with his brethren in the Bauddha faith, I was enabled to procure and transmit to Calcutta a large collection of Buddhist scriptures. [3]

However, Hodgson's meeting up with Amritananda may not have been quite such a matter of chance as he imagined. The pandit's own community was facing a crisis. Prior to the Gorkha conquest, Hinduism and Buddhism had co-existed in the Valley more or less amicably for centuries, even under several dynasties of Hindu kings. Hindu and Buddhist deities stood side by side on Buddhist shrines, and Hindu deities such as Bhairava had been accommodated within the tantric form of Buddhism followed by the Newars, who themselves had adopted their own version of the Hindu caste system. As the middlemen between India and Tibet, the Newars had prospered as traders. But following their subjugation by Prithvi Narayan Shah in 1768 they had become an oppressed underclass. Their lands were confiscated, their trading links with Tibet and India were cut and they lost the royal patronage that had supported their religious institutions and kept their temples in repair. To make matters worse, their new rulers were also ardent devotees of Lord Shiva who celebrated their devotion through such rituals as blood-sacrifice. This was anathema to most Newars, who felt their Buddhist way of life was increasingly under threat.

Prithvi Narayan Shah had made Kathmandu his capital and his successors had followed suit. This included the young Raja Rajendra Bikram Shah, who presided over all the rites and celebrations on the religious calendar as king of Nepal before retiring at the end of each day to the gilded cage that was the royal palace. This was the Hanuman Dhoka Durbar, dominated by the *Nautale*, or 'nine floored' tower, one of four watchtowers built by Prithvi Narayan Shah to dominate each of the Valley's four main towns. He and his successors made good use of the traditional skills of the city's Newar wood-carvers, metal workers and painters to further beautify Kathmandu with new shrines and statues, but nearly all were dedicated to Lord Shiva or his consort Parvati in their most terrible aspects as Bhairava and Kali.

Bhimsen Thapa, too, played his part in what amounted to a revival of Shaiva worship. It was he who organised the erection of the twelve-foot bronze mask of *Swet Bhairava*, the fierce manifestation of Shiva, at the Hanuman Dhoka Chowk, who donated doors of gold and silver to the great Shiva temple of Pashupathinath, and who erected new Shiva temples along the banks of the Vishnumati River, all in the name of the boy king.

Prior to the Gorkha invasion it was Pandit Amritananda's home town of Patan and not Kathmandu that, in terms of culture, had dominated the valley. Patan was known to its sixty-thousand Newar inhabitants as *Lalita-Patan* or simply *Lalitpur*, 'the beautiful city'. It was sited on the Bhagmati River's south bank opposite to Kathmandu, and was reputed to be the oldest town in the Valley, with a history that went at least as far back as that royal apostle of Buddhism, the Indian Emperor Ashoka, who briefly united much of the subcontinent under one government in the second quarter of the third century BCE. It was Ashoka who was said to have built the first Buddhist monuments in the form of stupas at the four cardinal points around the town, and Ashoka's Buddhist daughter and her Kiranti husband were said to have established the first two Buddhist monasteries in the Valley.

Patan was also the least Hindu and the most Buddhist of the major towns and had suffered because of it. Prithvi Narayan Shah had looted the town and then confiscated the *jagirs* or lands attached to its Buddhist *Bahals* or monasteries, so that they lost the revenues that paid for their upkeep. The town went into a rapid decline that was still very obvious when Dr Henry Oldfield took over as the British Residency surgeon in 1850. 'Patan has never recovered from the blow it then received,' he wrote:

It has lost all its social as well as political importance. The spirit of its inhabitants appears to have been completely crushed by the

A corner of one of the inner courtyards of the monastic complex of Uka
Bahal in Patan, the ancestral home of Hodgson's preceptor the Vajracharya
Amritananda – which makes one wonder if the group shown in the drawing
were members of his family. Also known as the Rudravarma Mahavihara,
it was one of the oldest monastic centres in Patan, although Hodgson's
caption states incorrectly that it was built by 'Dan Jyoti Bandya 801 of the
Newar era', corresponding to AD 1680. A pencil drawing probably by Raj
Man Singh. RAS Hodgson Collection 022.044. © Royal Asiatic Society.

loss of their independence, the overthrow of their royal house ...
and the plunder or destruction of all which they hold most sacred.
Its durbar, public buildings, and most of its temples have fallen
into a ruinous and dilapidated state; while the poor Niwars have
not the means to restore them, and seem stricken with a sort of
apathy which prevents their attempting even to check the progress of further decay.[4]

For Newars like Pandit Amritananda this oppression must have
seemed like history repeating itself. The Buddhist chronicles of
Nepal told how centuries earlier the Shaiva revivalist Shankaracharya had led an assault on Buddhism that had brought about its
extinction in India and had tried to do the same in the Nepal Valley.

This may not have been strictly true but that was what Amritananda and his fellow Buddhists believed – and now something very similar appeared to be happening in Nepal under Gorkha rule.

Only the British had stood up to the Gorkhas and this fact would not have been lost on the young Amritananda. In 1803, in circumstances still shrouded in mystery but which might well have put the pandit at serious risk, he had met the British envoy Captain William Knox and had subsequently prepared for him a copy of an ancient Buddhist text written in Sanskrit, the *Lalitavistara* – and no ordinary copy at that, for it carried on top and bottom two miniature paintings, both showing the pandit and Captain Knox (*see Plates 2 & 3 and page 38*). The fact that the second painting shows the horned moon in a dark sky in the background suggests that the presentation took place at night, perhaps for reasons of secrecy.

Whatever Amritananda may have hoped for, that first initiative came to nothing. Knox handed his manuscript over to Henry Colebrooke, at that time the President of the Asiatic Society. As a junior Bengal Civil Servant Colebrooke had sat at the feet of the great Sir William Jones and had come to share his love of Sanskrit. But, in common with his contemporary Horace Wilson, Colebrooke's interest lay in the Hindu classics. He accepted Knox's gift, noted that it was 'a life of the Buddha' written in Sanskrit and left it at that. The *Lalitavistara* was among the many Sanskrit manuscripts that Colebrooke subsequently donated to the HEICo's library in London after he returned to England in 1822. It took a Frenchman to realise the value of Pandit Amritananda's gift – but not until two decades later.

Brian Hodgson seems to have been entirely unaware of Pandit Amritananda's earlier association with Captain Knox and his singular gift. And he appears never to have questioned why Pandit Amritananda should have been so accommodating, attributing it to his own success in securing his trust. Indeed, it was some years before Hodgson himself came to understand how exceptionally fortunate he had been in his choice of informant. It was not simply that the pandit was among the best – if not *the* best – informed Buddhist teachers in Nepal. What made him quite exceptional was that he was prepared to break with centuries of custom to impart sacred knowledge that should have been passed only from *guru* to *chela*, or master to pupil, as part of a long and secret process of initiation. True, these revelations came by stages as the trust between the two parties grew over the years, but the intention to assist seems to have been there from the very start. Here was a quite exceptional man who, whether or not he had his own agenda, has never been given the recognition he deserves in making Vajrayana Buddhism known beyond the Himalayas.

Among the 108 volumes of manuscripts, papers and letters donated by Hodgson to the India Office Library in 1864 – the third and last of his donations to that institution – is a Newar Grammar complied by Pandit Amritananda and a book on the Newari language from the same source. The first is dated to 1831 and it is tempting to see these as the text-books from which Hodgson acquired his working knowledge of that language, with the pandit as his elbow.

Amrita's home town of Patan was a bastion of Vajrayana, or the Diamond Path, the form of Buddhism followed by the Newars and, with significant differences, by the Tibetans. What was quite unknown at the time was that this highly esoteric form of Buddhism had evolved out of mainstream Indian Mahayana, or Great Path, Buddhism as a result of the rich infusion of *tantra*, a means of achieving enlightenment through complex rituals that mixed the mystical with the magical, involving mantras (sacred utterances), *mandalas* (concentric shapes representing the cosmos) and *mudras* (hand gestures). This was Buddhism at its most arcane and least comprehensible – and it was here in Patan, its heartland, that Brian Hodgson's begin his serious enquiries into Buddhism.

The earliest evidence of this happy collusion between pandit and Assistant Resident is contained in a report of a meeting of the Asiatic Society of Bengal in Calcutta that took place in Calcutta on 21 December 1825, at which a Sanskrit manuscript 'illustrative of the Bouddh'ha religion' donated by Hodgson was discussed. Dr Horace Wilson took the floor to explain that he had translated the manuscript without difficulty: 'The Manuscripts he [Hodgson] has hitherto sent have been of little use, being written in languages with which we are not familiar. But he has now transmitted a book which is more available. The text is Sanscrit, interspersed with an interpretation of the Newaree language, which, although differing essentially in base and structure, borrows Sanscrit words so copiously, that the purport of many passages can be made out without the knowledge of the language itself.'[5]

According to Dr Wilson the manuscript was made up of three tracts: 'Rules for the religious observance of the eighth day of the lunar fortnight; the twenty-five stanzas propitiatory of the deities of Nepal; and the praises of the seven Bouddh'has.' However, Wilson's verdict on their value was scathing: 'Of these it would be tedious and uninteresting to give any analysis.'

For Brian Hodgson, this public disparaging of his efforts marked the start of a strained relationship with the Asiatic Society of Bengal that only ended in 1833 with the departure of Dr Horace Wilson to take up a prestigious lectureship at Oxford.

According to Hodgson's own lists of donated Sanskrit Buddhist manuscripts, in the course of what was to be his *annus mirabilis* of 1827 he sent 66 such manuscripts to the Library of Fort William College and 94 to the Library of the Asiatic Society of Bengal. He also donated to Fort William College what was thought at the time to be a complete set, amounting to over a hundred volumes, of the Tibetan *Kangyur*, being the 'translated words' of the Buddha Sakya-muni.[6] And yet, as Hodgson saw it, Wilson and his fellow Sanskrit-ists in Calcutta took no great interest in his donated manuscripts and showed scant appreciation for his efforts.

Years later he gave public vent to these frustrations in a foot-note attached to a reprint of one of his first papers on Buddhism: 'Nearly all (the Buddhist manuscripts on the pandit's list) were even-tually procured, chiefly, and in the first place, solely, for Calcutta. They were deposited first with the librarian of the College of Fort William, then with the Asiatic Society, but were for years utterly neglected, and still are so I fancy.'[7]

To describe these several rebuffs as deliberate is taking it too far, but it is hard to avoid the conclusion that Dr Horace Hayman Wilson was following his own agenda, which included publishing his own highly speculative accounts of Buddhism, and had little time for what he judged to be Brian Hodgson's enthusiastic but ignorant contribu-tions. That Wilson, for his part, did not think highly of Hodgson, can be deduced from his later description of him as a 'waspish animal'!

The better part of a year passed before Hodgson felt confident enough to come back to the Asiatic Society of Bengal, by which time he was well armed, for Pandit Amritananda was now acting both as supplier and mentor.

Soon after their first meeting the pandit had given Hodgson a list of what he considered to be all the important Buddhist scriptures and had then set about procuring them for him. Thanks to Bhimsen Thapa's change of policy the Newars were no longer having to fear 'the displeasure expressed by a Nepalese Government towards such of its subjects as are suspected of imparting to Europeans the knowledge they possess'. Indeed, the Chief Minister had even given his permission for the pandit to visit the British Residency, so that Amritananda now became a regular visitor, spending many hours closeted with the Assistant Resident.

Sanskrit manuscripts now began to accumulate at the Residency with gratifying speed, and with every delivery the 'old Bauddha' became ever more forthcoming – and it was always 'Bauddha' for Hodgson. Although eventually reconciled to the Western term 'Buddhism', Hodgson continued to take exception to 'Buddhist' and stuck to 'Bauddha', just as he stuck to Bhot and Bhoteas for 'Tibet' and 'Tibetans'.

'Let it not be supposed, because these works were procured in Nepal,' wrote Hodgson of his growing collection, 'that they are therefore of a local character. The contrary is asserted by the Bauddhas, and never disputed'.[8] According to the pandit, the sacred scriptures of Buddhism had originally amounted to no less than 84,000 volumes, of which only a small portion now existed, due to the persecution of the Buddhists both in India and in Nepal by the Indian zealot Shankaracharya – 'execrated by every Bauddha as a blood-stained bigot'.[9] This was the same Shankara so much admired as a great Hindu reformer by Sir William Jones in his writings forty years earlier. 'Let the exaggeration on either side be duly weighted,' Hodgson noted. 'The Bauddhas never had eighty-four thousand principal scriptures; nor did Sankara destroy more than a few of those which they really possessed when he came to Nepal.'

Yet the plain fact was that not a single Buddhist scripture had survived in India, which made these Nepalese and Tibetan texts all the more valuable.

These scriptures were known collectively as the *Dharma Ratna*, or Jewel of the Law, of which nine works known as the *Nava Dharma*, were regarded as particularly important by the pandit and his co-religionists in Nepal. 'Why the nine specified works have been selected to be thus peculiarly honoured, I cannot say,' Hodgson had to admit. 'They are probably the oldest and most authentic scriptures in Nipal.'

One of the nine was the *Lalitavistara*, which Hodgson believed – wrongly, but understandably – to be 'the original authority for all those versions of the history of Sakya Sinha which have crept, through various channels, into the notice of Europeans. I esteem myself fortunate in having been the first to discover and procure copies of these important works. To read and meditate them is not for me, but I venture to hint, that by so doing only can a knowledge of genuine Buddhism be acquired.' From this statement it is clear that Amritananda never told Hodgson of his earlier provision of a copy of the *Lalitavistara* to Captain Knox.

After further enquiry Hodgson learned from the pandit that there were other sets of texts just as important as the *Nava Dharma*. These were 'of a highly speculative character, belonging rather to philosophy than religion'. And no sooner had this second category of texts been made available to him than Hodgson became aware of the existence of a third category – to all intents, a secret teaching, involving highly esoteric rites 'which the more prudent Bauddhas chose to keep veiled from all but the initiated'. These the pandit had deliberately withheld from him. 'The Nipal Buddhists are very jealous of any intrusion into their esoteric dogmas and symbols,' Hodgson explained:

My old *Vajra Acharya* friend only recently gave me a peep at the esoteric dogmas; and my *Chitrakar* (Bauddha though he be) has only within these last twelve months brought me some esoteric pictures: nor probably should I have got at these secret things at all, if I had not been able to examine the Bauddha books, in some small degree, myself; and if a Bhotiya had not put into my hands a picture containing one of these naked saints. With these decisive means of questioning in my power, I at last got my Bauddha assistants to draw up the veil of the sanctuary, to bring me copies of the naked saints, and to tell me a little of the naked doctrines.[10]

Pandit Amritananda was patently a man of great learning, yet the more texts he produced and the more he expounded on the tenets of Buddhism, the greater his information appeared to be at odds with accounts of Buddhism as published in *Asiatic Researches* and other learned journals. In an attempt to clarify this disparity, Hodgson drew up a list of twenty questions on Buddhism as practised in Nepal. These were a mix of the highly speculative and the practical, ranging from Question 4, 'Is matter an independent existence, or derived from God?' to Question 18, 'What and from whence are the Newars, from Hindustan or Bhote? And what is the word Newar, is it a country or a people?'

Amritananda's twenty written answers gave Brian Hodgson his first outline of the nature of Buddhism, but also a glimpse of its extraordinary complexity. Some of the answers were short and to the point, as for example, the pandit's response to Question 18 above: 'The natives of the valley of Nipal are Newars. In Sanscrit the country is called *Naipala*, and the inhabitants *Naipali*; and the words *Newar* and *Newari* are vulgarisms arising from the mutation of 'p' to 'v', and 'l' to 'r'.'

The pandit's response to Question 7. 'What is Buddha?' was equally succinct:

> *Buddha* means, in Sanscrit, the wise; also, that which is known by wisdom; and it is one of the names we give to God, whom we also call *Adi-Buddha*, because he was before all, and is not created, but is the creator; and the *Pancha Buddhas* [Five Buddhas] were created by him, and are in the heavens. Sakya, and the rest of the seven human Buddhas are earth-born or human. These latter by the worship of Buddha, arrived at the highest eminence, and attained *Nirvana Pad* [i.e. were absorbed into *Adi-Buddha*]. We therefore call them all Buddhas.[11]

There were two distinct kinds of Buddhas: the celestial and the mortal. 'The practical Buddhism of Nepal,' explained Hodgson, 'has

(Left) The *Dhyani Buddhas*, or Celestial Buddhas: Vairochana, Akshobhya, Ratnasambhava, Amitabha and Amoghasiddhi. (Right) Their female equivalents: the *Dhyani Shaktis*. 'The images of the *Dhyani Buddhas*, which have been forwarded to the Society,' wrote Hodgson of these drawings, 'occupy the base of every *Manuchaitya*, or highest order of temples in Nepal.' These were the first representations of Vajrayana Buddhist iconography to be published in the West, based on drawings by an unnamed Newari *chitrakar*.

long admitted a marked distinction between those saints of mortal mould, who won the rank and powers of a Buddha by their own efforts, and the Buddhas of a celestial nature and origin'.[12] Both types owed their creation to 'a self-existent, infinite, and omniscient *Adi-Buddha*, one of whose attributes is the partial possession of five sorts of wisdom'. Out of these five sorts of wisdom the *Adi-Buddha* created the *Buddha Dhyani*, the 'Celestial Buddhas' – Vairochana, Akshobhya, Ratnasambhava, Amitabha and Amoghasiddhi – each of whom had a consort or female counterpart, known as *Dhyani Shaktis*. Images of these *Dhyani Buddhas* in stone or bronze, or carved in bas-relief, were to be found on every Buddhist edifice in Nepal and Tibet, with or without their *shaktis*.

The five *Dhyani Buddhas* created subordinate versions of themselves as a *Dhyani Bodhisattvas*, who were themselves the creators of finite existence: 'These creations are but perishable, and since the beginning of time, three of them have passed away. The present world is, therefore, the work of the fourth *Bodhisatwa* [i.e. Amitabha Bodhisattva], who is now Lord of the Ascendant, and his worshippers in Nipal are wont to invest in him all the powers of a Supreme and sole God.'

Within this present world there existed a second category of Buddhas known as mortal or *Manushi Buddhas,* who had lived out their lives as human beings. Although widely venerated in Nepal and Tibet, these human Buddhas were insignificant in comparison to the celestial Buddhas. And yet one of their number, Sakya Sinha, also known as Sakyamuni or *Tathagata*, was patently in a class of his own. According to Pandit Amritananda, this was because it was he who had first set down the *Dharma Ratna* in writing, in the form of sutras, or sacred verses:

In this important respect, Sakya is to Buddhism what Vyasa [supposed classifier of the Hindu *Vedas* and *Puranas*] is to Brahmanism ... That Sakya Sinha first collected and secured, in a written form, the doctrines taught by his predecessors, and himself, is a fact for which I cannot cite written authority, but which seems sufficiently vouched by the general belief by all the Bauddhas of Nepal and of Bhot.

As Hodgson understood it, Sakya Sinha was the seventh and last of the *Manushi Buddhas*. In fact, Mahayana Buddhism acknowledges twenty-eight mortal Buddhas, of whom five belong to the present aeon, Sakya Buddha being the fourth and Maitreya the Buddha still to come. Nor did Hodgson quite grasp the proper meaning of the term Bodhisattva – an enlightened being who seeks to achieve full Buddhahood – which he took to be some form of disciple. Given his circumstances, such misunderstandings were inevitable.

Pandit Amritananda's answers inevitably gave rise to more questions, resulting in ever more convoluted answers, that Hodgson did his best to comprehend:

The possession of the books led to questions respecting their relative age and authority; and, tried by this test, the Bauddha's quotations were not always so satisfactory. Thus one step led to another, until I conceived the idea of drawing up, with the aid of my old friend and his books, a sketch of the terminology and general disposition of the external parts of Buddhism, in the belief that such a sketch, though but imperfectly executed, would be of some assistance to such of my countrymen as, with the books only before them, might be disposed to enter into a full and accurate investigation of this almost unknown subject.

Brian Hodgson's first paper on Buddhism, 'An outline of the theocracy of the Bauddha system of Nepal', was completed in February 1827. He then took the precaution of sending it – not to the Secretary of the Asiatic Society of Bengal, Dr H. H. Wilson – but to his earlier patron, William Butterworth Bayley. The latter had just been re-elected as one of the Society's three Vice-Presidents but, more importantly, his standing as a member of the Governor-General's Supreme Council made him one of the most powerful men in Bengal. The outcome was that Hodgson's letter was read in full at the March meeting of the Asiatic Society of Bengal.

Those present heard the first recognisable account by a Westerner of Vajrayana as an esoteric extension of Mahayana Buddhism: 'Different innovations have been grafted on the primitive stem, and in none, apparently has this been carried further than in Nepal. The same modifications, probably, prevail throughout Tibet, and the regions which thence derive their creed, or China and Japan, in which we know a vast number of divinities share the populace's adoration with *Fo* [the Chinese term for Sakya Buddha] or Buddha.' [13]

Yet Hodgson was honest enough to admit that 'the vast extent and complexity of Buddhism', with its 'philosophy embracing a variety of very opposite opinions', had left him floundering: 'It becomes a very nice and arduous talk to estimate, with any degree of correctness, the meaning of such detached statements as are presented to us, either by personal communications with these religionists, or by reference to their voluminous written authorities.'

Hodgson must have hoped that that first paper would be published in the next volume of *Asiatic Researches*. However, that much admired journal tended to appear at irregular intervals after long delays and in bulky tomes that were hugely expensive to buy unless one was a member of the Asiatic Society of Bengal. In the meantime, his only other means of communicating the fruits of his researches among his peers in India was through *The Quarterly Oriental Magazine, Review and Register*. This was Calcutta's quarterly journal, founded four years earlier by the Reverend Dr Bryce, the Scottish Kirk's first chaplain in India and an active member of the Asiatic Society of Bengal.

To Hodgson's disappointment what the *Quarterly* published in its March 1827 was little more than a summary of his paper. He persisted, and three months later the same journal published a letter from Hodgson on the subject of 'The extreme resemblance that prevails between many of the symbols of Buddhism and Saivism'. He had examined a great many shrines and their attendant idols in the precincts of the Buddhist temples in Nepal and had initially taken them to be the result of 'an ignorant confusion of the two creeds by the people of this country'. A common feature of all these sites was the presence of solid stone structures that came in many sizes and varieties but which he had assumed to have their origins in the *lingams* of Hindu Shaivism – an error that his 'old Bauddha' had been quick to correct.

The proper name for these structures was *chaitya*, which he now understood to be the 'only proper temple of Buddhism'. These *chaityas* took many forms but all of them derived from the basic structure of a rounded dome resting upon a square base and surmounted by a pinnacle: 'Almost every Nipal *Chaitya* has its hemisphere surmounted by a cone or pyramid called *Chùrá Mani*. The small and unadorned *Chaitya* might easily be taken for a *Linga*.'

According to Pandit Amritananda, *chaityas* came in three distinct forms, ranging from the simple to the composite. Derived from the Sanskrit *chita*, or 'funeral pyre', the *chaitya* could incorporate a temple, a statue or even a sacred tree, but at its core there was always the *stupa*, from the root *stup*, meaning to 'heap', in the sense of a funerary mound heaped over cremated remains. This was the archetypical Buddhist memorial structure, intended to serve as an object of meditation and veneration, originally very simple in form but growing ever more elaborate over the centuries, particularly so in Nepal.

An important element of virtually every large *chaitya* in Nepal was the presence of the Celestial Buddhas in the form of sculptures or gilt effigies positioned round the base, often interspersed with their female *shaktis*: 'In Nipal the *Chaitya* is exclusively appropriated

The three main forms of the *chaitya* as found in the Nepal Valley,
according to Brian Hodgson, as published in *Asiatic Researches* in
1828. These were based on drawings by Hodgson's *chitrakar,* who
at this early stage was still following the traditional style of one-
dimensional representation. The second *chaitya* (top right) shows one
of the four supposed Ashokan stupas erected at the cardinal points
about the town of Patan. *Asiatic Researches*, Vol. XVI, 1828.

to the five *Dhyáni Búddhas*, whose images are placed in niches
around the base of the solid hemisphere which forms the most essen-
tial part of the *Chaitya.*' Vairochana, the most powerful of the five,

was considered the master of the structure and so occupied a place at or near the centre, while the other four each had their set positions at the cardinal points: Akshobhya faced east; Ratnasambhava south; Amitabha west; and Amoghasiddhi north.

Included in this same note on *chaityas* was a brief account of a pilgrimage made to India by Pandit Amritananda as a young man. The pandit had gone to a site near the Hindu pilgrimage town of Gaya in south Bihar that he knew of as Bodhgaya. A temple there, the Mahabodhi, was of special significance to Buddhists, although Amritananda was unable to explain why – more likely, Hodgson failed to understand what he meant.

At this time Bodhgaya was quite unknown, not only to Brian Hodgson but to every other Westerner – with the exception of one man: Dr Francis Buchanan-Hamilton, the same botanising surgeon who had spent a year in Nepal back in 1802–3. In 1811 in the course of surveying Bihar, Buchanan-Hamilton had visited the ruins of Bodhgaya and had learned from a local convert to Buddhism that the site was regarded as holy by the Buddhists because it had been the home of a great lawgiver named Gautama – another name for Sakya Buddha – who had sat in the shade of a pipal tree and meditated there. Buchanan-Hamilton had duly noted this all in his report but after a row with Governor-General Lord Hastings had left India in 1814 under a cloud, with all his notes and journals confiscated.

Dr Buchanan-Hamilton's discoveries at Bodhgaya and elsewhere remained unknown until an edited version of his survey report was published in 1838. So when Hodgson heard Pandit Amritananda account of his visit to Bodhgaya he missed its true significance as the site of the Buddha's enlightenment. What interested him far more were the pandit's references to the *chaityas* he had seen there and the way these had been appropriated by the Hindu ascetics who had taken over the site:

> This temple of *Mahà Búddha*, the Brahmans call the temple of *Jagat Nátha*, [Jaganath, Shiva] and the image of *Sàkya Sinha* they denominate *Mahà Múni*, and of the three *Lók Náths*, one they call *Mahà Déva* [Great God, Shiva], one *Párvati* [consort of

Hari-hari-hari-váhana Lokeshvara.

Lokeshvara, a manifestation of Avalokiteshvara, the Bodhisattva of
compassion and the protector of Tibet. As reproduced in *Asiatic Researches*,
Vol. XVI, 1828. Lokeshvara rides on the shoulders of the Hindu god
Narayan, who rides on the shoulders of a humanised Garuda bird, who rides
on a lion. The clear implication is that Buddhism overrides Hinduism.

Shiva], and the third their son [Ganesh]... At a little distance to
the North of the great Máhà Búddha temple are many small *Chaityas*, which the Brahmans call *Siva Lingas*, and as such worship

them ... Much astonished was I to find the great temple of my religion consecrated to Brahman worship, and Brahmans ignorantly falling down before the Gods of my fathers. [14]

The ideas contained in Brian Hodgson's 'Outline of the theocracy of the Bauddha system of Nepal' and his letter on *chaityas* were only half-formulated. But throughout the spring and summer of 1827 he reworked and revised these ideas as he continued to learn from his pandit. The end result took the form of two extended papers on Vajrayana Buddhism that were complementary to one another, written side by side and finished within months of each other in the late summer of 1827, even though published two years apart, in 1828 and 1830.

To illustrate his texts, Hodgson commissioned two sets of drawings of figures and religious edifices drawn by the same unnamed artist working under the guidance of Amritananda. The figures were examples of the 'innumerable deities' found within the Buddhist pantheon, dominated by the Celestial Buddhas, their female *shaktis* and their Bodhisattvas, but also including some of Vajrayana Buddhism's more esoteric icons.

Also illustrated in both papers were examples of Buddhist architecture showing the *chaitya* in its several forms and variations. Indeed, the *chaitya* became something of an obsession for Hodgson and over the next few years he caused his *chitrakars* to draw every possible variety of *chaitya* to be found in the Valley, and not just once but time and again, so that today many hundreds of examples can be found on scores of sheets in Hodgson Collections at the Musée Guimet in Paris, the Bodleian Library at Oxford, the British Library and the Royal Asiatic Society in London.

As well as the exclusively Buddhist *chaitya* there was also the *mandir*, or 'covered shrine', from which the town of Kathmandu partially got its name. Whereas the *chaitya* was solid and built of stone, the *mandir* was an open-sided wooden structure built to house one or more deities. To the Western eye they resembled Chinese pagodas, incorporating at least two and in some cases as many as five roofs, rising in tiers one above another and frequently metalled in copper and brass.

The larger versions of these *mandirs* were made all the more impressive by being set on raised platforms like stepped pyramids.

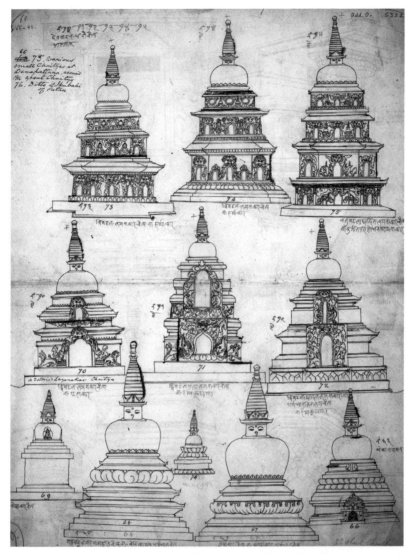

One of the many folios of Buddhist *chaityas* drawn for Hodgson by his *chitrakars*, each of them numbered. Hodgson's accompanying notes read: '66–75 Various small chaityas at Devapattana, around the great Chaitya', referring to the stupa of Deopatan. BL Hodgson Collection Add.Or.5332. © The British Library Board.

(Left) An engraving of an unidentified shrine, from a drawing by Brian
Hodgson's younger brother William, who stayed with him in Nepal
for some twenty months from March 1827. *Transactions of the Royal
Asiatic Society*, Vol. II, 1830. (Right) A drawing of a temple, captioned
in Hodgson's handwriting style 'Temple of Kumbheswara in Patan,
called in Newari, Kwonti'. Drawn in pencil, probably by Hodgson's
premier artist Raj Man Singh, it is executed in the three–dimensional
Company style possibly due to William Hodgson's influence.
RAS Hodgson Collection 022.024. © Royal Asiatic Society.

These were predominantly consecrated to Hindu gods and god-
desses, although in many cases Buddhist Bodhisattvas were also to be
found in attendance. Smaller *mandirs* were also a feature of many of
the buildings which the Newars called *Bahals* or *Bahis*, both words
being derived from the Sanskrit *Vihara,* or monastery. '*Chaitya,*'
explained Hodgson, 'is the proper and sole name for a Bauddha
abode of God. *Vihar*, the proper and sole name of a Bauddha abode
of the servant of God. In the former dwells the object of worship, in
the latter the professed.'

Both Kathmandu and Patan contained scores of these *Bahals*,
often discretely tucked away off the backstreets, each having the same
basic layout of an entrance door off the street flanked by a pair of
stone lions or elephants, which then opened into a paved courtyard

usually enclosed on all four sides, not unlike an Oxbridge university quad. Three sides of this surround were given over to living quarters, usually on two stories, while the fourth side, opposite the entrance, contained the main shrine or temple, also flanked by a pair of guardians in stone or metal. Hodgson preferred to use the word *Vihar* to describe these remarkable institutions, regarding *Bahal* as a corruption: '*Vihar* can never be construed "temple" – it is a convent, monastery or religious house, but never *templum dei vel Buddhae* ... The rule of these Vihars is a rule of freedom; and the door of every Vihar is always open, both to the entrance of newcomers, and to the departure of such of their old inmates as are tired of their vows.'

The most surprising feature of these *Bahals*, as Hodgson saw it, was that they were inhabited not by celibate monks but by householders with families, or, as Hodgson put it: 'These ample and comfortable abodes have long resounded with the hum of industry and the pleasant voices of women and children.' Whereas in Tibet the Buddhist monks and nuns lived lives of celibacy in their monasteries and nunneries, here in Nepal the original system had broken down, so that a superior class of Buddhists, the *Bandyas* – also termed *Vajra Acharyas* – married and lived with their families in the *Bahals*, while an inferior class of monks, *Bhikshus*, lived solitary lives as celibates.

For all his respect for his preceptor, Hodgson saw this as an abuse of the true tenets of Buddhism and part of the 'modern corrupt Buddhism of Nepal':

> Out of the gradual, and now total, disuse of monastic institutes, an exclusive minister of the altar, denominated *Vajra Acharya*, has derived his name, office, and existence in Nipal, not only without the sanction of the Bauddha scriptures, but in direct opposition to their spirit and tendency ... The superior ministry of religion is now solely in the hands of the *Bandyas*, entitled *Vajra Acharya* in Sanscrit ... These professions of the *Vajra Acharya*, and of the *Bhikshu*, have become by usage hereditary, as have all other avocations and pursuits, whether civil or religious, in Nipal.[15]

The first of Brian Hodgson's two major papers on Vajrayana Buddhism to be completed was 'Notices on the languages, literature and

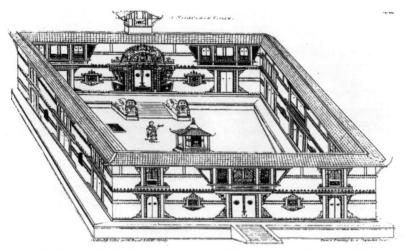

The Newari *Bahal*, more properly a *Vihara*, or monastery, usually built around a courtyard, with living and cooking quarters on three sides, a small temple on the fourth and a *chaitya* in the centre. An engraving based on an unnamed *chitrakar*'s drawing, as published in *Transactions of the Royal Asiatic Society*, Vol. II, 1830.

Bauddhas of Nipal and Bhot'. The second, 'A Sketch of Buddhism, derived from the Bauddha Scriptures of Nipal', was more tightly focused, based on Amritananda answers to his twenty questions together with Hodgon's additional notes.

'Notices' was despatched to Dr Horace Wilson in his capacity as editor of *Asiatic Researches*. However, Hodgson hedged his bets. Knowing that Dr Nathaniel Wallich was just about to return to England on extended sick-leave, Hodgson wrote to him in Calcutta on 11 August enclosing a draft copy of his 'Sketch of Buddhism' – evidently completed in a hurry, since it was followed by a series of corrections and amendments. Wallich was requested to take it with him to England and deliver it to Henry Colebrooke, the Director of the Royal Asiatic Society, in London.

In his accompanying letter Hodgson explained why he had felt compelled to write his 'Sketch':

When I conceived the design, I little suspected where it would lead me; I began ere long to feel my want of languages, and (to confess the truth) of patience, and almost looked back with a sigh to the tolerably full and tolerably accurate account of Buddhism which I had obtained so long ago, and with little comparative labour, from my old friend's answers to my queries. I also saw certain notices of Buddhism coming from time to time before the world, ushered by the talents and industry of Klaproth [the Mongolist Julius von Klaproth published *Leben des Budd'a* in 1823] and Rémusat [the Sinologist Jean Pierre Abel Rémusat published *Mélanges Asiatiques* in two volumes in 1825] ; and, so far as I had opportunity to learn what those notices contained, it seemed that the answers to my questions furnished much ampler and more accurate views of the subject than these distinguished men could extract from their limited sources of information.[16]

Hodgson's 'Sketch of Buddhism' was read in its entirety at a meeting of the Royal Asiatic Society in London on 28 June 1828. It was warmly received, the Society's Secretary, Sir Graves Houghton, writing to tell him how impressed he had been by its contents: 'You have helped fill up one of the most important blanks in Asiatic Antiquity.' It was subsequently published in 1830 in the second volume of *Transactions of the Royal Asiatic Society*, with Hodgson's later amendments attached as an appendix.

Hodgson's 'Notices on the languages, literature and Bauddhas of Nipal and Bhot' paper appeared in the sixteenth volume of *Asiatic Researches*, published in 1828. Both publications included engravings based on drawings by Hodgson's *chitrakar* artist.

More papers on Buddhism were to follow but it was these first two papers of 1827 that made Hodgson's name. He sent copies to his fellow hermit Csoma de Körös, by now living in a Tibetan monastery in the Western Himalayas north of Simla, who wrote back thanking him 'for making me acquainted with the names and contents of so many valuable works you have brought to public notice, and with many other things respecting Buddhism in Nepal', adding his great satisfaction at seeing 'the great coincidence of the Buddhistic faith in Nepal with that of Tibet. The figures on the Plates, the list of the Buddha scriptures and the whole sketch of Buddhism exhibit a wonderful agreement.'[17]

But it was the reaction of the savants in Paris that pleased Hodgson the most. 'You have laid out in a manner equally courageous and complete the ground plan of the edifice of Buddhism,' wrote the Pali and Sanskrit scholar Eugène Burnouf, Europe's foremost authority on Buddhism.[18]

Brian Hodgson did make some serious mistakes, most notably in declaring that that there were four philosophical schools of Buddhist thought. This information can only have come to him from Pandit Amritananda yet these four schools have never since been identified, whether in Nepal or elsewhere. [19] Given the circumstances, such misunderstandings were inevitable.

When in due course Burnouf came to publish the work that laid the foundations for the modern study of Buddhism, *Introduction à l'histoire du Buddhisme Indien*, published in 1844, Burnouf went out of his way to acknowledge his great debt to Hodgson, not only for his donations of manuscripts but also for his written contributions. Hodgson's 'Notices on the languages, literature and Bauddhas of Nipal and Bhot' gave an account of the different schools of Buddhism 'never since been surpassed or equalled'. It was 'full of ideas entirely new' and 'teemed with value as bringing to light, among other important discoveries, the grand and theretofore wholly unknown fact that in Nepal there existed numerous Buddhist works composed in Sanskrit'.

Not bad for a young man of twenty-six.

William Hodgson's drawing of the new 'Gothic' extension to the British Residency in Kathmandu, c. 1828, reproduced in W. Hunter's biography.

6

'Untutored eyes and ears, sedulously employed': Acting Resident, 1828–31

William 'Will' Hodgson was born four years after his brother. By the time he was sixteen it was clear that the family's continuing debts required that he, too, should seek employment in India. Mrs Hodgson again applied to her well-connected friend Mr Pattinson and again he obliged, although in this instance it was his sponsorship of a lesser value military cadetship in HEICo's Bengal Native Infantry rather than a civil Writership.

Will arrived in Calcutta in 1823 and did well for himself in his first four years in India, participating with his regiment in the ferocious assault that in January 1827 finally brought the mighty mud walls of Bhurtpore (today Bharatpur) tumbling down. But from that time onwards he was never an entirely well man. In March 1827 he was given permission to join his elder brother in Kathmandu on six months' sick-leave – and on half-pay. At the start of the Cold Weather he attempted to rejoin his regiment, but again his health broke down, so that he was back in Kathmandu in November of the same year. This time he stayed on for a full twelve months. Depressing as this inactivity must have been for him, it did at least provide his elder brother with a very welcome touch of family life.

A year before Will's arrival in Kathmandu Edward Gardner had set about enlarging the British Residency by adding an extension at the side, described by Brian Hodgson in a letter to Dr Wallich as 'gothics & I know not what besides'. The completed building presented a bizarre clash of styles: at the front, a neo-classical Regency facade in the grand style complete with triangular pediment, Doric columns and a white stucco façade; and now at the side, a tacked-on Gothic Revivalist structure more suitable to a high church vicarage, all arched windows and doorways, cranellations and battlements, topped off by a square, two-storey tower. At some point during his visits to Kathmandu Will Hodgson made a rough pen-and-ink sketch showing this new extension half hidden behind a wall of trees and shrubs. In the latter years of Brian Hodgson's tenancy of the Residency this surrounding shrubbery was cut back to allow the lawn to develop, its grass kept short by the various sheep, goats and deer that were allowed to wander freely within the confines of the Residency walls – as shown in a watercolour by Dr Henry Ambrose Oldfield, who joined the Residency staff as surgeon after Hodgson's final departure (*see Plate 9*).

Gardner's extension included a large central hall intended to provide the Resident with a suitable Durbar hall wherein he might receive the king of Nepal or his representative in proper state. After Brian Hodgson's departure from Kathmandu this became the Residency chapel, reflecting the greater show of piety associated with the Victorian era.

Like most of his British contemporaries in India, Hodgson wore his Christianity lightly. According to his biographer, he was 'not inclined to discuss religious subjects', and would discourage any attempts to raise the subject by declaring 'I do not care to talk about the unknowable'. His surviving letters contain no more than the conventional passing references to the deity in such forms as 'God bless thee' and 'with God's blessing'. But if Brian Hodgson had little time for religion increasing numbers of his compatriots at home certainly did.

Prior to Parliament's renewal of the HEICo's charter in 1813 the Company's Court of Directors had fought hard to keep Christian missionaries out of its Indian territories, believing that it was in the best interests of trade that Indian institutions should be left untouched, even encouraged. The Company had founded and funded a Moslem *madrassa* in Calcutta and a Sanskrit College in Benares, where all instruction was given in the vernacular. It also supported the Asiatic Society of Bengal, provided funds for the translation of Sanskrit, Persian and Urdu texts and actively encouraged such learning through Fort William College and the two so-called

Anglo-Indian colleges in Delhi and Agra. Muslim law officers sat as assessors in Sessions Courts and Brahmin pandits were consulted on points of Hindu law.

But after 1813 missionaries and evangelical Christians became increasingly vociferous and divisive fixtures of the Indian landscape, adding their voices to the demands of the utilitarians and the radicals in England that the Company abandon its easy-going paternalism in favour of direct interventionist reform, based on Christian values. And in July 1828 the reformers gained their most powerful champion with the arrival in Calcutta of Lord William Bentinck.

Lord William was no self-made man. His father was the third Duke of Portland, his mother the daughter of the fourth Duke of Devonshire. He had been gifted the governorship of Madras before he was thirty, only to be abruptly recalled in the wake of a brief but violent military mutiny, brought about chiefly by his signing an order that forbade the Indian sepoys from painting sectarian marks on their foreheads. His removal from office rankled and for the next two decades he made no secret of his desire to return to India as Governor-General, a wish that was finally granted when his relative George Canning became Prime Minister.

Lord Bentinck's admiration for the political philosopher James Mill and the views expressed in his *History of British India* stopped just short of idolatry. At a private dinner shortly before Bentinck's departure for India he was heard to remark to Mill, 'I am going to British India, but I shall not be Governor-General. It is *you* that will be Governor-General' – a remark overheard and recorded with great satisfaction by the utilitarian Jeremy Bentham. It was Mill's vision of Indian darkness and European civilisation that Bentinck brought with him to the sub-continent: 'a vast territory cursed from one end to the other by the vices, the ignorance, the oppression, the despotism, the barbarous and often cruel customs that have been the growth of ages under every description of Asiatic misrule'.

Bentinck arrived in Calcutta determined not only to reform but also to reduce expenditure. One of his first acts was to cut the salaries of the army and civil service, which goes some way to explaining why he became known as the 'Clipping Dutchman' and was so disliked by many of those who served under him – among

(Left) Governor-General Lord William Bentinck, a committed evangelical
bent on reforming India along British – and Christian – lines. (Right)
The man Bentinck most admired: the Scottish economist and political
philosopher James Mill, whose *History of British India*, completed
in 1817, was a major influence in shaping British policy in India.

them Henry Thoby Prinsep, who characterised him not so much
a reformer as a man 'deeply imbued with the love of change for
change's sake'.

Forced to spend two years at his side as the Governor-General
toured one province after another, Prinsep grew increasingly irritated
by Bentinck's 'incessant desire to meddle with everything, great or
small. Wherever he went he called for reports ... He was incessantly
writing minutes on all subjects and his private and military secretaries were employed all day in copying them out and sending them.'
Most maddening of all was the Governor-General's habit of turning
for advice not to his advisers but to his wife, Lady William, 'who was
always his confidential adviser on points of difference'.[1]

At the heart of Prinsep's grumbles was his dismay at the Governor-
General's contempt for his own service, which in Bentinck's view was
composed of men 'selected by no regard for qualification, possessing
appointments like an estate, as a matter of right; secure of promotion, because there are no competitors; and secured in their possession by the powerful patronage with which they are supported'.[2]
Taking his cue from James Mill, he considered the HEICo's rule in
India to be a 'monstrous absurdity' by which sixty million Indians

were governed by less than four hundred 'strangers in the land' who had secured for themselves 'all the honours and emoluments of the administration, to the exclusion of the native and natural agency of the country'. Indians should have a stake in their own government and to make that possible it was necessary, in Bentinck's words, to 'regenerate this degraded population', through a combination of reforms and education.

Many of the reforms pushed through during Lord Bentinck's seven years in office were indeed necessary, not least his measures against such basic denials of human rights as female infanticide, bans on widow remarriage, the immolation of widows known as *suttee*, and the strangler cult known as *Thugee*. Such reforms had the support of Prinsep and his colleagues but what they found deeply troubling was Bentinck's determination to reform Indian institutions by replacing them with British ones, driven by Bentinck's belief in British moral superiority based on Christianity. Here Bentinck had the vociferous support not only of the evangelicals at home but also the missionaries in India – men such as the Reverend Alexander Duff of the Church of Scotland, who argued that the only way to get Indians to abandon their heathen vices was to provide an English language-based education to high-caste Hindus and the Moslem landowning classes. They would then embrace Christianity and, by means what Duff called his 'downward filter theory', the uneducated Indians would follow.

The first targets of these Anglicists were the four prime agencies for the revival in Indian culture: the Asiatic Society of Bengal, Fort William College, the Sanskrit College in Benares and the Calcutta Madrassa. Government funds for the support of these institutions were administered by a General Committee of Public Instruction chaired by Dr Horace Wilson, with Henry Thoby Prinsep a prominent member. That body now became the subject of an increasingly bitter power struggle, with Wilson and Prinsep leading the Orientalists, while an opposing group fought to have the colleges closed and the funds redirected to the promotion of English-based education.

Up in Kathmandu it was Bentinck's pay cuts in the civil services that had the most immediate impact. Edward Gardner's salary as

Resident was halved and reduced to a meagre £4000 a year, which convinced him that there was little point in carrying on. In the spring of 1829 he left Nepal to proceed to Europe on what was officially deemed 'furlough', or extended leave. Once he had secured his passage home in Calcutta he submitted his letter of resignation.

Gardner's departure left Brian Hodgson ecstatic about his future prospects: 'My superior in office here left this Residency March 1st,' he wrote in a letter to his younger sister Fanny,

> since which time I have been *chargé d'affaires*, and they tell me I shall soon be confirmed in the new post in which I now only officiate. I am a great man, with a great house and great establishment, and, what is far better, possessed of a high and honourable charge. Whether all this is to last or not will depend on the Governor-General. Our dearest mamma bids me come home, but how can I leave my present glorious prospect of confirmation as Resident in full?[3]

Whatever Edward Gardner thought about his reduced salary, the prospect of earning what was still a very handsome sum as acting Resident meant a great deal to Hodgson, as it would more than double his earnings. He was still in debt to the Calcutta *banias* from whom he had borrowed substantial sums to support his parents and his still sickly brother William, and he was now also having to provide for his youngest brother Edward, who had just started his training at Haileybury with the intention of following him into the Bengal Civil Service.

The burden of family debt had hung over him ever since his earliest childhood and continued to colour his relations with his parents: 'Nor can it be otherwise,' he continued in his letter to Fanny, 'until with God's blessing, I have been enabled to take off entirely the load that has ever pressed on them since my reason and memory dawned – a day of liberation for them, how ardently longed for by me, and surely now not far off!'

Gardner's departure meant that Hodgson was able to move out of the modest Assistant Resident's bungalow in the grounds of the Residency and into that grand building itself. Assuming that his confirmation as

Resident was bound to come through in a matter of weeks, he took to calling it his new home – 'my garden, my grounds, my farmyard' – and himself as 'the very model of an English country gentleman'.

Hodgson had now for the first time to deal in person with the Nepal Durbar as the representative of the Governor-General. The most pressing issues were trade disputes and cross-border incursions – in part, because of continuing confusion over where exactly the border between Nepal and the HEICo's Northern-Western Provinces lay, but chiefly because the Durbar refused to co-operate. In one of his letters to his sister Fanny he gave two typical examples:

> Say ... how Gopi Mohun Das, a Nepalese, crossed the frontier, seized and carried off into this territory from under the shadow of the Company's wing, Deo Datt, Bengali, said Deo Datt having five years before bought some timber of said Gopi Mohan, and perseveringly excused himself from paying for the same. Or perchance (as has this very hour occurred) the Court scribe comes to me and explains how a Captain so-and-so, the Company's public agent for supply of timber, won't settle his accounts with one Girdhari Choudry, a Nepalese timber merchant. Meanwhile, in all probability, the said Captain has already paid and settled all that was due to said Choudry; and, moreover, has had the unheard-of effrontery and cruelty to bid said Choudry to produce his books before a set of arbitrers of both nations.[4]

Petty though these disputes were, little progress was made until Bhimsen Thapa himself came to Hodgson with a request for his co-operation. A large gang of armed robbers, known as 'dacoits', had ambushed a party of tax collectors in the Nepal Tarai. They had overwhelmed and killed the military escort and made off with a large sum of money into HEICo territory.

Hodgson's first reaction was to remind Bhimsen of the numerous occasions when his own requests for action on such border issues had been ignored. But he went on to say that if the Durbar was now ready to accept that the principle of mutual obligations then a plan of action might be worked out. 'The Durbar, smarting under its heavy loss, cordially agreed,' was how Hodgson summed up Bhimsen's response.

Hodgson's solution was highly original and, by today's standards, highly questionable. The Nepalis had captured some of the dacoits, who were now awaiting execution. At Hodgson's request, they were paraded before him and four of the most intelligent were selected for questioning. These four were told that their lives would be spared if they turned 'king's evidence' and betrayed their colleagues. They were only too eager to co-operate and in doing so revealed an extraordinary conspiracy that extended far beyond Nepal's borders: 'a system of plundering as wide in area as perfect in execution, spreading even to the Deccan, and upheld habitually by functionaries of native States, who regularly shared in the spoil'.

All this information was forwarded in conditions of great secrecy to the British Resident in Lucknow and on to the several British magistrates in the districts bordering Nepal – 'each officer being desired in a circular to read and take memorandas of the substance of the documents (originals being forwarded to save time), and then to pass them on, and to be ready for simultaneous movement in co-operation with all the Durbar's district officers.'[5] At a prearranged time a general round up of dacoits and their helpers took place on both sides of the border.

So successful was this break-up of the dacoit gangs and their accomplices that it became something of a model. One district officer in British India who applied Hodgson's technique of 'turning' leading criminals so that they informed on their fellow miscreants was Major Henry Sleeman, who achieved great fame in the 1830s as the suppressor of the secret society of murderers operating in Central India known as the *Thugees* or *Phansigars* ('stranglers').

In the Cold Weather of 1827–28 Brian Hodgson lost his two main advocates at the Asiatic Society of Bengal. The first was Dr Clarke Abel, who in October 1827 set out from Calcutta with the stated intention of carrying out unspecified research along the northern borders of British territory. He may well have been planning to enter Nepal at Brian Hodgson's invitation. In the event, he got no further than the military station of Cawnpore (Kanpur), where he died of unspecified causes.

Hodgson's second setback was the departure of Dr Nathaniel Wallich. At the request of the Governor-General, Wallich had followed the troops into Burma in order to report on its forest resources. He returned to Calcutta in such poor health that he had eventually to request permission to return to England. He took with him an enormous collection of eight thousand botanical specimens – nominally, to present them to the HEICo's Court of Directors, but, in reality, to bring about the publication of what was to be his *magnum opus*: his *Plantae Asiaticae Rariores*, the first volume of which was published in 1829.

With Dr Wallich went two giant Tibetan mastiffs sent down to Calcutta by Brian Hodgson. Over the years Hodgson kept a number of such spectacular beasts in his menagerie, all acquired from his Tibetan contacts, and he probably intended these particular specimens to be presented to the Zoological Society of London, of which he had very recently been voted a Corresponding Member. The two dogs survived the sea voyage and were duly handed over to the Zoological Society by Wallich on 20 July 1828. However, only three days later Wallich returned to take the dogs away, on the grounds that they had been handed over in error. He then presented them to King George IV.

It is quite possible that Hodgson never intended the dogs to go to the zoo but it is more plausible to suppose that Wallich acted alone, intent of securing the king's valuable patronage for his expensive publishing project – an endeavour in which he was indeed successful. In the event, the two dogs were returned to the Zoological Society of London by order of the monarch, only to die of distemper six months later.[6]

Dr Wallich's departure left Hodgson at the mercy of the whims of Dr Horace Hayman Wilson. However, in January 1829 a new monthly journal appeared in Calcutta. It was entitled *Gleanings in Science* and it had been set up by a group of like-minded individuals frustrated by the laboured proceedings of the Asiatic Society of Bengal, its Physical Committee having all but collapsed following the sudden death of Dr Abel. Regarding themselves as scientists rather than Orientalists, these rebels formed themselves into the Indian branch of the British Association for the Advancement of Science. This, in turn, led to a new committee being set up within the Asiatic Society of Bengal, designated the Class of Natural History

Two different types of Tibetan mastiff as drawn for Hodgson by one
of his *chitrakars*. It is unlikely these particular specimens were the ones
that accompanied Dr Wallich to England in 1828. NHM Hodgson
Collection 055 742. © The Trustees of the Natural History Museum.

and Physics. It was a sign of the times that among those reported
present at the second meeting of this new group were 'eight Hindoo
youths of the Anglo-Indian College'.

The stated purpose of *Gleanings in Science* was to make the discoveries and scientific advances now taking place in India known
beyond the confines of Calcutta. Two of its most enthusiastic advocates were Major George Everest, the Surveyor-General of India,
responsible for the mapping of India, and his deputy, Captain James
Herbert, an engineer and geologist who had spent the better part
of sixteen years mapping various regions of the Himalayan chain.
Herbert became the first editor of *Gleanings in Science*, with the
support of no less than four Prinsep brothers and one sister – including the eldest brother, Henry Thoby, and the youngest, James.

The September 1829 issue of *Gleanings in Science* carried Brian
Hodgson's first ornithological paper, based on yet another of the
specimens in the Kathmandu Residency's menagerie – this time a
hornbill, or rather, a pair of hornbills in the form of a parent bird and
its fledged young. These birds had been brought in to the Residency
by one of Hodgson's hunters and named by him *Buceros nipalensis*.
'This remarkable and very large species,' Hodgson wrote, 'which I

have the advantage of contemplating at leisure in a live specimen, measures from the point of one wing tip to that of the other, four feet five inches; and from the tip of the beak to the extremity of the tail, three feet six inches, whereof the beak is eight inches'.

One of the bird's most striking features was its call: 'The voice of the bird is usually a short, hoarse croak; but when angry, or alarmed, it utters a cry not unlike a dog's bark. If left alone it seldom speaks, but when once excited to utterance, is most pertinaciously noisy ... Its odious voice, awkward gait, frequently erected tail, and sombre plumage, proclaim its relationship to the Corvidae of the *Stirps corvina*: whilst its superior size, huge bill, gressorial feet, and tiny, triangular tongue, are family features that cannot be mistaken.'

Hodgson went on to describe the hornbill, together with its habits, habitat and diet, in the most scientific manner, taking his cue from George Shaw's sixteen-volume *General Zoology*, the last volume of which had appeared in 1826: 'Having no extensive or scientific knowledge of ornithology, I have been obliged to rely upon untutored eyes and ears, sedulously employed and assisted by careful reference to Shaw's zoology.' Even so, based on the information provided by Shaw, Hodgson was confident that he was describing a hitherto unknown species of hornbill, chiefly on account of its upper bill which appeared to be strengthened by 'six large prominent ribs, running obliquely down nearly the entire breadth of it ... giving it there an undulatory form'. Both parent and offspring had this same curious feature, so it was unlikely to be a malformation. Sadly, no reliable sighting of Hodgson's *Buceros nipalensis* has been reported since 1846.

This first ornithological paper appeared in *Gleanings in Science* without an accompanying illustration but a subsequent reprinting in the grander pages of *Asiatic Researches* did indeed include a fine hand-tinted lithograph of this clumsy but spectacular bird – a lithograph based, as always on a drawing by an unnamed Nepalese artist.

This first foray into ornithology was followed up by an account of a distinctive wader with a long decurved red bill and grey and white plumage which Hodgson named the Red-billed Erolia. However, he made the mistake of submitting his paper directly to Horace Wilson for publication in *Asiatic Researches*, together with a 'coloured

(Left) A hand-coloured lithograph as published in *Gleanings in Science* in 1829 to illustrate Brian Hodgson's first published paper on the Nepalese hornbill, *Buceros nepalensis*, now believed extinct. (Right) The Great Hornbill, which Hodgson named *Homrai buceros* after the Nepali name for the bird, now *Buceros bicornis*. *Asiatic Researches*, 1833.

drawing of natural size'. Both paper and drawing were put to one side and lost. This was the first known description of what is now known as the Ibisbill or *Ibidorhyncha struthersii* (*see Plate 24*), but fours years passed before Hodgson's resubmitted paper and accompanying illustrations were published, along with the profound apologies of the Asiatic Society of Bengal's new Secretary.

In the meantime, two specimens of the same bird had been found among a collection of bird skins from the Himalayas at the Zoological Society of London's museum. These were examined by the museum's newly-appointed curator and specimen preserver John Gould, who credited their discovery to an obscure Scottish physician, Dr Struthers of Glasgow, and named the bird accordingly.

Further evidence of Brian Hodgson's growing interest in ornithological drawings can be found in Sir Charles D'Oyly's *Oriental Ornithology*, published in Patna in 1829. Soon after his posting to Bihar Sir Charles D'Oyly had ordered a lithographic press from Edinburgh and in anticipation of its arrival had set up what he called the United Patna and Gaya Society or Bihar School of Athens for the Promotion of Arts and Sciences, with himself as President. Unfortunately for the Society, both the lithographic press and a large harp ordered for Eliza D'Oyly were lost when a sudden squall overturned the boat that was transporting them upriver. A second press had to be ordered and its arrival in 1828 led to the setting up of the Bihar Amateur Lithographic Press and a burst of publications of lithographs by D'Oyly and fellow artists drawn from the local European communities in Patna, Gaya and Benares – of whom one of the most talented proved to be James Prinsep.

Sir Charles D'Oyly's *Oriental Ornithology*, was ornamental rather than ornithologically correct, with a fellow Bengal Civil Servant, Christopher Webb Smith drawing the birds and D'Oyly adding the backgrounds. Among its plates was a coloured lithograph of a brace of woodcock pictured beside a river – with a Nepali temple on the far bank. According to the caption, this was a 'View of a Nepaulese temple near Katmandoo taken by B. H. Hodgson, Esq.' Both temple and woodcock were based on Hodgson's *chitrakar* drawings – graphic evidence of the D'Oylys' continuing interest in Brian Hodgson's activities.

In 1830 James Herbert left Calcutta to undertake a survey of the newly acquired mountain country of Dorje Ling, the Land of the Thunderbolt, which he Anglicised into Darjeeling. In his absence the editorship of *Gleanings in Science* was taken over by the youngest of the Prinsep brothers, James. Shortly afterwards Calcutta's leading journal, *The Quarterly Oriental Magazine, Review and Register*, folded – allowing *Gleanings in Science* to fill the gap, with James Prinsep in charge.

Reading through the February 1830 issue of *Gleanings in Science* Brian Hodgson came across an appeal from a prominent naturalist in England for more information on Indian zoology and, in particular, more information on the 'antelope (unicorn) of Bhutan', its author apparently unaware of Hodgson's earlier pioneering article. Hodgson responded with alacrity with an enlarged paper on the *Chiru*, or Tibetan antelope, published in the November 1830 issue of *Gleanings in Science*. 'This rare, new, and beautiful animal,' wrote Hodgson, 'though carefully and fully described by Dr Abel and myself, is still, after a lapse of five years, unknown to Natural History – both specimen and description having probably been wrecked by the untimely death of my friend Dr Abel'.[7]

Two of a number of watercolours of the Tibetan antelope in the Zoological Society of London's Hodgson Collection match the published lithograph. One carries a note in Hodgson's hand-writing, '*Chiru* antelope Raj Man Singh 1829', which confirms that the artist was Hodgson's principal *chitrakar*, Raj Man Singh. The other has a line written in Devanagri script which translates as 'the deer is roaming in the king's jungle', showing that it was drawn from life, which suggests that this was done back in 1825 when the *Chiru* was briefly the Raja of Nepal's menagerie, or that further live specimens were subsequently brought down to Kathmandu from Tibet.

These and other watercolours show how well Raj Man Singh had learned to adapt his traditional two-dimensional Newari style of drawing to accommodate European tastes, in the manner of Indian artists from Benares and Delhi working for British patrons, who had developed the style known today as 'Company Painting'.

Seven months later *Gleanings in Science* carried Hodgson's account of what he termed the 'Bubaline Antelope, the *Thar* of the Nipalese', also known as the *Jharal*. 'It is a large, coarse, heavy animal,' Hodgson wrote in his account,

> with bristly thin set hair, not unlike that of a buffalo, and as the female is distinguished by the singular (and, as far as I know, unheard of) circumstance of having four teats, I propose to name it Bubaline Antelope ... The Nipalese call this animal the *Thar*: and the chase of it is a favourite diversion, with the Gooroong [Gurung] tribe especially, who usually kill it with poisoned arrows. It is not speedy, as might be inferred from what has been said of its make. Its flesh is very coarse and bad. But there is plenty of it and these mountaineers, who are apt to look at the quantity, more than the quality, of such flesh, as a Hindoo Government deems licit for them, prize the *Thar* very highly and hunt him very eagerly.

Hodgson believed he had identified a new species but his *Thar* or *Jharal* was subsequently shown to be a Serow, *Naemorhedus sumatraensis*, the first specimen having been discovered in Sumatra in 1799.

It was much the same with his next two papers on Nepalese mammals, also published in *Gleanings of Science* in that same year of 1832. One of these was a description of a new species of wild cat,

(Above) A watercolour of a group of *Thar* or *Jharal*, afterwards found to be Serow. NHM Hodgson Collection 069561. (Below) A watercolour of a pair of Hodgson's Moormi wild cats, which he named *Felis moormentis*, afterwards identified as the Asian Golden Cat, *Felis temmickii*. NHM Hodgson Collection 055742. © The Trustees of the Natural History Museum.

one of no less than five kinds of jungle cats that were by then housed in the British Residency's menagerie. This, too, had been a gift from Bhimsen Thapa, presented to Hodgson soon after being captured by hunters in a dense forest in central Nepal. According to Hodgson, it was 'entirely unknown to the natives and had consequently no name', so he had called it Moormi, after the tribe in whose territory it had been found – today better known as the Tamangs.

(Above, left) A pair of Hodgson's Speckled Pigeons, *Columba hodgsonii,*
presented to the Zoological Society of London in January 1832.
(Above, right) The Drongo Cuckoo, *Surniculus lugurbris*, also new
to science, which Hodgson described as combining the characters
of the cuckoo and the drongo. © Zoological Society of London.

(Below) Five years later Hodgson submitted a second paper on
this new sub-species, what he now termed the Fork-Tailed Drongo
Cuckoo (*Surniculus dicruroides*), together with a greatly improved
illustration. *Journal of the Royal Asiatic Society*, Vol. VIII, 1839.

Hodgson found his Moormi cat to be of a 'tractable disposition and cheerful unsuspicious temper' and the only time he ever saw it angry was when one of his pets, a 'huge Bhoteah dog', had approached its cage. It lived in the Residency's menagerie for some six months before dying of some unspecified disease.[8] He named it *Felis murmensis*, but it was in fact the Asiatic Golden Cat, *Catopuma temmickii*. It is now believed to be extinct in India and no specimen has been seen in Nepal since 2009.

In the meantime, summaries of Brian Hodgson's papers on the Tibetan antelope and the wild dog of the Himalayas had appeared in that august journal *Proceedings of the Zoological Society of London* – a society of which Hodgson was now an elected corresponding member at the proposal of Dr Wallich.

It was also through the kindness of Dr Wallich that those attending a meeting of the same Zoological Society on 24 January 1832 were able to examine the skins of seven mammals of Nepal and eight birds that been despatched from Nepal eight months earlier. They included two wild dogs, one *Thar* goat, one Tibetan antelope, one wild cat, a pair of hornbills, a pair of Khalij pheasants, a pair of speckled pigeons, one Nepalese cuckoo and three birds of the thrush family. These specimens were accompanied by 'coloured figures and accounts of the several animals from the pen of Mr Hodgson'.

On the basis of Hodgson's information and after careful examination of the pair of specimens supplied, it was proposed at that same meeting of the Zoological Society that the speckled pigeon, known in Nepal as *Banbajura* and termed by him *Columba nipalensis*, be declared a newly discovered species and named *Columba hodgsonii* – which it still is.

The Gurung Tribe of Nepal

A group of Gurungs, with some of their everyday utensils
in the foreground. Undated and unsigned watercolour.
BM Ethnographic Library Hodgson Album.
© Trustees of the British Museum.

7

'The truth is that these are saving times': Assistant Resident again, 1831–33

Brian Hodgson could never quite make up his mind as to whether Nepal's strongman, Bhimsen Thapa, was a friend or an enemy, a check on the warmongers among his countrymen or an impediment to Nepal's progress. His views swung frequently from one extreme to the other. In July 1833 we find him writing to Lord Bentinck complaining of Bhimsen's arrogance and declaring that 'at the bottom of Bhimsen's profound character I have at last discerned, as I conceive, an intense hatred of us'. Yet three months later Hodgson is full of praise for the 'internally vigorous and just and externally pacific administration of Bhim Sen'.[1]

These fluctuating opinions were largely due to Bhimsen Thapa's own attitudes, which changed according to his political circumstances, so that one day Hodgson might complain of the 'degree of shyness towards the Residency originating in the Premier's anomalous situation' and on the next find himself invited to ride out with the Chief Minister and exchange confidences with him on the friendliest of terms.

Brian Hodgson's period of office as the Acting Resident passed relatively peacefully. The young king was still a minor and his step-mother, the Queen Regent Lalita Tripura Sundari, still very much alive, so that the Pandya Brahmans – the most powerful faction at court opposing Bhimsen and his Thapa alliance – remained powerless. This made for relatively untroubled dealings with Bhimsen and the Nepal Durbar. In a letter to his sister Fanny, written in May 1830 when she was aged twenty, Hodgson described his very leisurely daily routine:

I usually ... rise at eight o'clock, go to breakfast at nine, get up from the breakfast table at ten. Then, alas! indite a public letter to Government acquainting the Right Honourable the Governor-General of the continued disposition of the Court of Kathmandu to maintain the relations of amity and concord for some time past so happily established. Or turn over some of my heaps of raw materials fore the future investigation of the manners and institutions of the Nepalese, and sigh to see how far from sufficient those materials still are, after ten years of search. Or mount my horse and follow the strenuous idleness of woodcock-shooting; or take up my Cuvier [Baron Georges Cuvier, eminent French naturalist, whose *La Règne Animal* was published in four octavo volumes in 1817] and seek in him how to dispose some of my now numerous and valuable ornithological specimens; or pore over some book taking a general and scientific view of the subject of law.

By such means the Acting Resident passed the day till four o-clock, when he took a turn round his garden before returning to dress for dinner, served at six: 'Eating and drink and chat, or billiards or backgammon, till nine, when my two guests' – the commander of the Residency escort and the Residency surgeon – 'retire, and I draw up my chair to the fireside, and, taking up the last work that has reached me from my bookseller in Cornhill, read and meditate till midnight, or haply till one o'clock. Then to bed and so ends the day.'[2]

But fourteen months after Gardner's departure Hodgson's promotion had still not come through. In that same letter to his sister quoted above he grumbled that Lord Bentinck had refused to promote him, this despite the best efforts of his friends the D'Oylys, still marooned in Patna:

As the Governor-General lately passed up the country, he stayed three days with the D'Oylys and that excellent woman Lady D'Oyly (for mama says I must not call her Eliza) attacked the great man upon his usage of me, making me do the Resident's work and giving me only half the pay. The Right Honourable the Governor-General said I was a proper person enough, and applauded the

talent manifested in a recent report made by me, and added what
a thousand pities it was I was so very young ... He showed my said
report to the Lord Bishop, and the Church joined the State in
applauses, as the Church told Lady D'Oyly (for the Church too
is migratory in India) when recently the Church personified, alias
the Bishop, passed Patna on his or its way down to Calcutta. Yet
I only get half pay ... The truth is that these are saving times, and
the Governor-General the prince of political economists. And
verily, if he does not supersede, he will keep me *chargé d'affaires*
for another year for the sake of the saving.

The report that had been so well received by Church and State
alike had been on the subject of Nepali militarism and how it might
be curbed without provoking another war. 'This was a nation of warriors and conquerors,' Hodgson had written to Henry Thoby Prinsep
in September 1829. Bhimsen Thapa, his fellow-ministers and his generals were all Parbatiyas drawn from Nepal's warrior caste, whose
sole hereditary function was military service. In Hodgson's view,
Edward Gardner had never taken this continuing threat of Gorkha
militarism seriously. Year on year the numbers of troops under arms
or in rotated reserve had risen steadily:

> I have often said, and now repeat, that when in 1816 we drew a line
> round the territory of these men ... we should either have crippled
> them effectually or have insisted on a change in their institutions,
> giving the surplus soldiery employment in our own armies. We
> did neither ... Since the war we have seen nothing but drills and
> parades, heard nothing but the roar of cannon or the clink of the
> hammer in arsenal or magazine. Soldiers have been and are heads
> of the law and finance at Kathmandu, and administrators of the
> interior. Soldiers have been and are everything, and they have been
> headed by a plenary viceroy [Bhimsen Thapa] of that old stamp
> which must support its habitual aggression at home by pandering
> to the soldiery, and teaching them to look to aggression abroad.[3]

Part of the solution, Hodgson suggested, lay in turning the 'martial
propensities of the Gorkhas' to the HEICo's advantage. Back in 1815,

having seen at first hand how well they had fought in the first round of the war, General Sir David Ochterlony had recruited four battalions of surrendered Gorkha soldiers in Kumaon and Garhwal. These subsequently became the nucleus of the Indian Army's Gurkha regiments. A decade later, when it was suggested that more troops from Nepal should be enlisted, the idea was fiercely opposed by Edward Gardner, who argued that 'even on entering our service the Gorkhas would not separate themselves entirely from their native country', and that in the event of a rupture with Nepal their strong sense of patriotism would lead them to side with their native land.

Hodgson, on the other hand, was all for recruitment, not only to reduce the threat of Gorkha militarism but also on the grounds of sheer military efficiency, since the flexibility of the Gorkhas was in stark contrast to the mostly Brahman sepoys of the Indian plains who made up the bulk of the Bengal Army's Native Infantry:

> These Highland soldiers, who despatch their meal in half an hour, and satisfy the ceremonial law by merely washing their hands and face and taking off their turbans before cooking, laugh at the pharisaical rigour of our sepoys [of the Bengal Native Infantry] who must bathe from head to foot and make *Puja* [religious rituals] ere they begin to dress their dinner, must eat nearly naked in the coldest weather, and cannot be in marching trim again in less than three hours – the best part of the day. In war the former [the Gorkhas] carry several days' provisions on their backs; the latter [HEICo's sepoys] would deem such an act intolerably degrading. The former see in foreign service nothing but the prospect of gain and glory; the latter can discover in it nothing but pollution and peril from unclean men, and terrible wizards and goblins and evil spirits.[4]

Hodgson argued the case for Gorkha recruitment with passion, having no qualms over their loyalty:

> Such are their energy of character, love of enterprise, and freedom from the shackles of caste, that I am well assured their services, if obtained, would soon come to be most highly prized. In my

humble opinion they arc by far the best soldiers in India, and if they are made participators of our renown in arms, I conceive that their gallant spirit, emphatic contempt of Madhesias [Madheshis, people of the plains] and unadulterated military habits might be relied on for fidelity; and that our good and regular pay, and noble pension establishment, would serve to counterpoise the influence of nationality.

However, the final report that Hodgson submitted to Calcutta was much more than an argument for Gorkha recruitment. It was, as he himself entitled it, an account of the origin and classification of the military tribes of Nepal, complete with charts – quite rightly seen today as Hodgson's first entry into ethnography. 'The great aboriginal stock of the inhabitants of these mountains, east of the river Kali, is Mongol,' the report begins. 'The fact is inscribed in character so plain, upon their faces, forms, and languages.' Of this stock three tribes provided the bulk of the martial classes: 'The Khas, Magar and Gurung, each comprising a very numerous clan or race, variously ramified and each subdivided.'

The most powerful of the three racial groups were the Khas (*see Plate 31*), originally Hindu refugees from the Indian plans who had been driven into the hills by what Hodgson declared to be 'the tide of *Musulman* [Muslim] conquest and bigotry'. Some of these newcomers were Rajputs of the Kshatriya warrior caste – known in Nepal as Chhetris – made up of Thakuris, princes whose kingdoms had fallen to the Muslims, and Ekthariahs, their knights and squires. However, the most influential element among these newcomers were Brahmans, known locally as Bauns, about whom Hodgson had plenty to say, particularly on their manipulation of the Hindu caste system to suit their needs:

They saw that the barbarians had vacant minds, ready to receive their doctrines, but spirits not apt to stoop to degradation; and they acted accordingly. To the earliest and most distinguished of their converts they communicated, in defiance of the creed they taught, the lofty rank and honours of the Kshatriya tribe. But the Brahmans had sensual passions to gratify, as well as ambition.

They found the native females – even the most distinguished – nothing loath; but still of a temper, like that of the males, prompt to repel indignities. These females would, indeed, welcome the polished Brahmans to their embraces; but their offspring must not be stigmatised as the infamous offspring of Brahman and *Mlechha* [barbarian without caste] – must, on the contrary, be raised to eminence in the new order of things introduced by their fathers. To this progeny, also, the Brahmans, in still greater defiance of their creed, communicated the rank of the second order of Hinduism; and from these two roots, mainly, sprang the now numerous, predominant, and extensively ramified, tribe of the Khas – originally the name of a small clan of creedless barbarians, now the proud title of the Kshatriya, or military order of Nepal.

These Khas saw themselves as a new warrior caste, distinguished by 'that masculine energy of character and love of enterprise which distinguish so advantageously all the military races of Nepal'. They were Hindus, but by habit rather than conviction: 'They agreed to put away their old gods, and to take the new; to have Brahmans for *Gurus*; and not to kill the cow; for the rest ... their active habits and vigorous character could not brook the restraints of the ritual law; and they had the example of licentious Brahmans to warrant their neglect of it.'

Under the guidance of their priestly Bauns and the Thakuris, the Khas became a powerful fighting force: 'They availed themselves of the superior knowledge of the strangers to subdue the neighbouring tribes of aborigines, were successful beyond their hopes, and, in such a career continued for ages, gradually merged the greater part of their own habits, ideas, and language (but not physiognomy) in those of the Hindus. The Khas language became a corrupt dialect of *Hindi*, retaining not many palpable traces (except to curious eyes) of primitive barbarism.'

Although the Khas claimed Gorkha as their ancestral seat, this was only because it was from this hilltop bastion that they had sallied seventy years earlier under the leadership of Prithvi Narayan Shah. They were now to be found in every corner of the existing kingdom of Nepal, having subdued the two martial tribes who occupied the higher mountain country of Nepal: first the Magars (*see Plate 30*) and then the Gurungs (*see page 132*):

> The attachment of the Magars to the house of Gorkha is but recent and of no extraordinary or intimate nature. Still less so is that of the Gurungs, whose native seats occupy a line of country parallel to that of the Magars, to the north of it and extending to the snows in that direction. From lending themselves less early and heartily to Brahmanical influence than the Khas they have retained, in vivid freshness, their original languages, physiognomy, and to a lesser degree, habits ... As they have, with such grace as they could muster, submitted themselves to the ceremonial law of purity, and to Brahman supremacy, they have been adopted as Hindus. But they have been denied the thread [sacred thread accorded to Brahmans and Kshatriyas] and constitute a doubtful order below it, and yet not Vaisya [agriculturalist caste] nor Sudra [trader caste] but something superior to both.

All three martial tribes were, in Hodgson's opinion, admirably free of religious prejudices, which made them ideal soldier material, even if Hodgson had reservations about the Khas as a potential threat to British interests.

As a work of anthropology, Hodgson's work was inevitably flawed, and marred by his strong prejudices against the Hindu Brahmans, possibly as a result of his dealings with Pandit Amritananda and other Newars. However, Hodgson's main purpose was to make a case for Parbatiya recruitment as a means of dealing with Nepal's rampant militarism – and it was only half of his proposed solution.

Prior to the Gorkha conquests there had been considerable commercial activity between India and China through Tibet, with the towns of the Nepal Valley acting as trading marts where goods were bartered and exchanged. This had to all intents collapsed thanks to the Gorkha treatment of the Newars but it might still be revived: 'Should we win or gently coerce the Gorkha to steadily peaceful ways the commerce of the Newars with India, Bhote and China might be fully revived and infinitely increased by means of the introduction into it of British commodities.'[5]

Hodgson believed these trade-links could be reopened, as much to the advantage of John Company as Nepal. To this end he began to collect commercial statistics: 'I have secretly and carefully applied,' he wrote in a subsequent despatch to Government, 'to some of the oldest and most respectable merchants of Kathmandu and other chief towns of the valley.' His enquiries revealed that in the Nepal Valley there were currently fifty-two local and thirty-four Indian merchants engaged in cross-border trade, most of the latter having come to Nepal since the establishment of the British Residency in 1816. With their co-operation he was able draw up a detailed account of Nepal's main trade routes from the plains of India through Kathmandu and on into Tibet, together with statistics on 'the manner and expense of conveying goods, the amount and nature of the duties levied thereon by the Nepal Government, and the places where they are levied'.

One of Hodgson's most forthcoming informants was a Tibetan named Amta, whom he described as 'a Cashmiro-Bhotiah by birth, and by vocation an interpreter to the Traders'. Amta travelled regularly along the trade route that ran from Kathmandu right across Tibet as far as the Chinese customs post at Tezedo in far north-western Tibet, a journey made up of forty-nine stages, of which the twelfth involved the crossing of the Central Himalayan Range by way of a high pass across 'a huge mountain called Yellum-thung-La, the ascent of which is five *cos*, and the descent as much. The snow never melts on this mountain and the wind is so violent that the Bhotias are wont to say that "He who never wept for his father would weep here". Yaks, and mules and sheep alone can pass the mountain, and they only by having the snow strewn with ashes to prevent their slipping'.

However, once this formidable barrier had been crossed travellers found themselves on the edge of 'a finer verdant plain, enamelled with beautiful flowers', across which 'scour vast numbers of fleet animals resembling the mule, and called by the Bhotias, *king* [*kiang*, the Tibetan wild ass]'. From here the route followed the great river of Tibet eastwards: first to the great monastic and political centre of Tashi Lhumpo – 'the especial residence of the Grand Lama presiding over that part of Tibet' – reached on the twenty-third stage, and then northwards to Lhasa – 'seat of the great lama resident in the Putla [Potala]... very magnificent, the roof tops being gilt and the pillars of silver' – reached on the thirty-sixth stage.

Amta's itinerary was duly published as 'Route from Cathmandu in Nepal to Tezedo, on the Chinese Frontier, with some occasional allusions to the manner and customs of the Bhotiahs', in *Asiatic Researches* in 1832. It makes fascinating reading, much of it being a mix of the factually correct and the fantastical, as in the following account of the self-mortification practiced by some lamas in the town of Sakya, reached on the twentieth stage of the journey:

Day and night, winter and summer, their clothes consist of merely a pair of black trowsers [sic], and a narrow band of red cloth circling diagonally round the body, and passing over the right shoulder and under the left arm. These lamas never sleep with their limbs extended at ease, like ordinary mortals, but in the same erect cross-legged attitude which they maintain throughout the day. The better to enable them to keep the erect attitude at the times when they are involuntarily overcome by sleep, they pass the diagonal body-band under their feet at night ... In one of their apartments are placed two leather bags filled with sand, and having a couple of eyes painted on the outside of each of them. The name of these bags is *Upke*, and it is said, whenever any of the followers of these Lamas is about to die, some of the lesser Lamas takes one of the bags to the abode of the dying man, and, emptying it of the sand, places the mouth of it over the mouth of the man, so as to receive his last breath – which thus secured in the bag, is carried away to a mansion called *Ukin*, or 'the house of breath', for such is the meaning of the word. *Ukin* is an immense structure, whence issues at night a horrible din of ghosts and demons, so no man hath courage to approach it.

All this extraneous information was intended to bolster Hodgson's main argument, which was that if Russia could export British woollen goods, glassware and cutlery to China by way of Siberia why should those same goods not be exported by way of Calcutta through Nepal and Tibet? And Tibet itself had a lot to offer: 'With her musk,

her rhubarb, her borax, her splendid wools, her mineral and animal
wealth, her universal need of good woollens, and her incapacity to
provide herself or to obtain supplies from any of her neighbours,
Tibet may well be believed capable of maintaining a large and valuable exchange of commodities with Great Britain, through the
medium of our Indian subjects and the people of Nepal.'[6]

In the event, Hodgson's advice of Gorkha recruitment was set
aside but his report on improving trade, completed in December
1831, went down well with the Governor-General. As a consequence,
serious efforts were made to improve trade relations with Nepal, particularly in the easing of border restrictions and the levying of duties.
Even so, Hodgson's hopes for establishing a trade route through
Tibet and China were not so much far-sighted as far-fetched and
came to nothing, not least because of the Nepal Durbar's fear of
upsetting China – a fear that continues to this day.

In January 1832 Hodgson learned that his reward for acting as
British Resident in Nepal for the best part of three years was to be
passed over.

Lord Bentinck had instead appointed Herbert Maddock, a more
experienced political officer ten years Hodgson's senior. Maddock's
previous appointment had been the highly prestigious one of British
Resident to the Kingdom of Oude in Lucknow. However, while in
Oude Maddock had blotted his copybook by accepting an offer from
the Nawab of Oude to serve on retirement as his agent in Britain.
Even though Maddock had subsequently turned down the proposal,
this had been enough to convince Lord Bentinck that he had laid
himself open to corruption.

Maddock's effective demotion to British Resident in Kathmandu
was thus intended to serve as a rebuke and a public warning. Not
surprisingly, on his arrival in Kathmandu in late March 1832
Maddock made no secret of the fact that he found the posting
disagreeable. Hodgson's biographer afterwards made much of Maddock's high moral character and his warm regard for Hodgson,
but the plain fact was that Hodgson was ousted from what he had
come to think of as his home, together with all the privileges and
political responsibilities that he had so long enjoyed. This was certainly a huge blow for Hodgson, but, with no surviving record of

how he felt at the time, we can only imagine his disappointment and his frustration.

Hodgson's response seems to have been to return to the several *shokes* that his extra responsibilities had forced him to drop. One of these was his study of the wild dog of Nepal. His further observations led him to conclude that this was indeed a quite separate subspecies that should therefore be known by its Nepali name, *Buansu*, rather than the Indian *Dhole*. His revised and enlarged paper reveals that Hodgson maintained a pack of wild dogs in the Residency's menagerie specifically in order to observe their behaviour over an extended period:

> I have myself been acquainted with the existence and general character of the Wild Dog of Nepal for a long time past, and some years ago I sent to M. Devaucel two very fine specimens alive; which, however, probably met the fate too often attending presents of this sort. But having since obtained many individuals, alive, some of which lived in confinement many months and even produced young, having been enceinte when they reached me, I considered it my duty to keep memorandums of such traits of character and manners as I was enabled to observe; and, as I see no prospect of the task falling into abler hands, I shall now record the substance of those memorandums, embodying them in such a description of the essential characters, aspect and habits of this most rare animal, as my small conversancy with the science will permit me to give.

This new attention to scientific detail did not stop Hodgson from adding the odd human touch. 'One of the finest males I had broke lose,' he writes of one of his wild dogs, 'and leaping a six-feet wall, attempted to make off; but being instantly appraised of the fact, I gave him chase with greyhounds and a horse ... After a run of about a mile, we suddenly came up with him and found him quite dead! The violent exertion after long confinement proved too much for him; he broke his heart!'

What his published paper also reveals is that Hodgson had by now acquired a *camera lucida*, of the sort patented by the scientist and inventor William Wollaston in 1812, with a meniscus lens that

(Above) The Avalokiteshvara or Machhendranath temple in Patan, as outlined in pen-and-ink with the aid of the *camera lucida*. RAS Hodgson Collection 022.052. © Royal Asiatic Society. (Below) The finished drawing, with detail added and finished off in watercolours. BL Lawrence Collection Add.Or.5251. © The British Library Board.

allowed an image to be projected on to a sheet of paper and adjusted to any size. 'To my description,' wrote Hodgson, 'I shall add drawings of the *Buansu* and of his skull, together with (for the sake of comparison), others of the Jackal and Fox, and of their skulls. These drawings are upon a uniform scale, reduced with the Camera, from others of the natural size.'

Two linked sets of drawings – thirteen pen-and-ink outline drawings in the Royal Asiatic Society's Hodgson Collection and a corresponding number of finished watercolours in the British Library's Lawrence Collection – demonstrate how Hodgson's *camera lucida* was employed in the initial stages to set the shape of a picture, which was then traced in pencil and the detail and colour added (*see page 144*).

Another feature of his studies that first emerged at this time was Hodgson's increased knowledge of anatomy. This was because he had acquired a new friend and valuable ally at the Residency: the new surgeon, Dr Archibald Campbell, M.D., who most probably accompanied Maddock when he arrived in Kathmandu in March 1832.

Archie Campbell was the son of a scion of the Campbell clan from the remote Scottish island of Islay who had tried and failed to set up the island's first commercial whiskey distillery. Like so many beneficiaries of Scotland's pioneering education system he could find no genteel employment in his homeland and so joined John Company's Bengal Army, serving for three years as a surgeon in the horse artillery before fate directed him to Kathmandu. He was only four years younger that Brian Hodgson and, crucially, he had the same sort of enquiring mind. The two got on well together and remained the best of friends, initially in Kathmandu and afterwards in Darjeeling.

Hodgson's 'Description of the Wild Dog of the Himalaya', complete with anatomical drawings of the dog's skull alongside other canine species, was published in *Asiatic Researches*. There were now good reasons for Hodgson's return to the organ that had previously done him few favours. One was that his friend Dr Nathaniel Wallich had returned from England and was once more in a position to champion him in Calcutta. But far more significant was the great change that was now taking place at the Asiatic Society of Bengal, initiated by a bequest of a retired Bengal Army officer who believed that by establishing a Sanskrit professorship at Oxford he would help convert the benighted natives of India to Christianity.

Dr Horace Hayman Wilson duly applied for the Boden Chair of Sanskrit and on 15 March 1832 was elected by a narrow majority of the graduates of Oxford. In anticipation of Wilson's election and departure the Asiatic Society appointed a joint Secretary to work alongside him – none other than his deputy at the Mint, James Prinsep, who at this stage of his career saw himself first and last as a scientist and showed not the slightest interest in Sanskrit.

It may have been no more than coincidence that Brian Hodgson's name was put forward for election as a member of the Asiatic Society of Bengal just at the time when the news of Horace Wilson's departure from Bengal was announced. He was duly elected a corresponding member a month later.

One of James Prinsep's first actions as Joint Secretary was to persuade the Society that it had to publish more frequently and more widely, and that the best means of achieving this was through his own journal, *Gleanings of Science* – to appear monthly and to be renamed the *Journal of the Asiatic Society of Bengal*.

Its first number, published in March 1832, duly carried an article by Brian Hodgson – not on Buddhism or birds but on the unlikely subject of the manufacture of paper. He had seen an article in *Gleanings of Science* on the commercial possibilities of the large scale production of so-called 'Nepalese paper' and had at once set out to show why it was 'incomparably better than any Indian paper ... and ought to be generally substituted for the flimsy friable material to which we commit all our records'.

In this article, 'On the Native method of making the paper denominated in Hindustan Nipalese', Hodgson explained that the manufacturers of this high-quality Nepalese paper were actually Bhotias living in Nepal, providing further proof of his growing enthusiasm for anthropology:

> It is manufactured exclusively in Cis-Himalayan Bhote, and by the race of Bhoteahs denominated (by their own tongue) *Rangbo*, in contradistinction to the Trans-Himalayan Bhoteahs, whose vernacular name is *Sokhpo*. The *Rangbo* or Cis-Himalayan Bhoteahs are divided into several tribes who do not generally intermarry and who speak dialects of the Bhote or Tibetan language so diverse that, ignorant as they are, several of them cannot effectually communicate together. They are somewhat ruder, darker,

and smaller than the *Sokhpos* or Trans-Himalayan Bhoteahs, by whom they are all alike held in slight esteem, though most evidently essentially one and the same as themselves in race and language, as well as religion.

Many more articles by Hodgson appeared in subsequent issues of Prinsep's *Journal of the Asiatic Society of Bengal*, and when the eighteenth and what proved to be the final volume of the now outmoded *Asiatic Researches* was published in 1833 – now under James Prinsep's sole editorship – it was dominated by no less than ten zoological papers from Brian Hodgson, many of them illustrated by high quality lithographs based on drawings by one or more of Hodgson's Nepali *chitrakars*.

One of these articles was a revised version of Hodgson's earlier published paper on the Rufous-necked Hornbill (*Aceros nipalensis*), but it was followed by five new ornithological papers: 'On a Species of *Aquila*'; 'On a Species of *Circaetus*'; 'On a Species of *Dicrurus*'; 'On the migration of *Natatores* and *Grallatores* as observed in Kathmandoo'; and 'Description of the *Buceros Hormai* of Himalaya' (the Giant Hornbill).

The paper on bird migrations was particularly significant because his long residence in the Nepal Valley had allowed Hodgson to observe and to record, for the first time, the regular seasonal comings and goings of the local bird populations:

> The Grallatorial and Natatorial birds begin to arrive, from the *North*, towards the close of August, and continue arriving until the middle of September. The first to appear are the common snipe, and jack snipe and *Rhynchoea*; next, the *Scolopaceous* waders (except the woodcock); next the great birds of the heron and stork and crane families; the *Natatores*; and, lastly, the woodcocks, which do not reach us till the November. The time of the reappearance of these birds, from the *South*, is the beginning of March, and they go on arriving till the middle of May. The first which thus return to us are the snipes; then come the teal and ducks; then the large *Natatores*; and, lastly, the great cranes and storks.

Two of the lithographs of birds published in *Asiatic Researches* Vol. XVIII
in 1833, based on original watercolours by an unnamed artist. (Left)
Hodgson's Nepalese Eagle, which he called *Aquila nipalensis*, now better
known as the Steppe Eagle. (Right) Hodgson's *Circaetus Nepalensis,*
today known as Hodgson's Mountain Hawk Eagle, *Spizaetus nipalensis.*

Three of the four remaining papers dealt with species of ungulates;
'The *Jharal* or Wild Goat of Nepal' (essentially an enlargement of his
earlier paper on the *Thar*); 'The *Nyaur* or Wild Sheep of Nepal'; and
'The *Ratwa* Deer of Nepal'. The last article, unsurprisingly, was what
proved to be Hodgson's final observations on the *Buansu* or wild dog
of Nepal.

Hodgson's identification of what he initially called the *Nyaur,*
after the animal's Nepali name, as a new species was proved correct.
It is better known today as the *Bharal* or Blue Sheep, *Pseudois nayaur,*
found throughout upper regions of the Himalayas and the Tibetan
plateau and regarded as an intermediate between the sheep and the
goat.

These papers were of an entirely different order from Hodgson's
first efforts. They were the fruits of prolonged study and observation,
even if greatly facilitated by the fact that several of their subjects were
occupants of the Residency menagerie. These included Hodgson's
goat-like *Thar/Jharal* (more properly the Serow) and the sheep-like

(Left) The *Ratwa* Deer of Nepal. (Right) The *Nyaur* or Wild Sheep of Nepal
with its skull and horns, better known today as the *Bharal* or Blue Sheep.
Lithographs published in *Asiatic Researches*, Vol. XVIII, 1833, based on
drawings which for the first time were publicly credited to Raj Man Singh.

Nyaur (more properly the *Bharal* or Blue Sheep). These two creatures were of very different disposition and Hodgson quite evidently
warmed to the more spirited character of the first:

> Soon after his capture (if he be taken young) he becomes content
> and cheerful: and, within a year, may be safely let out to graze and
> herd with the tame sheep and goats. Intelligent and observant, he
> gives the keeper little trouble; and is an annoyance to the flock
> only by reason of his wantonness: but, ever and anon, as it were
> in sheer contempt of sobriety, he will display the most amazing
> feats of activity, and the most fantastic freaks of humour. He is
> very wanton; and so ardently courts the tame females he may be
> turned amongst, that it is often necessary to deprive him of the
> tips of his horns, lest he gore them to death.

Even so, Hodgson could never quite make up his mind over whether
he was dealing with goats or sheep:

> Though I have kept and petted the *Jharal* and the *Nyaur* for years, I
> could never have affirmed that the former was a goat, and the latter
> a sheep, but for the moral characteristics of the *genera* furnished

me by the graphic Buffon! [Compte de Buffon, eminent naturalist, author of the multi-volume *Histoire Naturelle*]. I have mentioned that the *Jharal* is a saucy, confident, capricious, clambering animal, whose freaks of humour and of agility are equally surprising. The *Nayaur*, on the contrary, is a staid, simple, helpless thing, which never dreams of transgressing the sobriety of a sheep's nature.[7]

What was also abundantly clear both from the texts and the accompanying illustrations was that Hodgson was now conducting serious anatomical investigations involving dissection. His article on the wild dog of Nepal was illustrated by a series of drawings of the skulls of various canines which were themselves hugely impressive both in their detail and their accuracy. Similarly, Hodgson's final paper on the *Chiru* or Tibetan Antelope exhibited an acute understanding of the several adaptations that the creature had undergone in order to thrive in the high altitude and hostile environment of the Tibetan plateau, most notably in the curious protuberances behind its nostrils, which Hodgson correctly surmised to be 'designed to assist this exceedingly fleet animal in breathing, when he is exerting all his speed'.

Although nothing survives to support the claim, it is impossible to believe that Hodgson learned these skills from Shaw's *General Zoology* or other such text books. They must surely have come to him from his good friend the Residency Surgeon, Archie Campbell.

Another new feature was the illustrations accompanying the papers on the *Jharal, Nyaur, Ratwa* and *Buansu*. All bore the name of the *chitrakar* who would remain Hodgson's premier illustrator, of zoological, architectural and religious subjects alike, for the remainder of his time in Kathmandu: Raj Man Singh.

Very little is known about Raj Man Singh other than what Hodgson happened to mention in passing in letters or in his papers, which was that he was a Newar, a Buddhist and illiterate, born to a family of hereditary painters of the religious works known as *paubha,* who at an early stage of his connection with Hodgson took direction from Pandit Amritananda and subsequently broke away from the local painting styles under Hodgson's direction.

In the course of this break Raj Man Singh learned to draw with the pencil and with pen and ink rather than sticks of charcoal, to work

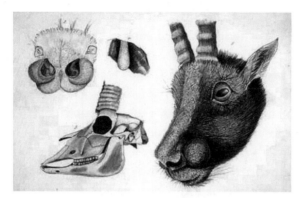

An engraving of a meticulously executed drawing by one of Hodgson's artists of the head and skull of an adult male *Chiru*, showing evidence of careful dissection. *Journal of the Asiatic Society of Bengal*, Volume 1, 1832.

on smooth Europe-derived watermarked paper rather than a mix of buffalo horn glue and white clay laid on canvas, to abandon the single hair brush of the miniaturist for the less fine European paintbrush, to paint with European watercolours in place of the more limited local palette of colours derived from minerals and plants, and to employ the *camera lucida*. But the greatest leap of all – which says a great deal for Raj Man Singh's versatility – was that he learned to draw and paint to suit the Western eye, combining accuracy of detail with the ability to give the picture depth through shading and the use of perspective. It has to be admitted, however, that Raj Man Singh never really learned to draw people with any degree of accuracy.

How Raj Man Singh learned to paint in the Company style is still a mystery, because he could not have done so in a vacuum. Brian Hodgson was no artist but his brother William certainly was, and could well have played a part. As the several examples of his known drawings included in this book demonstrate, he was a solid amateur artist and he had plenty of opportunity to pass on some of his skills and techniques during his extended stay in Kathmandu. Either William Hodgson, or some other visitor to Kathmandu during the late 1820s adept in the tastes and techniques of the *Feringhi*, must surely have passed on his skills to the talented Raj Man Singh, who learned so well that he became Nepal's first modern artist – to be commemorated two centuries later in the form of two postage stamps: one bearing an imagined portrait and the other a reproduction of his painting of the national bird of Nepal, the *Monal* pheasant, *Lophophorus impejanus*, also known as the Impeyan pheasant, although Nepalis know it better as *Danphe*.

It is worth noting that in his identification of mammals and birds Hodgson always gave precedence to local custom by keeping the local Nepali name where one existed, going out of his way to chose an appropriate name if no such name could be found. A blue-bearded bee-eater he named *Bucia nipalensis* after the local term *Bukay chera* (now *Nictoyonris athertoni*); a purple thrush he named *Cochoa purpurea* (which it still is) after the local term *cocho*; a small brown forest bird of the babbler type became *Cutia nipalenis* (which it still is) after the local term *cutia* – and so on down through the alphabet, all the way to a little spotted tree-creeper which he named *Vivia nipalensis* after the local term *wiwi*, now the Spotted Piculet, *Picumnus innominatus* (*see Plates 17–28*).

This use of local nomenclature did not go down well in some ornithological circles. It led Dr Thomas Jerdon, who became an increasingly influential figure in Indian ornithology during Hodgson's time, to publicly express his regrets 'that Mr Hodgson, who ... has shown his talent in the formation of classically compounded words, should in general adopt unmeaning (to most readers) and cacophonous generic names from the vernacular dialect of Nepal'.[8]

For some years Hodgson resisted the pressure, calling the practice of using only classical names in the naming of genera 'absurd and pedantic', but eventually he was forced to fall into line. He did so with characteristic ill-grace, writing to the *Journal of the Asiatic Society of Bengal* that he acted under protest: 'As I am told that continued non-compliance therewith on my part will be considered by most persons as a sort of excuse for past and future appropriations of my discoveries in this branch of science, as described in your *Journal*, I have now the pleasure to transmit to you a series of classical substitutes for my previous local designations.'[9]

Within a week of his arrival in Kathmandu in the spring of 1832 Herbert Maddock found himself having to deal with the fallout

Plate 1 (top). The ratification of the Treaty of Sugauli at Makwanpur in March 1816, as imagined by Lieut. Samuel Tickell in 1849. Courtesy of Lok Bhakta and Kabita Rana.

Plates 2 and 3 (above and left). The inside cover and the last folio of the copy of the *Lalitavistara Sutra* presented by Pandit Amritananda to Captain Knox in 1803. In both miniatures the Pandit is shown kneeling on the left and Captain Knox seated on a chair on the right, in his hand a prayer-wheel.

Plates 4 and 5. Two portraits in oils of Brian Hodgson separated by seven decades: (left) at the time of his graduation from Haileybury; (right) at 89 or 90, after receiving his honorary doctorate from Oxford. Detail of a painting by C. Alexander.

Plates 6. Two rulers of Nepal: (left) Raja Rajendra Bikram Shah, king of Nepal from 1816 to 1847, who ascended the throne at the age of three but even after coming of age in 1832 was ruler in name only.

Plates 7. Bhimsen Thapa, the real ruler of Nepal, who rose to power in 1806 and remained Chief Minister of Nepal until his deposition and subsequent suicide in jail in 1839. A commemorative miniature by an unknown artist painted shortly after Bhimsen's death.

Plate 8. Kathmandu viewed from the road to Patan, with the city in the middle distance and the Himalayan snows to the north-west. A watercolour by Dr Henry Oldfield, April 1853.

Plate 9. The British Residency outside Kathmandu, showing the original Regency style building with the gothic extension behind it. Watercolour by Dr Henry Oldfield, March 1850.

Plate 10. Part of the royal palace area in Kathmandu with worshippers at the shrine of Kala Bhairava, drawn by an unnamed *chitrakar* artist for Brian Hodgson c. 1842.

Plate 11. The stupa of Swayambhu with surrounding temples and *chaityas*, also drawn by an unnamed Nepali artist for Hodgson, one of many left behind when he had to leave Kathmandu in 1843.

Plate 12. A Tibetan *thangka* presented by Brian Hodgson to the Royal Asiatic Society in 1825. It shows the tantric master Guru Rinpoche, credited with introducing Vajrayana Buddhism to Tibet in the ninth century.

Plate 13. A Tibetan painting of the great monastery of Tashi Lhunpo, near Shigatse, recently rediscovered in the Map Room of the British Library. This was probably the 'View of the *Goombu* [*gompa*, monastery], or Lama's Residence' presented by Hodgson to the RAS in 1825.

Plate 14. A group of Tibetan traders together with their mastiffs, captioned in Hodgson's writing 'Bhootiyas from Digurchee [Shigatse], Province of Utsang, Central Tibet'.

Plate 15. A group of Newar types, set against a composite background associated with their religious affiliation as Buddhists c. 1843. One of a number of unfinished drawings left behind in Kathmandu in 1843 which were afterwards claimed by Hodgson's successors at the British Residency.

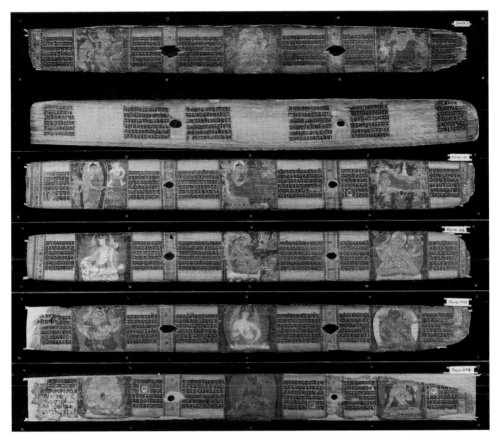

Plate 16. Leaves from the twelfth century copy of the *Astasahasrika Prajnaparamita Sutra*, 'The Perfection of Transcendent Wisdom', a key text of Mahayana Buddhism and one of 80 Buddhist Sanskrit manuscripts presented by Brian Hodgson to the Royal Asiatic Society in 1835 and 1836.

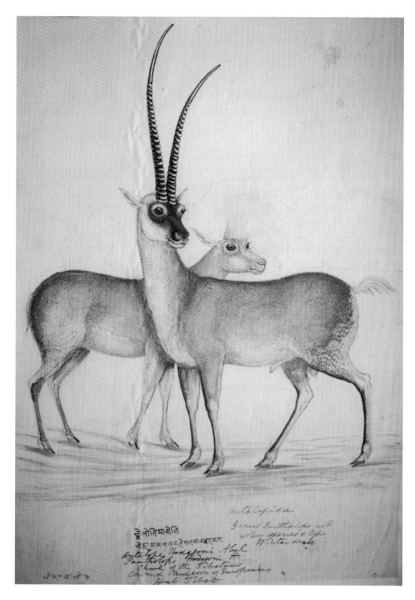

Plate 17. One of a number of drawings of the *Chiru* or Tibetan antelope (*Pantholops hodgsonii*) made over the years following Brian Hodgson's discovery in 1826 that this was not a Tibetan unicorn. This and subsequent plates show a few of the mammals and birds 'discovered' by Brian Hodgson in Nepal—in that he was the first to identify them and write about them scientifically. Many of the drawings carry the name of his premier artist, Raj Man Singh. Hodgson presented one set of working drawings with notes to the Zoological Society of London, from which this selection of drawings is made. A second set of more finished drawings went to the Natural History Museum.

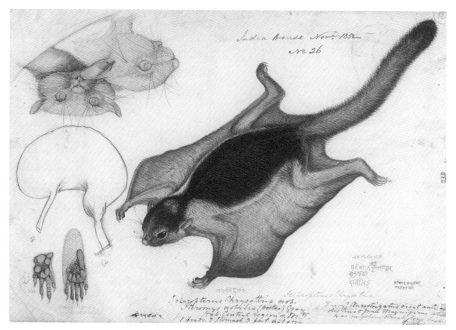

Plate 18. The Giant Flying Squirrel or Hodgson's Flying Squirrel (*Peraurista magnificus hodgsonii*), one of three varieties of flying squirrel bearing Hodgson's name, identified by him in 1836 and now under severe threat from loss of habitat.

Plate 19. The Greater Himalayan Leaf-nosed Bat (*Hipposideros armiger*), one of two previously unknown species of bat identified by Hodgson in 1835. His accompanying note states: 'Nov 4 Valley, skimming rice fields at evening'.

Plate 20. A sub-species of Pallas's Cat (*Felis manul nigrepecta hodgsonii*) known to the Tibetans as the *Risim*, which Hodgson named *Felis nigipectus mihi*. A first specimen was sent to him in 1843 by the Chini Lama, an important Tibetan abbot from Sikkim. This live specimen came from eastern Tibet.

Plate 21. The Tibetan Sand Fox (*Vulpes ferrilata Hodgsonii*), found only on the Tibetan plateau, first identified by Hodgson in 1842 from a skin and skull sent to him from Lhasa.

Plate 22. The Crab-eating Mongoose (*Herpestes urva*), an expert swimmer, one of two species of mongoose identified by Hodgson in 1836.

Plate 23. A folio from one of six volumes of ornithological drawings with notes from the Hodgson Collection at the Zoological Society of London, showing several varieties of sunbird, including two first identified by Brian Hodgson: the Fire-tailed Sunbird (*Aethopyga ignicauda*) and the Green-tailed Sunbird (*Aethopyga nipalensis*), both shown in the foreground.

Plate 24. The Ibisbill (*Ibidorhyncha struthersii*), the discovery of which Hodgson felt should have been credited to him. 'Very rare below,' his notes read, 'hardly known to most expert Shikaris; seen only in cold weather in hills'.

Plate 25. Ferruginous Flycatchers (*Muscicapa ferruginiea*) and their nest, one of four species of Flycatchers first identified by Hodgson in Nepal.

Plate 26. The Tibetan Partridge (*Perdix hodgsoniae*), a specimen obtained from the picturesque Kyirong Valley in Tibet, north of Kathmandu in 1857.

Plate 27. The Bay Woodpecker (*Blythipicus pyrrhotis*), first identified by Hodgson in 1837, seen here with its mate in their nest, with another woodpecker, the Lesser Goldenback, nearby.

Plate 28. A pair of Green Cochoa (*Cochoa viridis*), a brightly plumaged member of the thrush family, first identified by Hodgson in 1836.

Plate 29. The women's quarters of the house of a Gorkha general. A watercolour credited to Dr Henry Oldfield but more likely the work of one of Brian Hodgson's *chitrakars*.

Plate 30. A group of Magars, some dressed in military uniform with their weapons on display. Like other *chitrakar* drawings now in the Lawrence and Oldfield collections, these were originally drawn for Hodgson's anthropological studies of the Himalayan peoples.

Two of a number of anthropological drawings recently discovered
in the Ethnographic Library of the British Museum,
showing various tribes and communities of Nepal.

Plate 31. 'The Khas tribe of Nepal', showing the ruling warrior group of
Nepal, with a rural dwelling and Hindu temple added to show their religious
affiliation.

Plate 32. 'The Murmi tribe of Nepal', showing the Tamangs who occupied
the hills surrounding the Nepal Valley. The Buddhist stupa drawn in the
background indicates their Buddhist leanings.

Plate 33. The Balaju water-garden outside Kathmandu. Brian Hodgson regularly passed this way on his way to and from his summer house in the hills. Since the work was left unfinished when he left Kathmandu in December 1843, the horseman in the blue jacket of the Indian Political Service was probably Brian Hodgson.

Plate 34. The British Residency, Kathmandu, showing a political officer in his blue jacket with his family on the grounds. This was assumed to be Hodgson's successor Henry Lawrence and his family, but new evidence points to it being Brian Hodgson with his Muslim wife Begum Mehr-ul-Nissa together with their older children Henry and Sarah and their new-born third child, a daughter c. 1843-5.

from a major political upheaval, resulting from the death of the Queen Regent.

Rani Tripura Sundari Devi had been Bhimsen Thapa's main ally for the best part of two decades and her death suddenly left him very exposed. The young king, Raja Rajendra Bikram Shah, had turned eighteen just four months earlier, which constituted the official age of majority. He now found himself able to flex his own political muscles for the first time, so that the Durbar became the stage for a new round of power struggles, with the young king, his two wives, various Thapa factions and the descendants of Bhimsen Thapa's old enemy, the Brahman Damodar Pande, all conspiring in various combinations to depose the now elderly Chief Minister.

Bhimsen Thapa's response was to declare a month of public mourning, during which all public business was suspended, and to redouble his measures to isolate the young king from all potential allies. 'The Raja is hemmed into his palace,' reported Hodgson in a letter to Government, 'from which he cannot stir unaccompanied by the Minister, and even then only to the extent of a ride or drive. Even within the walls of his palace the Minister and his brother reside, the latter in the capacity of "dry nurse" to His Highness.'[10]

At this same time Bhimsen Thapa became markedly less friendly in his relations with the British Resident, exhibiting 'a degree of shyness towards the Residency', which Hodgson ascribed to a fear that the appointment of Maddock was 'the prelude to some material change in the style of our intercourse with the Durbar'.

However, Maddock's real test came in September 1832, when a complaint was received from the Durbar about an outrage committed on a Nepali subject by an Indian *mehtar* or low-caste sweeper attached to the British Residency. The complainant was an aggrieved Nepali Chhetri whose wife had allegedly committed adultery with the *mehtar*. Under Nepali customary law this gave the husband the right to exact retribution in person by chopping off his head, not so much because of the adultery but because the sweeper was of the lowest caste and had thus polluted the higher-caste woman. The complaint was seized upon by those bharadaris at court opposed to Bhimsen Thapa, who demanded that the sweeper be handed over to face Nepali justice. This Maddock refused to do, on the grounds that the sweeper was a subject of the HEICo. After a tense two-month stand-off a compromise was reached by which the unfortunate sweeper was tried at the Residency according to Company law and sentenced to five years rigorous punishment, to be served in India.

Brief as it was, the crisis over the two conflicting judicial systems led Hodgson to look more closely at Nepal's legal system, which he did with the thoroughness that was now becoming his mark. He began by enquiring into Nepali law as it affected the case of the adulterous *mehtar*, which he afterwards drafted into a report entitled 'On the law and legal practice of Nepal as regards familiar intercourse between a Hindu and an outcast'. This initial enquiry then led him to look deeper still into the whole issue of Nepali jurisprudence. He drew up another of his questionnaires; in this case, ninety-three questions, which he first put to the Indian Brahmans attached to the Residency and then to a number of Nepali Brahmans and law officers contacted through secret channels.

This second report, 'Some account of the systems of law and police as recognised in the state of Nepal', provides a unique glimpse into Hindu law based on the ancient *Shastras*, largely abandoned in India itself but still practised in Nepal, where it had continued to be applied for centuries untainted by foreign influence. In such matters as capital offences, the law was rigid and unbending: 'Destruction of human life, with or without malice, and in whatever way, must be atoned for by loss of life. Killing a cow is another capital crime. Incest is a third. Deflowering a female of the sacred tribe [i.e. Brahmans] subjects a man of lower-caste to capital punishment and the confiscation of all his property. Robbery is a capital crime. Burglary is punishable by cutting of the burglar's hands ...'

Yet in the matter of civil disputes a complicated series of checks and balances sought to ensure that a kind of justice was arrived at, sometimes by the application of *nyaya*, or trial by ordeal, which could be resorted to where both parties in dispute agreed to it. It was a complicated process that was played out in the large tank or reservoir on the edge of Kathmandu known as the *Rani Pokhari* or Queen's Tank, beginning with the names of the two parties in dispute being written on two pieces of paper which were then rolled into balls and stuck on the ends of two lengths of reed:

The reeds are then entrusted to two of the *havildars* [beadles] of the Court to take to the Queen's Tank; and with the *havildars*, an examining officer of the court, a Brahman, and the parties proceed thither, as also two men of the *Chamakhalak* [*Chamars*, low-caste leather-workers] caste ... If they continue to insist on the ordeal, the two *havildars*, each holding one of the reeds, go, one to the east and the other to the west side of the tank, entering the water about knee-deep. The Brahman ... performs worship to Varuna in the name of the parties, and repeats a sacred text, the meaning of which is that mankind knows not what passes in the minds of each other, but that all inward thoughts and past acts are known to the gods Surya, Candra, Varuna, and Yama; and that they will do justice between the parties in this case.

When the *puja* is over the Brahman gives the *tilak* [sacred mark on the forehead] to the two *Chamakhalaks*, and says to them, 'Let the champion of truth win, and let the false one's champion lose!' ... The *Chamakhalaks* separate, one going to each place where the reed is erected. They then enter the deep water, and at a signal given, both immerse themselves in the water in the same instant. Whichever of them first rises from the water, the reed nearest to him is instantly destroyed, together with the scroll attached to it. The other reed is carried back to the court, where the ball of paper is opened, and the name read. If the scroll bears the plaintiff's name, he wins the case; if it be that of the defendant, the latter is victorious.[11]

The most forthcoming of Hodgson's informants he described as 'an eminent old *bichari* or judge of the chief court, to whom I am indebted for an excellent sketch of the judicial system of Nepal'. Hodgson had got to know this judge in the course of his dealings with the law courts over the matter of the Residency *mehtar* and he proved to be remarkably helpful, confiding to Hodgson that he and his fellow Parbatiyas held the Madheshis of the plains in contempt for not being better Hindus:

Below [in the plains] the *Shastras* [Hindu scriptures] are things to talk of, here [in Nepal] they are acted up to ... Below let men and women commit what sin they will, there is no punishment provided, no extirpatory right enjoined. Hence Hinduism is destroyed; the customs are Mohammedan; the distinctions of caste are obliterated. Here [in Nepal] on the contrary. All these distinctions are religiously preserved by the public courts of justice, which punish according to caste and never destroy the life of the Brahman. If a female of the sacred order go astray, and her paramour is not a Brahman, he is capitally punished; but if he be a Brahman he is degraded from rank, and banished. If a female of the soldier tribes [i.e. Khas] be seduced, the husband, with his own hand, kills the seducer, and cuts off the nose of the female, and expels her from his house

Satisfactorily resolved though it was, the crisis over of the adulterous sweeper seems to have been too much for Herbert Maddock. In December 1832, after less than nine months in post, he applied for sick leave and immediately set out for the plains, leaving Brian Hodgson once more in charge as Acting Resident.

Hodgson lost no time in lobbying Charles Metcalfe, William Bayley and Henry Thoby Prinsep – and quite possibly to others, too – begging for their support. But in fact his recent reports on Nepali jurisprudence, trade and militarism had already done the trick. 'His conduct when recently in charge of the Residency has given great satisfaction to the Government,' wrote Lord Bentinck, in explaining to his own Council his decision to promote Hodgson. 'The reports that he has from time to time transmitted upon the laws and usages of the Nepalese with other statistical information do him much credit ... which makes me confident that this important charge may be advantageously conferred to his hand.'

At long last, in January 1833 the Governor-General wrote to Hodgson to inform him that he was about to invest him with the full powers of British Resident at the court of the Raja of Nepal, declaring that 'I will confirm whatever you may transact with the Raja in my name and on my behalf according to the instructions with which I shall have furnished you for that purpose.'[12]

In February 1833 that appointment was finally confirmed. Brian Houghton Hodgson was now aged thirty-two. He had served John

Company for fourteen years, the last nine spent in Nepal without a break.

The powers of the Governor-General at this time were trimmed by his need to defer to the HEICo's Court of Directors in London and, to a lesser degree, to Parliament. But in India itself his authority was supreme, tempered only by a requirement to consult with his Supreme Council, composed on solid men like Sir Charles Metcalfe and William Bayley. One tier below the Supreme Council were the three heads of the executive branches. In 1833 these were Henry Thoby Prinsep, Secretary of the General, Commercial and Finance Departments; Henry Shakespear, Secretary of the Judicial and Revenue Departments; and William Hay Macnaghten, Secretary of the Foreign and Political Departments. All three were avowed Orientalists who believed that Company rule in India depended on their respecting and working with existing local institutions.

The youngest and the cleverest was undoubtedly the Ulsterman William Macnaghten.[13] Like Metcalfe and Bayley and other political high fliers before him, Macnaghten had cut his teeth in the Sadr Diwani Adalat, the highest court of appeal in Bengal, after which he published two major works on Indian jurisprudence, one of which becme a handbook for generations of ICS magistrates and judges. His talents caught the attention of Lord William Bentinck, who appointed him to be his personal secretary, culminating in Macnaghten's elevation in 1832 to Secretary of the Foreign and Political Departments.

It was in this capacity that William Macnaghten became Brian Hodgson's chief conduit to the Governor-General. Within a week of his elevation to Resident Hodgson was writing to Macnaghten setting out his views on British policy – views that had had plenty of time to harden during his time as acting Resident. It was his conviction that the Government of India had been too accommodating towards Bhimsen Thapa in allowing him to isolate the young king and in failing to insist that the British Resident should be shown all the ceremonial courtesies due to him as the representative of the Governor-General.

More letters in a similar vein followed, with Hodgson insisting that all their difficulties stemmed from the Chief Minister's 'intense hatred of us'. At the same time Hodgson began to receive overt overtures from various factions opposed to Bhimsen Thapa, particularly from the Brahmans who acted as the young king's religious advisers. This meddling did not go down well with Lord Bentinck, who commanded Macnaghten to write back that His Lordship thought it best to avoid 'unnecessary irritation' and that they should do nothing until the situation at the Durbar had stabilised.

This inaction infuriated Hodgson, who grumbled to his sister Fanny that for all his new honours, he was still having to deal with 'barbarians' who treated the British Government in India and its local representative with contempt: 'They are insolent and hostile, and play off on us, as far as they can and dare, the Chinese etiquette and foreign polity'. By contrast, China was shown far too much respect:

> As I write, the [Nepalese] sovereign himself is passing the Residency in all royal pomp in order to receive a letter which has just reached Nepal from Pekin. There they go! Fifty chiefs on horseback, royalty and royalty's advisers on elephants, and three thousand troops before and behind the cavalcade! They have reached the spot. The Emperor's letter, enclosed in a cylinder covered with brocade, hangs round the neck of a chief; the Prince descends from his elephant to take the epistle, a royal salute is fired, the letter is restored to the chief, who, mounted on a spare elephant, is placed at the head of the cavalcade, and the *cortège* sweeps back to the capital.

In this same letter, written in October 1833, Hodgson set down for his sister a useful summary of his growing body of work as a scholar of Nepal and how it was being received abroad:

> Zoology in the branches of birds and quadrupeds amuses me much. I have three native artists always employed in drawing from nature ... and my drawings now amount to two thousand. The antiquities, too, of the land afford me much entertainment. I pore over the pictorial, sculptural, and architectural monuments of Buddhism by the light of the ancient books of the sect; and the learned Thebans of your isle appear to gather up my gleanings

with eagerness. But the past chiefly interests me as [far as] it can be made to illustrate the present – the origins, genius, character, and attainments of the people.

I have published a good deal already in the Asiatic Socie-ties' *Transactions* of London and of Calcutta. In the *Journal des Savants* there is a review of my sketch of Buddhism by a famous scholar of Germany, in which I am given all sorts of laudation and placed at the head of all who have treated of the subject. I sent home for you my diploma as Ambassador, and also the Court of Directors' public thanks for my papers researching into the insti-tutions, laws, and resources of this kingdom.

But for all the plaudits that were now coming his way, Hodgson lamented his continuing state of isolation, heightened by the news that his little sister was now married: 'I am thirty-three – the last thirteen years passed in the wilderness without wife, children, or the presence of a female. No change, no society! What think you then I am likely to be? Something, at least, sweet Fan, standing in need of more of your affection than I have yet experienced. So entirely are we strangers to each another's habits and occupations, that I feel the awkwardness of a stranger in attempting to interest you in what concerns me, and in asking you to repay me in kind.'

Hodgson closed his letter with news of his two brothers in India, for whom he had high hopes: 'William has been ill again, but is now well in the Western Hills ... Edward is well and strong, and his promise as good as you could wish. He has reached Meerut, and com-menced his public career. The Governor-General's secretary [Henry Thoby Prinsep] who was very kind to him in Calcutta, speaks most highly of him.'[14]

But at least Hodgson now had convivial company at the Resi-dency: three 'very pleasant folks in their various ways'. The first was his new assistant and secretary, twenty-three-year-old Andrew Bell, whom he described as 'a brother-civilian, young, sceptical and gay'. Then there was the long-standing commander of his escort, Captain George Robinson, an older and more complex character: 'a worthy captain of foot, selfish but discreet, and whom scientific pursuits form an odd contrast to the plain and unformed character of his mind'. Lastly, there was the Residency's surgeon, 'about my own age, and is sensible, spirited and amiable'. This was his good friend Dr Archie Campbell, who was quietly making himself indispensable to Hodgson as his right hand man.

It was Campbell who now began to stretch his own wings by sending in to the *Journal of the Asiatic Society of Bengal* an account of a violent earthquake that struck the Nepal Valley late on the afternoon of 6 August 1833, its epicentre just to the south-east: 'The shock was preceded by a rumbling noise,' he wrote. 'The motion of the earth was undulatory, as of a large raft floating on the ocean, and the direction of the swell was from north-east to south-west. The shock lasted about one minute.'

A second shock followed two and half hours later and then a third and far more violent one: 'At first, it was a gentle motion of the earth, accompanied by a slight rumbling noise: soon however, it increased to a fearful degree, the earth heaved as a ship at sea, the trees waved from their roots, and houses moved to and fro from the perpendicular. Horses and cattle, terrified, broke from their stalls, and it was difficult to walk without staggering as a landsman does on ship-board. This shock lasted for a full three minutes.'

Lesser tremors followed but it was this third shock that did the damage. The Residency suffered only one collapsed building, but the capital and the other towns and villages in the Valley were much harder hit, with the town of Bhatgaon, also known as Bhaktapur, the City of Devotees, suffering the worst damage: eight of its finest temples reduced to rubble, and over two hundred dead.[15]

Hodgson and Campbell toured the Valley noting the damage. Several large mansions newly built by Bhimsen Thapa and other senior members of his family had suffered severe damage, as well as two large towers erected by Bhimsen Thapa. A newly built temple to Lord Jaganath erected by the young king was also destroyed. However, the great Shiva temple at Pashupatinath – 'containing Pusputi Jee, the patron deity of the Brahminical inhabitants of Nipal' – came through unscathed, 'to the great joy of the rulers and people of the land, who attribute the circumstances solely to the interference of the blind goddess, in behalf of their favourite god, rather than to the stout deposition of bricks and mortar'.

At this same time a very different kind of earthquake was starting to shake the foundations of British Orientalism. It began with a private letter written by a comparatively junior member of the Bengal Civil Service – but one who had already made his mark in a most dramatic fashion. His name was Charles Trevelyan, the son of a West Country archdeacon with strict evangelical principles.

'Missionary Influence', or 'How to make Converts': an anti-missionary cartoon by Thomas Rowlandson from 1816. Christian missionaries from four denominations are confronted by a group of Hindus and Muslims. The Catholic with papal mitre declares, 'Infidel barbarians! We are come to convert you to the European faith.' The Sadhu in the loin-cloth responds in broken English: 'Master, you very fine Gentleman got very fine Topy [hat] but not speak too much good sense ... What for Barra Sahib Bahadur [Very Great Lord, ie Governor-General] send master for black man. Not become Christian being, got one God already. What can I say more?' Illustration from *The Grand Master, or the Adventures of Qui Hi in Hindostan*, 1817.

8

'Reason over barbarism': British Resident, 1833–1835

Charles Edward Trevelyan was only six years younger than Hodgson but utterly different in temperament and outlook – a man so driven by his convictions that he had no time or patience for anything else, the very model of stern Victorian rectitude. Trevelyan had done well at Fort William College but had been so offended by what he saw as the college's moral laxity – in the year of his graduation thirteen of his fellow students were expelled for idleness – that he had left convinced it had outlived its purpose and should be closed down. His scholarship had earned him a post in January 1827 as a junior assistant to Sir Charles Metcalfe in Delhi, where the Resident's responsibilities had been enlarged to include the commissionership of Delhi.

Trevelyan had thrown himself into various city improvement schemes, but none more significant than those involving the Delhi Anglo-Indian College, a new institution set up to educate the sons of the local Muslim landowning class with the emphasis on Western learning. Having joined the college committee, Trevelyan played the leading role in the drafting of a quite remarkable paper that proposed a complete rethink of educational policy, not just for Delhi but for the whole of British India. Its central arguments were two-fold: that Indian learning, and science in particular, was so backward that it had to be replaced by Western learning; and that the only efficient means of imparting this new learning was through the medium of English:

Before an uneducated and half barbarous people can be improved by their adoption of a foreign Literature in their vernacular

Tongue, a general taste and inclination for it must be diffused by
the best educated people among them making it their study in
the original. From this will follow a diffusion of the knowledge
of the new literature – a general assimilation of Ideas towards it,
and, what is of equal importance, assimilation of the Vernacular
tongue.[1]

Just as the Romans had acquired Greek learning through the
Greek language, so the Indians would acquire Western learning
through English, leading to better relations between rulers and ruled,
the breaking down of barriers of caste and religion between the different Indian communities, and, ultimately, to a people united by a
common language. A new and more efficient civil service would be
created and morals would be improved, to 'the real and lasting glory
of our Nation'.

Despite his tender years Trevelyan had had no hesitation in
sending his paper direct to the Governor-General and in writing to
him privately urging him to act. Bentinck had been sympathetic but
it was not until after Trevelyan had been transferred to the political
department in Calcutta in 1831 that he was able to join forces with the
Reverend Alexander Duff and others who shared his views and aims.

In the meantime, Charles Trevelyan had made his mark in a most
dramatic manner. A year after his arrival in Delhi Charles Metcalfe was promoted to the Governor-General's Supreme Council
in Calcutta and his place as Resident and Commissioner was taken
by Sir James Edward Colebrooke, the elder brother of the distinguished Sanskritist, Edward Colebrooke, but a man of very different
morals. Sir Charles, 3rd baronet, was aged sixty-seven but had failed
to enrich himself in India to the degree that he thought fit, despite
his ownership of large sugar plantations in Antigua along with all
their slaves. To Charles Trevelyan's amazement and growing disgust,
Colebrooke, his wife and their young son now set about exploiting
their positions in the most blatant manner.

According to Indian custom, those who called on the Resident
as representative of a sovereign power made a token offering by
presenting him with one or more gold coins, known as *nazr*. The
Resident then either remitted the *nazr* by returning it to the donor

The single-minded reformer Charles Trevelyan, the man behind
Macaulay's notorious *Minute on Education*. A pen-and-ink sketch
by a friend, 1835. Courtesy of the late Raleigh Trevelyan.

or accepted it in the name of the Government and placed it in the
Residency *toshakana,* or treasury, where it and all other gifts were
lodged and recorded. It was strictly forbidden for any Government
officer to accept *nazr* or any gift for himself or his family unless it
was perishable, such as fruit or flowers. Trevelyan was astonished to
see the Colebrookes not only helping themselves to every coin and
gift that came their way but very deliberately setting out to extort
further sums of money from those with whom they were supposed
to be working in alliance, such as the local Indian princes.

Within weeks of his arrival Trevelyan began to record what was
happening and to gather material evidence. In June 1829 he submitted a long letter to the Governor-General that listed more than fifty
acts of embezzlement or corruption on the part of Sir Edward, his
family and his personal servants.

This was an extraordinary act of courage considering Trevelyan
was only twenty-two years of age. In the uproar that followed he was

ostracised by most of the other Europeans in Delhi and subjected to a stream of abuse and vilification by the Colebrookes, who sought to lay their own counter charges against what they described as 'the clandestine whisper of a stripling'. But a board of enquiry was set up and in December 1829 the most serious of Trevelyan's charges were found proven. Sir James Colebrooke was declared 'unworthy of the confidence of Government and unfit for further employment' and dismissed from service. He took ship with his family before criminal charges could be brought against them.

Sir James Colebrooke's behaviour confirmed Bentinck's poor opinion of his civil servants. As for Charles Trevelyan, he received the warmest approbation of the Governor-General and the HEICo's Court of Directors for having 'ably, honourably and manfully discharged his duty as a public servant, and by his zealous and unremitting exertions, performed a most painful and invidious task'. From this time on he could do no wrong in the eyes of Lord Bentinck and was promoted to become an under-secretary in the Foreign and Political Department.

On 18 March 1833 – just weeks after Brian Hodgson had been confirmed as the British Resident in Kathmandu – Charles Trevelyan again wrote to the Governor-General. Not through his official conduit, Henry Thoby Prinsep, as propriety demanded, but again in a private capacity, reiterating some of the proposals for the Anglicisation of education that he had first articulated in Delhi two years earlier. His letter began:

> I long to see established under your lordship's auspices a system of education so comprehensive as to embrace every class of public teachers, so elastic as to admit of it's being gradually extended to every village in the country and so interwoven with the constitution of the state ... In short, I long to see such a system of education established in India as already exists in the state of New York, in the New England states and in Prussia and such as it [is] now proposed to establish in France & England. This would form the crowning measure of Your Lordship's administration. In 25 years it would entirely change the moral face of the country and countless millions in their successive generations would bless the

memory of the man who called them to a higher & better state of existence.[2]

This flattery hit its mark. Within a month Trevelyan was given a seat on the General Committee of Public Instruction, now chaired by Henry Shakespear following the departure of its long-time chairman Dr Horace Wilson. A seat on the board of the Native Medical Institution Committee as its Deputy Secretary followed. With the tacit support of the Governor-General, Trevelyan began a press campaign against what he termed the 'rage of Orientalism' and the 'ivory-towerism' of its proponents, writing under the pen-name 'Indophilus'. He again called for Fort William College to be closed down and for all educational funding to be redirected only to those institutions where English took precedence, with no more money to be spent on the translation of Sanskrit, Persian and Arabic texts:

> Let us not suffer ourselves to be persuaded ... that we are instructing the Indians, while we are only gratifying the peculiar literary taste, and I fear, too generally, the vanity of a few European scholars who happen to have turned their attention to the Sanscrit and Arabic languages. Our business is not with Europe, but with India; and our object is to instruct the people of India by the united means of English and of the popular languages, and not to gain a reputation in Europe by a patronage of the learned few who have leisure and inclination to devote themselves to the study of Sanscrit and Arabic.[3]

The General Committee of Public Instruction now split down the middle, five against five, with the Orientalists, led by Henry Thoby Prinsep and William Macnaghten, on the one side and the Anglicists, led by Charles Trevelyan, on the other. From Oxford Horace Wilson gave the Orientalist faction what support he could, writing to his *protégé* and friend Ram Kamal Sen[4] at the Asiatic Society in Calcutta urging him to resist the changes on the grounds that 'neither Lord William nor Mr Trevelyan know what they are doing' and that it was 'a visionary absurdity to think of making English the language of India'.

Divisions grew as each party set out to make its case. Initially, the Governor-General presented himself as above the fray. However, on the Supreme Council Sir Charles Metcalfe and William Bayley now found themselves increasingly sidelined, their advice overruled. 'He appears to prefer everyone's opinion to mine,' declared Metcalfe of Lord Bentinck in a letter to a friend. What swung the balance was the arrival of Thomas Babington Macaulay.

Macaulay owed his position to a speech he had made in the House of Commons on 10 July 1833 seconding a motion to move a bill for the better government of His Majesty's Indian territories. Largely thanks to his oratory, the motion was carried without a division and duly passed into law as the Government of India Act. The speech was indeed remarkable, with Macaulay calling for Indians to be so well educated in European knowledge that they might one day be fit to govern themselves:

> Whether such a day will ever come I know not. But never will I attempt to avert or to retard it. Whenever it comes, it will be the proudest day in English history. To have found a great people sunk in the lowest depths of slavery and superstition, to have so ruled them as to have made them desirous and capable of all the privileges of citizens, would indeed be a title to glory all our own ... Those triumphs are the pacific triumphs of reason over barbarism; that empire is the imperishable empire of our arts and our morals, our literature and our laws.

Macaulay's reward was a brief period of office as Secretary of the Board of Control with responsibility for Indian affairs followed by his advancement to India as Law Member on the Governor-General's Supreme Council. His main grounds for accepting the post were financial rather than ideological. It paid £10,000 a year (say, a quarter of a million pounds today) and the Macaulays – just like the Hodgsons and from the same cause of unwise investment – were in dire financial straits.

When Macaulay stepped ashore in Madras in June 1834 he was welcomed as a much needed ally by Lord William Bentinck. They proceeded to the hill-station of Ootacamund and then travelled together through South India. However, Macaulay had come to

India with his twenty-four-year-old sister Hannah, and she proceeded directly to Calcutta without her brother.

It was at this point that Charles Trevelyan played another of his astonishing blinders. When the Governor-General's cavalcade finally arrived in Calcutta in September 1834 Macaulay was dismayed to find that Hannah – a plain young lady without prospects whom he had expected to remain by his side as his housekeeper – had accepted a proposal of marriage from an equally plain and very intense young Civilian with no obvious charms. 'He has no small talk,' wrote Macaulay of his future brother-in-law to another of his sisters. 'His mind is full of schemes of moral and political improvement, and his zeal boils over in his talk. His topics, even in courtship, are steam navigation, the equalisation of the sugar duties, the substitution of the Roman for the Arabic alphabet in the Oriental languages ... He is quite at the head of that active party among the younger servants of the Company who take the side of improvement.'[5]

These views softened when Macaulay was informed by Lord Bentinck that his sister's suitor was 'the ablest young man in the service and the most noble-minded man he had ever seen'.[6] Within days of his arrival in Calcutta Macaulay had been steam-rollered into a much talked about *ménage a trois*: Hannah Macaulay married Charles Trevelyan and William Macaulay moved in with them. The Governor-General was then persuaded by Trevelyan to appoint Macaulay President of the General Committee of Public Instruction in place of a demoralised Henry Shakespear.

Macaulay at once made it plain to his fellow committee members that he had no time for its existing policy: 'We are at present a board for printing books which are of less value than the paper on which they are printed when it was blank, and for giving artificial encouragement to absurd history, absurd metaphysics, absurd physics, and absurd theology.' He proposed that no more public money should be spent either on translations of Sanskrit, Persian and Arabic texts or in funding the Sanskrit College in Benares and the Calcutta Madrassa – 'temples of darkness that were falling of themselves into decay'. After protests from the Orientalists on the General Committee, each party agreed to make its case before the Governor-General.

Two reformers united by marriage. (Left) Charles Trevelyan, drawn
by Colesworthy Grant, who captioned the lithograph 'The Zealous
Promoter of European Literature among the Natives of India', 1838.
(Right) The essayist and lawmaker Thomas Babington Macaulay,
who allowed his judgement to be swayed by his brother-in-law,
leading to his writing of the notorious *Minute on Education*.

At this juncture Macaulay by-passed the General Committee and
submitted to Lord Bentinck his now notorious *Minute on Education*,
ridiculing India's culture, languages and civilisation – a *Minute* that
in its uncompromising call for Anglicisation was in every respect but
rhetoric the work of his brother-in-law:

Of all foreign tongues, the English tongue is that which would be
the most useful to our native subjects. The question now before us
is simply whether, when it is in our power to teach this language,
we shall teach languages in which, by universal confession, there
are no books on any subject which deserve to be compared to
our own; whether, when we can teach European science, we shall
teach systems which, by universal confession, wherever they differ
from those of Europe differ for the worse; and whether, when we
can patronize sound philosophy and true history, we shall countenance, at the public expense, medical doctrines which would
disgrace an English farrier, astronomy which would move laugh-
ter in girls at an English boarding school, history abounding with

kings thirty feet high and reigns thirty thousand years long, and geography made of seas of treacle and seas of butter.

According to Henry Thoby Prinsep's son (also, and confusingly, named Henry Thoby), Macaulay threatened to resign if his proposals were not implemented. Lord Bentinck had only weeks to go before the end of his tenure as Governor-General and his health was giving way. He was content to give his approval, writing at the top of Macaulay's *Minute* 'I give my entire concurrence to the sentiments expressed in this Minute'. He then sent it across to Henry Thoby Prinsep's office with instructions to bring it before the Supreme Council.

Prinsep was shocked by what he read and called for an emergency meeting of the General Committee of Public Instruction, at which Macaulay's *Minute* was fiercely criticised by himself, William Macnaghten and his youngest brother, James Prinsep – all threatening to resign if Macaulay went ahead and published his *Minute*. According to Trevelyan, harsh words were exchanged on both sides. 'The blow had gone straight to the sources of their habitual feelings and the effect that followed was highly remarkable,' he afterwards wrote in seeking to explain the Orientalist's hostility:

> They felt as if the world were given to understand that they had spent their strength for nought and that their learning was altogether vanity. The axe seemed to them to be laid at the root of their reputations. This was more than human nature could bear. Men who had been remarkable for self-restraint completely lost their temper, and those who had been unaccustomed to give free expression to their feelings showed unusual warmth on this occasion. It was a striking exhibition of character.[7]

The meeting broke up in disorder. Both Macnaghten and the older Prinsep then sat down to write their own counter-submissions, arguing that Macaulay's proposals were based on his 'superficial knowledge' and were 'useless, wasteful and cruel', and that the imposition of English as a medium of instruction would be counterproductive: 'If we wish to enlighten the great mass of the people of

India we must use as our instrument the Languages of India ... Our object is to impart ideas, not words, and it must be much more easy to acquire these through the medium of the mother tongue than by a foreign one.'[8]

At this point one of the Anglicists on the Committee, probably John Colvin, leaked at least part of Macaulay's *Minute*. This was the last straw for Henry Thoby Prinsep. Although he always denied it, there is little doubt that it was he who then leaked the rest. 'The report,' he afterwards wrote in a private memoir, 'was too widely circulated and too well vouched to be checked [i.e. stopped] and the whole town of Calcutta was in a ferment. In the course of two days a petition, respectful in language but strong in the points to which it averted, was signed by upwards of eight thousand educated Mahomedans and a similar petition in regard to the Sanscrit College was under preparation by the Hindoos.'[9]

Calcutta's English-language newspapers now entered the fray, the *Friend of India* and the *Calcutta Englishman* arguing in favour of Macaulay's proposals, while other papers such as the *Bengal Hurkaru* [Messenger] defended the Orientalist position.

On 7 March the Governor-General's Supreme Council met with the city of Calcutta in an uproar. Prinsep and Macnaghten's submissions were declared by Lord Bentinck to be out of order and set aside. 'I was met by a rebuke,' recorded Henry Thoby Prinsep, 'for having taken upon myself so much, accompanied by the declaration that Secretaries are the organisers and not the advisers of Government and that their submitting *Notes* at all was under sufferance and an irregularity.' To add further insult to this rebuff, Prinsep's submission was returned to him with Macaulay's pencilled comment attached, brief and to the point: 'I remain not only unshaken, but confirmed in all my opinions on the general question. I may have committed a slight mistake or two as to details, and I may occasionally have used an epithet which might with advantage be softened down. But I do not retract the substance of a single proposition I have advanced.'

Some members of the Supreme Council did indeed speak against Macaulay but he had the Governor-General's support and a formal resolution was duly passed stating that 'His Lordship in Council is of opinion that the great object of the British Government ought to be the promotion of European literature and science amongst the natives of India: and that the funds appropriated for the purposes of education would be best employed on English Education alone.' No more money was to be spent on the printing of 'oriental books' and the money saved should be devoted to 'imparting to the native population a knowledge of English literature and science through the medium of the English language'.

Two weeks later Lord William Bentinck left for England, his six-year term of office completed and his place in history as a reforming proconsul assured.

At a meeting of the Asiatic Society of Bengal held on the evening of 6 May 1835, a despondent James Prinsep informed those present that he had received an order from Government suspending the printing of all oriental works and disbanding the printing establishment. He then read out a list of the works then in the process of being printed and now to be 'consigned to sudden destruction'. They included the *Mahabharata* – 'to form five quarto volumes, and printed nearly to the middle of the second volume' – the *Rajatarangini* chronicle of Kashmir – 'comprising one quarto volume of 620 pages, of which about 200 remain to be published' – and a great many other works in Sanskrit, Arabic and Persian either partly printed or being prepared for publication. 'The interdiction,' added Prinsep, 'extends to all the oriental classics selected by the Committee and by Mr Wilson as eminently fit to be preserved in a printed form: the *Ramayana* and some of the *Puranas*; the *Mugdabodha*, with commentary, and other works on Grammar; various standard treatises of Law, Rhetoric and Logic; and, eventually, the *Vedas* themselves; also the various standard Bauddha works in Sanscrit brought to light by Mr Hodgson ... and a vast number of others.'[10]

Prinsep then called upon the Society 'not only to remonstrate but in every way to exert its influence to save the venerable fabric of Indian literature from such a catastrophe, and to rescue our national character from the stigma of so unjust, unpopular, and so impolitic an act, which was not so far outdone by the destruction of the Alexandrine library itself!' He proposed a series of resolutions that in essence called upon the Government of India to reverse its policy.

Only one member present expressed his opposition. That was Charles Trevelyan, who chose to lighten the proceedings with an ill-timed joke, reported without comment in the minutes: 'He had himself had a narrow escape of being a great orientalist, for he had obtained some credit for his progress in Sanscrit at [Haileybury] College, but his dictionary fell overboard during his voyage to this country, and thus he was saved from the bias which an enthusiastic devotion to this ancient tongue might have given to his views on education.' In the circumstances the remark must have fallen very flat indeed.

An appeal, written by James Prinsep and the Bengali intellectual Ram Camal Sen, set out in fifteen clauses and addressed to Sir Charles Metcalfe in his capacity as acting Governor-General, was read out for approval at the next meeting of the Asiatic Society of Bengal, held on 3 June 1835. This time the Anglicists came to the meeting better prepared. Led by John Colvin and Sir John Grant (brother of the President of the Board of Trade, Charles Grant), they did their best to water down Prinsep's draft but were soundly defeated The memorial was duly presented to the acting Governor-General.

But it was a Pyrrhic victory only. A month later the Asiatic Society was informed that the original order issued by Lord Bentinck in Council must stand, and that it was the opinion of Sir Charles Metcalfe, as acting Governor-General, that 'the funds appropriated for the purposes of education would be best employed in English education alone'. The only sop was that the collection of oriental books and manuscripts in the library of Fort William College should be made over to the Asiatic Society, since the college would have no further need for them.

James Prinsep announced the news of the Orientalist's defeat at the Asiatic Society's next meeting in July 1835. But he also had some good news, which was the Society's acquisition of a complete set of the Tibetan *Tengyur* in 108 volumes: 'Mr Hodgson proposes, with his usual munificence, to present this copy to the Calcutta Asiatic Society, while he destines another complete copy of the printed *Kangyur* for the Royal Asiatic Society in London.'

This was indeed a magnificent gift that lifted the spirits of the demoralised Orientalists in Calcutta, and James Prinsep went on to place on record the Society's gratitude that 'good chance had placed a man of Mr Hodgson's zeal in the residency of Nipal, in lieu of one of the *new school*' – the italics were Prinsep's own. 'But for him the 300 volumes of Indian literature, preserved beyond the snows in a foreign dress, might still have been unknown, or, if known, despised and unrecovered.'[11] To this James's brother Henry Thoby Prinsep added his own thanks in a private letter. 'This is indeed glorious,' he wrote, 'and will redound on your immortal fame. I have told Csoma [de Körös] that he must on no account run away until he has read the whole of the *Stangyur* [*Tengyur*] and made known its contents'.[12]

According to Hodgson's biographer this complete set of the Tibetan religious canon had come to Hodgson from no less a person than the Tashi Lama of Tibet, apparently as an expression of thanks for his work on Buddhism.

In Kathmandu Brian Hodgson had followed the battle between the Orientalists and those he called the 'Anglomaniasts' with growing frustration. He had been kept fully in the picture by William Macnaghten and the Prinseps, but had felt unable to publicly take sides without jeopardising his position as British Resident. Furthermore, he had his own views, which meant that he was unable to offer the Orientalist faction his full support.

A letter in which Hodgson set out his own position over seven tightly-written pages survives among the papers of James Prinsep. Dated 29 April – which places it a matter of days before the fateful Supreme Council meeting – it shows every sign of having been scribbled in a state of agitation, the words scarcely formed in places, sloping down at the end of every line and with lots of underlining. But the gist is clear: the imposition of English language as the prime medium of education might help the few but not the masses – and much the same could be said for Sanskrit, Persian and Arabic.

Hodgson had had plenty of opportunity to examine the way in which the Newars conducted themselves. Caste-ridden though they were, they nevertheless met in small assemblies to sort out disputes among themselves and to share information. Known as *panchayats*, these local assemblies also provided a means of education, chiefly in the form of religious instruction passed on by gurus such as Pandit Amritananda.

A group of Nepalis enjoying an outdoor feast in front of the ancient
temple of Balkumari on the southern outskirts of Patan, known to
Hodgson as the Kwachha Dewal. Detail of a signed drawing by Raj Man
Singh. RAS Hodgson Collection 022.021. © Royal Asiatic Society.

Hodgson's argument was that if education was to extend beyond
the privileged few in India it had to be in the vernacular languages and
through such long-established local institutions as the *panchayat* and
the village pandit, whose traditional role was to provide some form of
rudimentary education to the children of the village: 'Unless I mistake
much,' runs one of the more lucid passages in Hodgson's letter, 'it may
be demonstrated from history & Reason that the <u>intellectual</u> faculties
of the <u>many</u> never get more cultivated with success save through the
vulgar speech ... My object is to inspirit & instruct the <u>many</u> in the qui-
etest but most operative manner, & consistently with the present & permanent weal, <u>none</u> of which can be found in English indoctrination.'

Hodgson's letter closed with an exhortation to Prinsep and his
brothers not simply to oppose Macaulayism but also to promote the
vernacular cause: 'Unless we are up & stirring, the Enemy will carry

it by talk. The Press is their ally because so far as English prevails, so far are the gentlemen of the Press at home – & <u>no farther</u>. Ditto, ditto, all views come from England. G.G. [Governor-General], Heads of Law, Commission etc etc.'[13]

Hodgson lost no time in developing these views, which grew in time into 'a plan and outline of a system of general education for the people of India'. One of the English language newspapers in Calcutta that had supported Macaulay's Anglicisation programme was the *Friend of India*, edited by an English missionary. Five months after Bentinck's pronouncement the paper's editor received the first of seven letters written by Hodgson attacking what was now official Government policy. The first two letters appeared under the pseudonym of 'Junius' but their authorship was soon known and when they were published with two more letters in 1837 under the title of 'Preeminence of the Vernaculars, or the Anglicists Answered: being four letters on the Education of the People of India' they bore Hodgson's name – and with good reason, for by then the tide had turned against the Anglicists and in favour, not of the Orientalists, but of Hodgson's cause: education in the vernacular.[14]

'You have,' Hodgson charged the newspaper at the start of his first letter, 'with the majority of the Anglomaniasts, whilst disclaiming all express purpose of annihilating the indigenous literature, advocated the justice as well as expediency of the so-called negative course of withdrawing all public patronage from it. But Sir, have you considered … the extent to which the spread of British rule from province to province, and kingdom to kingdom, has had the effect of closing the native seminaries throughout India, either by the political extinction of their patrons, or by the absorption of their resources?'

The present policy of Anglicisation could only make the situation worse. 'Macaulayism,' Hodgson predicted, 'will help to widen the existing lamentable gulf that exists between us and the mass of people' – and it was that mass of people that he cared about. Macaulayism called for the 'exclusive learning' of the favoured few, leading to the creation of what Macaulay had called 'a class of people who can act as intermediaries between us and the millions we govern: a class of persons, Indian in blood and colour, but English in taste, in opinions, in morals and in intellect'.

But the dangers of creating this new class of Anglicised officials were already becoming apparent:

> The new class are leaning Shakespeare and Milton, Bacon and Newton; and with that sort of training they are despatched into the interior to become officials, possessed of but a poor and mimicked resemblance of our own peculiar knowledge, though purchased at the expense of their own ... The Europeans cannot possibly dispense with the old class of functionaries; cannot possibly get through the work with the new class: and thus the scheme which looks so well in Calcutta, finds no serious approver in the interior.

Macaulay had declared that the Indians were 'a people who cannot at present be educated by means of their mother-tongue' – this in defiance of the fact that 'Bengalee, the language of twenty-seven millions, has good dictionaries and grammars, as well as works which exhibit a respectable share of precision and compass; whilst its connection with Sanscrit, and the peculiar genius of the latter, afford extraordinary means of enrichment by new terms competent to express any imaginable modification of thought.' The same could be said of Hindi in Northern India outside Bengal: 'You have an indigenous system of vernacular instruction which has slowly and naturally grown out of the wants of the people. Build upon it.'

It was not a question of choosing between English or India's classical languages: 'Sanscrit, Arabic, Persian, have proved the curse of this land ... by reason of the administrative mystery they have created and upheld; and I hold it to surpass the wit of man to demonstrate that that terrible mystery will not be perpetuated by English.' English certainly had a role to play in promoting Western knowledge, but if education was to include the Indian masses it had to be through their mother-tongues.

What Hodgson proposed was a 'middle way', one that was neither Anglicist nor Orientalist. He called for the setting up of what he called Normal Colleges, where the vernacular languages would take precedence over English:

Though I give the mother-tongues of the people the first and second place, I give English the third; and in my Normal College, which is not so much an educational establishment as an indirect means of making all such establishments efficient, I would have the *alumni* equally versed in both tongues – theirs and ours ... I want to locate therein a set of able men of the West, who shall be competent to give to India the essence of our indisputable knowledge; and to associate with them other men of this land, English and Native, who shall transfer this essence into the vulgar tongues of India in the most efficient and attractive manner.

This call went down surprisingly well with the Christian missionaries, who had made it their business to set up their own vernacular schools, with Hodgson taking care to invoke the name of the Almighty:

We seek to regenerate India; and to lay the foundations of a social system which with time and God's blessing on the labours of its founders shall mature perhaps long after we are no longer forthcoming on the scene. Let then the foundation be broad and solid enough to support the vast superstructure. Let us begin in the right way, or fifty years hence we may have to retrace our steps and commence anew! Sound knowledge generally diffused is the greatest of blessings; but the soundness of knowledge has ever depended and ever will on its free, and equal, and large communication.

One of the first to support Hodgson's appeal was his fellow Civilian and contemporary Frederick John Shore, whose father Sir John Shore (Lord Teignmouth) had been a very able administrator and noted Orientalist in his day. Shore waded in with a series of newspaper articles against Macaulayism under the *nom de plume* of 'Friend of India'. But it was the intervention of the missionaries that really counted, among them the much respected Dr John Wilson, founder of Wilson College, which became the nucleus of Bombay University. 'Mr Hodgson's advocacy of the vernaculars is most convincing,' he wrote. 'They must be the medium of the regeneration of India, as they have been in every country on the face of the globe.'[15]

Growing public disquiet, stoked by Hodgson, Shore, Wilson and others, now gave greater urgency to a commission on Indian education that had originally been set up by Lord Bentinck before his departure. Leading that commission was the Baptist missionary turned maverick journalist William Adam, and what Adam discovered in the course of his enquiries in Bengal and Bihar was that a widespread system of indigenous education in the vernacular already existed in the form of 'hedge schools'; in virtually every village there was a schoolmaster who provided at least some form of rudimentary education to its children. Adam estimated that there were a hundred thousand such schools in the Lower Provinces of Bengal alone and he recommended that they should not only be recognised but supported by Government.

Sir Charles Metcalfe was still acting Governor-General, pending the arrival of the next Governor-General. He had refused to annul Lord Bentinck's Resolution on Education, but he was no admirer of Charles Trevelyan and saw to it that he was moved sideways to become the Secretary of the Sudder Board of Revenue. As for Thomas Macaulay, all his energies were now focused on the drafting of the Indian Penal Code, intended to replace the existing patchwork of Hindu, Muslim and East India Company laws with a single standard of justice that could be applied equally to all throughout British India.

This was to be Macaulay's most lasting legacy. Although not fully implemented until 1862, the first draft of Macaulay's Indian Penal Code was delivered to the Governor-General in Council in October 1837. A month later its author, together with his sister and his brother-in-law set sail for England.

Trevelyan passed the home voyage in a frenzy of writing, setting out at length the case for Anglicisation, published in England in 1838 as *On the Education of the People of India*. He claimed a great victory, in that Persian was no longer being promoted as the language of diplomacy and Sanskrit no longer a required subject at Haileybury, but he had also to acknowledge that his victory was not complete, in as much that 'every body is now agreed in giving the preference to the vernacular language'. The tide had turned against him.

Adam's Indian Education Commission Report of 1838 greatly strengthened Hodgson's case, as the Government of India acknowledged in its response: 'No one has more earnestly urged the duty of communicating European knowledge to the natives than Mr Hodgson; no one has more powerfully shown the importance of employing the vernacular languages for accomplishing that object; no one has more eloquently illustrated the necessity of conciliating the learned and of making them our coadjutors in the great works of a nation's regeneration.'[16]

There was by now a new Governor-General in post, who in his *Minute* of 1839 announced a watering down of his predecessor's policy with vernacular instruction to be given equal weight with English. Even those elements of the Calcutta press that had previously supported Trevelyan now gave their support of Hodgson's vernacular education scheme, urging the HEICo's Court of Directors to increase the existing education budget so as to make this possible.

This foot-dragging on the part of that body so exasperated Brian Hodgson that in 1842 he publicly offered to put down five thousand rupees from his own purse towards the setting up of one of his Normal Vernacular Schools. In 1854, after more than a decade of dithering, the Court of Directors published a *Despatch on Education* that proposed 'a scheme of education for all India'. So the principle of vernacular education was at least established, even though it was not until 1883 that primary education, 'through the vernacular, in such subjects as will best fit them for their position in life', began to be implemented in schools and colleges in British India.

Historians will continue to argue over the degree to which Brian Hodgson's intervention influenced events but he undoubtedly helped to make vernacular education respectable as Government policy – and he had the satisfaction of seeing that great change brought about, however slow it had been in coming.

Yet it must be added that Brian Hodgson also lived to see the extinguishing of the spirit of British Orientalism that had so revitalised the language and culture of Bengal in his day, and which was greatly diminished as a consequences of the narrow-minded nationalism of Trevelyan and the Macaulayites. And as Orientalism declined so a new attitude towards India and Indians began to take its place, a growing sense of British superiority that only served to widen the existing gulf between the two peoples.

Brian Hodgson's summer house, perched on Kakani ridge some six miles north of Kathmandu, gifted to the Resident by Bhimsen Thapa. Detail of a watercolour by an unknown artist showing the summer house and attached tent as it was soon after Hodgson's departure in 1843. The British Embassy still owns a summer house on Kakani but on a different site.
BL Lawrence Collection Add.Or.5253. © The British Library Board.

9

'Nepal has real and rational charms for me': British Resident, 1835–40

When things were going his way Bhimsen Thapa could be extremely generous. In addition to his donations of beasts and birds to the Residency's menagerie his gestures of friendship included the making over of an acre of land on a top of a steep-sided ridge to the north of the Nepal Valley, just wide enough for a summerhouse. At an elevation of seven thousand feet above sea-level it provided a welcome refuge in the summer months and Hodgson relished the greater sense of freedom it gave him. 'I write to you from a cottage on one of the boundary ridges of the valley, built for my convenience,' he wrote in one of his letters to his sister Fanny:

> The cottage is a pretty domicile, though small, and commands a double view of the valleys of Nepal proper and of Nayakot, to the east and west respectively ... There is not much level space, but the undulations of the hill's summit are graceful, and covered by a superb forest of rhododendron, oak, and numberless Laurifolias. The sward is emerald, and the familiar tokens it displays of England in its daisies, fern, thistle and colewort, are dear to the exile! Parallel to the course of the ridge, one can walk and ride a native pony with ease and pleasure. But there is no transverse development of flat ground; and in the direction of either valley, a lusty bound from the door might carry you a good way towards either![1]

Here in his elevated summer cottage Hodgson was able to let his hair down in a way that was impossible to do down in the Valley: 'I am felling, and digging, and sowing potatoes and oats – yea, with my own proper hand. Somewhat to the admiration of the Court gentry, who, however, have very little of the pompous inanity of Asiatic high-breeding about them, and, I believe, value me for my simple habits.'

Bhimsen Thapa's summer house at Kakani remains to this day one of the perks of the British Ambassador in Kathmandu, although Hodgson's original cottage is long gone and the new building stands on a slightly higher ridge.

By the start of 1835 Brian Houghton was well into his stride. He was close to securing agreements with Bhimsen Thapa on outstanding disputes concerning commerce and trade, the common boundary and customs duties – even if forced to suffer the pinpricks of censorious Charles Trevelyan, writing in his capacity as Secretary to the Governor-General, warning him time and again that he was not to 'force a more intimate intercourse with the Raja' and that he was not to exceed his authority: 'Whether the Raja rules the Minister, or the Minister rules the Raja, your business is with the Government as you find it ... Your duty is strict neutrality and conciliatory and inoffensive conduct towards all.'

Dr Archie Campbell was now proving to be an invaluable ally, so much so that on Hodgson's recommendation he was promoted to an additional role as Assistant Resident. In this capacity he took over the responsibility of keeping up the Resident's political diary in Hodgson's name, recording all the twists and turns in the Nepal Durbar as Bhimsen Thapa strove to limit Raja Rajendra Shah's powers to ceremonial duties and to promote his own nephew Matabar Singh. But it was Hodgson himself who noted that Bhimsen Thapa was now starting to show his age, even though there was 'no statesman in Nepal with a tithe of his weight of character or reputation to succeed him'. A power struggle over the succession was bound to ensue: 'Power is wholly on one side, right on the other. But ... the whole stay of the stronger party is an old man of 65 whose health and even sickness will be the instant signal for a struggle between the several grown members of his family, during which struggle the amiable & intelligent young prince can scarcely fail to redeem his own with the voice and aid of the nobles.'[2]

Hodgson was now earning £4000 a year – far less than his predecessor had earned but a princely sum all the same, and it allowed him to finally clear his own and his family's debts and to start putting something into his pension pot. In a letter written to his ever-loyal sister Fanny in December 1834 he gave a brief account of his situation and his hopes of retiring in five years: 'This is my 17th year's service: at the close of the 22nd I become free to retire on a furlough of three years, the expiry of which at home will entitle me to stay there on the pension of £1000, to which I may perhaps be enabled to add another thousand of my own, or £500 at all events.'[3]

He was hoping that his adored Fanny, then aged twenty-five and still unmarried, would remain so in order to act as his house-keeper on his retirement: 'We shall, therefore, dear Fan, have enough to keep house upon and room enough in the house for our beloved parents occasional or permanent abode at their pleasure. Five years more, God willing: and all may be realised, unless (as I fear) some sensible fellow shall cheat me, in the interim, of my house-keeper!'

Hodgson's continuing poor health in the form of his 'liver derangement' featured regularly in his letters but his main concern was for his military brother William, now in such a bad way that he had been advised to take a year off to recover in the less debilitating climate of the Cape of Good Hope – although Hodgson was also hoping to secure Government permission to have him posted to Kathmandu as his escort commander when Captain Robinson finally retired in a year's time.

That same letter shows how much his relationship with Fanny meant to him and how desperately – for all the solid friendships of Campbell and Robinson – he missed female company:

When your letter reached me I happened to be in low spirits and fancying that no one cared for me; conceive what a cordial to my heart was your outpouring of affectionate devotion and too partial praise! Love me, ever with your whole heart and be assured of my entire devotion! Remember always that if cold England affords you no worthy mate, my house will ever be a home to you, since it is pretty clear that a bachelor's lot must be mine. I cannot leave India before I am two and forty, the last sixteen of which I have spent in a monastery and have contracted no doubt the monastic wont of celibacy!

A combination of two Hodgson family marriages seem to have played a part in helping Brian Hodgson put an end to his celibacy. The first was the marriage of Hodgson's second eldest sister Ellen to a Dutch military officer and widower, Major-General Baron Hubert Gerard Nahuys van Burgst. The eldest sister, Catherine, had already married and gone to live in Canada, and now Ellen went to live abroad with her husband, first in Holland and subsequently in the Dutch East Indies. That left the youngest sister, Fanny, with the responsibility of staying at home to look after her parents.

The second marriage was that of William Hodgson to a Miss Mary Tickell whom he had met in Dinapore, which was solemnised in Patna in July 1835. Soon afterwards Hodgson wrote to Fanny that he still hoped to bring the newly-weds to live with him in Kathmandu: 'I want William and his little wife to join me and I think I shall be able to affect this object in December. He will command my bodyguard of two hundred soldiers and his wife may perhaps help to wean me of some bad bachelor habits.'[4]

What exactly Hodgson meant by 'bad bachelor habits' is open to speculation, but it was at just about this time that he secured for himself a common law wife or *bibi*. He had no prospect of acquiring an English bride and, besides, there was a supposed prophecy going the rounds among the Nepalis that the arrival of a casteless *Firingi* woman would bring an end to Nepal's independence. He therefore fell back on what was by now the unfashionable – and increasingly disapproved of – practice of Company servants acquiring a local *bibi*, the Persian word for a lady of distinction but which in this context meant a kept woman. Yet even in this respect there was a further complication, which was that the strict caste prejudices prevailing in Nepal made it impossible for Hodgson to take a Nepali *bibi* without provoking a major diplomatic incident, as he well knew from his encounters with Nepali law.

According to one local legend, the solution was provided by Hodgson's Bengali clerk. A less probable story has Hodgson's 'old Bauddha' Pandit Amritananda playing the role of procurer. What is much more likely is that Hodgson looked hard at the limited options open to him and found his *begum* among the small Muslim community of camp-followers who provided laundry, tailoring and other services to the British Residency. These camp-followers had come to Kathmandu along with the Resident's military escort, probably at the time of Edward Gardner in 1816. They had settled on a patch of land between the British Residency compound and the east bank of the Vishnumati River, which had afterwards been made over to them by the Durbar.

The descendants of this small Muslim community still occupy some of that land to this day (part of which now lies within the boundary of the Indian Embassy) and they still provide *dhobi* services to the British Embassy. However, attempts to probe them for information about this now ancient – and, from their point of view, highly objectionable – alliance between a woman of their faith and a English *Nazrani* have always been met by a wall of silence. What is incontrovertible is that Hodgson's *bibi* was a Muslim, her father a humble *rajaka,* or 'washerman', and her name Begum Mehr-un-Nissa, or 'Sun among Women' – a name that became popular among Indian Muslims from the time of the Mughal Empress of that name, also known as Nur Jahan, wife of Emperor Jahangir and for many years the power behind the throne. One theory, based upon supposed local lore, is that Mehr-un-Nissa was a widow or a divorcee.

Whatever her past history, Hodgson knew her as Meharunnisha, and their relationship appears to have begun early in 1835. If Hodgson followed the example of other Britons known to him, then he and Mehr-un-Nissa would have gone through a simple ceremony that made them married under Islamic law. According to the tombstone erected by Hodgson in Darjeeling, their son Henry was born on 18 October 1835 and died on 3 April 1856, which would make him twenty when he died. However, the memorial erected subsequently by his father in Petersham parish church states that he was twenty-one years old when he died on 3 April 1855, which would make his year of birth 1834. But then we have further uncertainty over the exact date of the birth of Hodgson's second child, his daughter Sarah. That same Petersham memorial gives Sarah's age as fifteen at the time of her death on 12 September 1851, which puts her birth anywhere between September 1837 and September 1838.

The suspicion has to be that Brian Hodgson was one of those fathers not very good at remembering their children's birthdays.

How the news of this alliance and its consequences was delivered to or received by his family is not known. No mention of Hodgson's children can be found in any surviving correspondence before December 1839, the date of a letter partially quoted by his biographer in which Hodgson states that his children are well 'and make my heart glad and soft amid all the rough obstructions of life'. This letter was to Hodgson's beloved Fanny, who was now Mrs Frances Nahuys van Burgst, having married her elder sister's step-son Petrus Cornelieus Nahuys van Burgst in St George's, Hanover Square, London, on 14 May 1839.

That same letter offers one more fragment of information: 'I touch not meats or wines, and find the Indian habits of food well suited to the climate'. Coupled with a local tradition that Hodgson took to wearing some form of native dress, this suggests that Mehr-un-Nissa may well have played a part in 'Indianising' her partner's tastes and habits.

All this is reading between the lines, except that very often there are no such lines. The four albums of Hodgson's correspondence in the Bodleian Library show clear signs of filleting, with gaps where the original letters pasted in have been cut from their pages. These may have been Hodgson's letters to his sister Fanny from which William Hunter drew extracts in his biography of 1896 – and, of course, we have no idea what Hunter omitted from those letters, because the originals are lost. All that he has to say on the sensitive issue of sexual companionship is contained in one rather terse paragraph: 'Of Hodgson's domestic relations at this period I shall only say that he communicated them frankly to his own family, and watched with a father's care over his children ... It is characteristic of him that there was no concealment on the subject either at the time or when he subsequently married, and it would have been his wish that I should deal with the matter in the same candid spirit.'

But there is one Hodgson letter that his biographer included which may relate to his marriage and how it affected him. Written in Hodgson's hill-top eyrie of Kakani at the height of summer in May

1835, it was addressed to his dear friend and patron Eliza D'Oyly. Hunter's purpose in publishing excerpts was to show how gratified his subject was by the way things were going politically in Nepal and how much his efforts were appreciated by the Nepalis. Hodgson begins by admonishing Lady D'Oyly for remarking that she would 'as soon be a cabbage as live in Nepal' and for urging him to apply for a posting outside Nepal that would do more for his career. He then explains that what keeps him at his post is the knowledge that by 'unwearied kindness and confidence' he has 'melted the rock of Gorkha alienation and jealousy' and so saved Nepal from itself: 'Whilst I live I shall reflect with delight that I saved a gallant and ignorant people from the precipice on which they were rushing'. He cites the example of 'an amiable old chief' who had embraced him in tears and called him the 'saviour of Nepal' and he wishes only that his correspondent could show him the same degree of sympathy.

But at this point the letter changes tack to become a paean in praise of Nepal and its charms:

Nepal has real and rational charms for me – for any one of cultivated mind and self-resource. What say you to its delicious climate, its glorious scenery, with the enduring, accessible, and healthful gratifications inseparable from them? What say you to the possession of leisure by a servant of the public? What to duties free from all tedious and petty routine labour? ... As I sit at this moment in my study with my cheeks fanned by the most temperate of breezes, and my eye filled with the splendid garniture of Mount Arjun, I could almost consent to live and die here and should never cast a longing look towards the third-rate society of all our Indian stations, Calcutta excepted. I am naturally of too eager [and too infirm?] a temperament for either the fiery clime or the killing labours of office below; and many a time have I blessed God that He was pleased to cast my official lot in Nepal.

Nowhere else in Hodgson's surviving writing does he allow himself to be quite so lyrical. Is it reading too much between the lines to see this as a letter written by a man who has at last found domestic happiness?

Among other Hodgson letters quoted by Hunter is one written to his sister Fanny just three months after the above, but utterly different in tone – understandably so, since it concerned the sudden and unexpected death of their Civilian brother Edward in Meerut on 3 July 1835. 'Do not mourn unduly,' Hodgson writes, 'Happy, thrice happy they who quit this troubled scene ere the bloom of their virtuous feelings has been rubbed off! . . Already had he given evidence of such talents and dispositions as made his immediate superiors forward to employ and to advance him. In his private capacity he had won so much respect from the society of Meerut that all the station combined to honour his remains. Let these things be your consolation.'[5]

Edward's death had left Brian Hodgson having to deal with the aftermath: 'Poor boy, he dreamed not of fatal consequences and of course left no will. The Registrar of the King's Court will administer: his debts will become mine, and I have taken measures to secure the possession of whatever may serve to remind us of him, such as his prize books, trinkets etc.'

Despite the family tragedies and, indeed, despite the Anglicist triumph of March 1835, these were good years both for Brian Hodgson and for Orientalist scholarship in India. The Asiatic Society of Bengal was once again breaking new ground as it had done in the days of Sir William Jones, very largely due to the energy of its Secretary and his editorship of the Society's *Journal*. James Prinsep's personal achievements as the man who laid the foundations of Indian numismatics and as the 'code-breaker' who restored Emperor Ashoka to Indian history through his deciphering of the Brahmi script have been chronicled elsewhere.[6] But the key to this brief second golden age of Orientalist scholarship was Prinsep's management of an ever-growing circle of correspondents throughout India and beyond.

Among the most enthusiastic and prolific of those correspondents was Brian Hodgson in Kathmandu, whose further articles on Buddhism continued to appear in the monthly issues of the *Journal of the Asiatic Society of Bengal*. They were often published side by side with those from Csoma de Körös, now settled in Calcutta in a room found for him by Prinsep at the Asiatic Society, but with many new contributors joining in from as far afield as Kabul and Colombo:

most notably, George Turnour of the Ceylon Civil Service, whose translations of the island's ancient Buddhist chronicles, written in Sanskrit's sister language of Pali, threw fresh light on early Buddhist history as a counterbalance to the Sanskrit texts obtained by Hodgson and de Körös.

Hodgson's main contribution to Buddhist studies now chiefly took the form of responding to objections to some of the claims made in his *Sketch of Buddhism* and his *Notices*, which he did by supplying translations of Sanskrit texts with the help of his old friend Pandit Amritananda, now lauded by Hodgson as 'the most learned Buddhist then, or now, living in this country'. He also followed every twist and turn of the steady uncovering of Buddhist history as it appeared month by month courtesy of James Prinsep and his *Journal of the Asiatic Society of Bengal*, making frequent interventions when he had something to add.

One such intervention followed the report on an excavation at a site outside Benares carried out by a young engineer officer named Alexander Cunningham. Supported by funds from James Prinsep, he had taken local leave to examine some ruins where the local maharaja, in the course of excavating the site for its bricks and stones, had come across some heretical sculptures, leading him to abandon the dig. Unknown to all, these was the remains of the deer park at Sarnath where Buddha Sakyamuni had preached his first sermon, a key moment in Buddhist history known to its adherents as The First Turning of the Wheel of the Dharma. Cunningham had transported the best of the recovered statues down to Calcutta for presentation to the Asiatic Society, including one that carried an incomplete inscription at its base written in early Sanskrit: *Ye dharma hetum-prabhava hetum tesha tathagata*.

Tathagata was an honorific term for Buddha Sakyamuni but the line made little sense to the Sanskritists in Calcutta. However, when published in the *Journal of the Asiatic Society of Bengal* it provoked an immediate response from Hodgson. 'Your enigma requires no Oedipus for its solution in Kathmandu,' he wrote back to Prinsep, 'where almost every man, woman and child of the Bauddha faith can repeat the *confessio dei* inscribed in the Sarnath stone'. He went on to explain how central this phrase was to Buddhism:

As I was looking over your *Journal* my Newari painter came into the room. I gave him the catch word, '*Ye Dharma*,' and he immediately filled up the sentence finishing with *Tathagata* ... The passage occurs in numberless places, sometimes containing but half of the complete dogma of the inscription ... Nothing is more complete or more fundamental than this doctrine. It asserts that Buddha revealed the causes of mundane existence, as well as the causes of complete cessation, implying by the latter translation to the eternal quiescence of *Nirvritti* [Nirvana], which is the grand object of all Buddha vows. It explains especially the manner in which, according to the scriptures, a devout Buddhist may hope to obtain cessation from mundane existence.[7]

However, in this same letter Hodgson revealed in passing that he had only recently lost his Newar friend and teacher: 'Whenever, in playful mood, I used to reproach my old friend Amritananda (now alas! no more) with the atheistic tendency of his creed, he would always silence me with, "*Ye Dharma* ..." insisting that Tathagata referred to the supreme self-existent (*Swayambhu*) Buddha.'

This letter dates Amritananda death to before March 1835[8] and accords with Nepali records which place his death in the year 955 according the Nepali calendar, or 1835. This is one of the few details known about this remarkable Newar Vajracharya. It is a puzzling fact that until very recently his work remained unacknowledged among his own community, perhaps because he broke with centuries of tradition in making this most esoteric form of Buddhism understood outside his own circle of adepts. That he won the respect of the local British community at the Residency is shown by the fact that two decades on his grandson was being employed as official Residency Pandit, a role usually filled by a Hindu Brahman from India.

It was almost entirely due to Amritananda that Hodgson was able to procure so many Sanskrit manuscripts to be sent down to India and on to Europe. In addition to the sutras presented to the Fort William College Library, the Asiatic Society of Bengal and the Royal Asiatic Society in London, Hodgson also presented manuscripts to France – prompted by the warmth of the French savant Eugène Burnouf, the most supportive of the many scholars who began writing to Hodgson following the publication of his two papers on Buddhism.

Hodgson despatched a first tranche of twenty-four such manuscripts from Nepal in November 1835. These included the *Lalitavistara* and some of Buddhism's earliest and most important sutras, such as the *Prajnaparamita* or 'Perfection of Wisdom', regarded as one of the earliest and most influential teachings of the Buddha, and the *Saddharmapundarika*, or 'Lotus Sutra', which Eugène Burnouf afterwards used as the title for the second of his major works on Buddhism, *Le Lotus de la Bonne Loi*.

The enthusiasm with which the French acknowledged this donation was in marked contrast to the lukewarm responses of some of the British institutions and Hodgson made no bones letting Burnouf know how he felt. 'Our British Zoological Societies,' he told him in a letter in May 1837, 'are saucy and ticklish and would fain draw from us all our materials for their sole compounding.'9

Burnouf's response was to write to Hodgson to inform him that the Societé Asiatique intended to present him with a gold medal for his efforts, to which Hodgson reacted by despatching a further collection of Sanskrit manuscripts – sixty-four in all, and 'of inestimable value', according to Burnouf. These were formally handed over to the Societé Asiatique by Burnouf at a meeting held in Paris on 14 July 1837.

Once again, the French were quick to express their appreciation. Hot on the heels of Hodgson's receipt of the Societé Asiatique's gold medal came a letter forwarded by Burnouf from the Grand Chancellor of the Royal Order of the *Légion d'Honneur* informing him that he had been appointed a Chevalier of that order by King Louis Philippe of France. A bizarre chapter of accidents followed, including the fall of a French government and a US consul in Algiers also named Hodgson, which meant that the honour was withdrawn, reinstated and then sent to the wrong man, so that it was not until October 1841 that Hodgson finally received his *Légion d'Honneur* medal with its distinctive red ribbon. He was understandably proud of this award, not least because it was the only national recognition he ever received for his services.

For Brian Hodgson the death of his preceptor and supplier of Buddhist material in the spring of 1835 marked the end of an era. He continued to accumulate manuscripts and to employ his artists to draw religious structures, both Buddhist and Hindu, but he all but ceased to pursue his studies in Buddhism beyond adding the occasional amendment to his earlier work. The main emphasis now was on the more accessible field of zoology, and from this time onwards Hodgson began to write papers on various species of mammals and birds at a quite astonishing rate – at an average of just over one a month – as part of a prodigious output that would amount to 146 zoological papers written between 1826 and 1858.

That these papers were good enough to arouse the admiration of eminent naturalists in Europe is demonstrated by a letter James Prinsep sent to Hodgson at some point in 1836 asking him to send in 'more zoological papers as well as duplicates of those the printer has mislaid, for Professor Royle [of the Zoological Society of London] writes to me from London that your papers are held to constitute the principal value of my journal among the folks at home.'[10]

Thanks to the industry and artistry of Raj Man Singh and at least two of his fellow *chitrakars*, Hodgson was now accumulating an ever-expanding portfolio of zoological drawings and watercolours that, in his opinion, could be matched against the best of the European artists. 'Have you got the latest batch of drawings – twenty-two sheets', we find him writing to James Prinsep in April 1836 – 'and are they not wondrous work for a Nipalese? I have some more now executing which I dare any artist in Europe to excel and they are rigidly correct in every detail.'[11]

Following the long-standing Company practice of duplicating everything, Hodgson required two copies to be made of every drawing or painting, the more experienced artist producing the original, which was then copied by his less skilled assistants. Many of these paintings were subsequently lost, most notably those Hodgson sent to the Asiatic Society of Bengal and the library of Fort William College. However, such was the scale of production that impressive collections of Hodgsonian drawings and paintings survive in five major institutions in England and France. Of these, the most spectacular are the two sets of paintings, each made up of six large albums of ornithological drawings and notes and of mammals, insects and reptiles, that form the basis of the Hodgson Collections at the Natural History

Museum and the Zoological Society of London. Hitherto inaccessible to all but serious scholars, both sets are now in the process of being digitised prior to making them available to view on the internet.

Some of these paintings and their accompanying notes were intended to provide the material for a major illustrated work on the mammals of Nepal which Hodgson first began to contemplate as early as 1831, inspired by reading the first edition of *A Century of Birds from the Himalaya Mountains*. This was mostly the work of the artist John Gould, whose sidelines as a taxidermist and curator at the Zoological Society of London gave him privileged access not only to the many specimens that Hodgson and others had been sending in from the Indian sub-continent but also to the expertise of the ornithologist Nicholas Vigors, one of the co-founders of the Zoological Society of London and its first Secretary.

Hodgson, however, was determined to concentrate on mammals, where there was less obvious competition, and in 1835 he wrote to the Scottish naturalist Sir William Jardine, who had begun to produce a series of what proved to be immensely popular illustrated books on various branches of zoology under the generic title of *The Naturalist's Library*. Jardine warmed to Hodgson's idea and advised him on how to proceed. This led to an appeal appearing in the June 1835 issue of the *Journal of the Asiatic Society of Bengal* from 'a gentleman who has been, for some years past, fixed in a favourable situation for observing nature, with more leisure than usually falls to the lot of the Servants of Government in India'.

This said gentleman, the appeal went on – in the long-winded style that any of Hodgson's correspondents would have instantly recognised –

has amused himself by the formulation of a large stock of drawings and notes, calculated to illustrate the zoology of the district in which he resides, and he proposes by placing these drawings and notes in the hands of some true minister and interpreter of nature at home: and by establishing a system of reference between such a one and himself to complete his observations during the next two or three years, under the counsel of ripe science. The object of this gentleman is not to exhibit himself as a zoologist, which he is not; but to aid zoology, by marrying opportunity to skill.

Examples of the zoological drawings referred to were available for inspection at Asiatic Society's rooms in Upper Park Street, Calcutta. Clumsily put though it was, the purpose of the appeal was to open a subscription list by which signatories pledged themselves to support the cost of printing a limited edition, of which they themselves would be entitled to one or more copies, depending on the amount pledged. This was the usual means at the time of enabling the publication of an expensive book of the sort that Hodgson intended.

At this same time Hodgson wrote to Sir Alexander Johnston, Vice-President of the Royal Asiatic Society, asking for his support, stressing the importance he placed on scientific accuracy and the care he had taken to ensure as much in his drawings:

> My drawings amount to several hundreds, and almost every subject has been again and again corrected, from fresh specimens, in respect to colour and figure. Sexual differences, as well as those caused by nonage, have been fixed and portrayed when it seemed advisable; and various characteristic parts, external and internal, have been separately delineated. In regard to the latter ... the use of the camera has been resorted to, to insure rigid accuracy; and when it has not been employed, the draughtsmen have been perpetually recalled to the careful exhibition of characters by my supervision ... I have myself continued to draw from the same source notes of the structure of stomachs and intestines, of habits in regard to food, as indicated by the contents of the stomachs, and of other habits, of manners, location, and economy, derived either from observation or report.[12]

A detailed synopsis of Hodgson's planned work subsequently appeared in the *Journal of the Asiatic Society* listing all the species of mammals that were to be included. The Prinseps, the D'Oylys, Dr Nathaniel Wallich and many others duly came forward with pledges of support – but not enough to cover the considerable costs involved. In desperation, Hodgson wrote to John Gould suggesting that they collaborate on a book on the zoology of Nepal that would combine birds and reptiles with mammals – and, of course, using his Nepali drawings. But Gould was insistent that the book should be done only on his terms, which were that it cover the birds of Nepal only, and that Hodgson was to confine himself to writing about the birds' habitats and behaviour, leaving him to write the scientific descriptions. Furthermore, Gould was convinced that no work executed by a local artist would sell, so he proposed redrawing all Hodgson's *chitrakar* drawings himself. Not surprisingly, Hodgson withdrew.

However, Hodgson had not given up and later that same year he sent Sir William Jardine a large parcel of drawings and bird-skins. Jardine responded with enthusiasm, claiming to have discovered some thirty to forty news species among these specimens. Again, Hodgson's hopes were raised. But, for reasons unknown, Jardine withdrew his support. Subsequently, Hodgson approached a third naturalist, William Swainson, and the two of them even got so far as drawing up a contract – but, again, the project came to nothing.

A single sentence from a letter Hodgson sent to James Prinsep in 1836 sums up not only Hodgson's frustration at these setbacks but also his sense of grievance over what he saw as the failure of others to appreciate his efforts: 'By my soul it is a d___d bore to be compelled to fawn and entreat for subscribers as if one was obliged instead of the obliging party, when one undertakes to labour with pains and cost for the love of science.'[13]

On 20 March 1836 Calcutta celebrated the long-delayed arrival of the new Governor-General: the convivial George Eden, second Baron Auckland, together with his two equally sociable sisters Emily and Fanny, all three of them unmarried. Lord Auckland was a jobbing Whig politician, previously employed at the Board of Trade and as First Lord of the Admiralty. Like every other pro-consul, he arrived full of good intentions, declaring that 'he looked with exultation to the new prospects before him as affording him an opportunity of doing good to his fellow creatures, of promoting education and knowledge, and of extending the blessings of good government and happiness to millions in India'.

The popular but fatally obliging Lord Auckland, who by listening
to bad political advice brought about the greatest military disaster
in British history. Lithograph by Colesworthy Grant c. 1838.

However, Auckland also came bearing a memorandum for the
HEICo's Court of Directors bidding him to 'watch more closely
than has hitherto been attempted the progress of events in Afghanistan' empowering him to 'interfere decidedly in the affairs of
Afghanistan' and to take any measures he thought desirable 'to
counteract Russian advances in that quarter' – a memorandum that
was to haunt Auckland, leading to the destruction of a lot more
than his reputation.

The Edens' informal style went down as well with the administration as it did with Calcutta society. 'He had many amiable qualities and his two sisters, especially the elder, contributed much to
establish his popularity,' recorded Henry Thoby Prinsep, now at the
top of the Bengal Civil Service ladder as the Chief Secretary. 'He
was a good man of business, an assiduous reader of all papers, and
very correct and careful in avoiding to commit himself in any of the
drafts he approved and passed.'

But there were weaknesses to Lord Auckland's character that soon became obvious to those who had to work closely with him: his inability to make up his mind coupled with an 'overwheening dread of responsibility, which caused the instructions he gave, which were often penned by himself, to be so unsatisfactory that his agents had generally to decide for themselves what to do in any difficulty.' Auckland liked to be told what to do and for others to do it.

What was gratifying for the Orientalists was Lord Auckland's overt support for the work of James Prinsep and his colleagues at the Asiatic Society of Bengal. His predecessors had accepted the position of the Society's President as essentially honorary but Auckland took the role seriously, ordering an exhibition of the Society's work to be held in Government House itself. 'On the round tables of the drawing room were spread out numerous beautiful drawings,' noted the Society's *Journal* for November 1836. These included 'Mr Hodgson's Nipal Zoology, Dr Canton's collection of Indian snakes, and Dr McClelland's Assamese Zoology'. Other tables displayed collections that ranged from Indian, Greek and Roman coins, fossils and Buddhist sculpture to 'a beautiful apparatus belonging to Mr James Prinsep by which water was decomposed by the magnet; a candle was lighted by it, and an electric shock was administered to many of the spectators, among whom the native gentlemen in particular betrayed considerable astonishment at its effects'.

Despite the favourable climate, Hodgson's subscription list still failed to take off. In July 1837 he was writing to his father that he had secured the backing of the Musée d'Histore Naturelle in Paris and enough sponsors to make the project viable: 'I make sure of three hundred and fifty to four hundred subscribers, and if we say £10 per copy of the work that list should cover all expenses.' The quality of the illustrations had also greatly improved: 'Granted my first drawings were stiff and bad, but the new series will challenge comparison with any in existence.'[14]

But Hodgson was mistaken. Despite the best efforts of his friends, the subscription list failed to reach the numbers he needed to risk publication. He tried various compromises in an effort to bring in more names, but was eventually forced to postpone his scheme. Yet the collecting of specimens, the drawing and the careful observation

The last portrait of James Prinsep, whose six-year tenure as the
presiding genius of the Asiatic Society of Bengal greatly advanced
Indian studies. A lithograph drawn by Colesworthy Grant in
1838 when Prinsep's fatal illness was already well advanced.

and note-taking, all these continued unabated – always in the hope
that at some point Hodgson would find a way of publishing his
Nepal Zoology.

That hope was never realised, not least because younger and
better qualified zoologists – and ornithologists, too – were entering
the field, none of them better placed than Edward Blyth, appointed
curator of the Asiatic Society of Bengal Museum in 1841. Blyth very
soon began to make a name for himself as an outstanding zoologist
and ornithologist – and he began to challenge Hodgson's claims and

his outmoded system of naming his specimens. Worst of all, he put to one side the descriptions of new species that Hodgson submitted for publication, often for months and even years – while publishing what were essentially the same descriptions under his own name.

When Hodgson complained, Blyth countered with a complaint of his own. 'Of the new species which I am now describing,' he wrote to a friend in 1845, 'Hodgson has furnished a good many, which I have had all this time in hand: he was, and is, terribly eager to have them all published, no matter how crudely: being fond of the credit of making discoveries of this kind, and leaving to others the labours of reducing and determining his species, of which I have done in an immense number of instances, quashing his new species altogether.'[15]

Things might have been different had James Prinsep lived, but after six years of quite breathtaking industry and achievement, that warm-hearted and much-loved genius contracted an inflammation of the brain that by October 1838 rendered him a speechless, helpless invalid. His death in England six months later at the age of forty-one robbed the Asiatic Society of Bengal of its main driving force. Good men came and went thereafter as Secretaries of the Asiatic Society of Bengal and as editors of its journal but none with the energy and intellect required. With each decade that followed the Society's authority as the centre of Indian studies dwindled – to the point where today it is little more than a dusty and sadly underfunded relic.

In 1836, the year of their closest co-operation, Hodgson contributed fourteen articles to Prinsep's two publications, chiefly on birds and mammals; in 1837, the year of Prinsep's increasing debilitation, nine; in 1838, the year of his death, just one – 'On a new species of pheasant: *Phasianus crossoptilon* from Tibet'.

It is just possible that these two men met in Calcutta a matter of months before the latter's sickness overwhelmed him. Early in 1838 Hodgson became so unwell with another bout of his liver complaint that he was brought down to the Indian plains by *doolie* and then on to Calcutta to seek medical advice. Nothing more is known about this brief visit, except that Hodgson suffered some kind of medical crisis after the bursting of a tumour or ulcer in his liver, and that he recovered and was back in Kathmandu before the onset of the Hot Weather in March 1838. In that same year Hodgson's oldest and dearest friends on the sub-continent, Sir Charles and Eliza D'Oyly, left India for good, first moving to England and then to Italy. William Bayley also retired, later to become a Director and subsequently Chairman of the HEICo.

At this same time Hodgson's plans to bring his surviving brother William back to live with him in Kathmandu came to nothing. Early in 1838 William's first-born child died as an infant in Mhow and then only months later, on 12 June, William himself followed her to the grave. It became Brian Hodgson's responsibility to pay off his debts and to make arrangements for his young widow to return home. His great comfort at this time would have been the presence of his own little family. That summer Henry must have been about three and Sarah about two years old.

Initially, Lord Auckland's willingness to take advice worked well. He was happy to support the promotion of vernacular education, which became the one major reform instituted during his term of office. But his obliging nature also made him prey to those closest to him. Had he remained in Calcutta all might have been well, since he would then have been obliged to listen to Sir Charles Metcalfe, Thomas Macaulay, Henry Thoby Prinsep and the other members of his Supreme Council. However, on completing a tour of the North-Western Provinces in April 1837 Auckland proceeded direct to the hill station of Simla – taking with him as his advisers only his personal secretary, John Colvin, and the Secretary of the Foreign and Political Department, William Macnaghten – both of them strong-minded individuals with decided views. A pattern was established whereby for six months every summer the Governor-General and his closest advisers were distanced from Calcutta and the bulk of the civil and military administration by a thousand miles and a time-lapse of four-to-five weeks.

On 30 April 1837 the then ruler of Kabul, Amir Dost Moham-mad, launched an attack on the Punjab in a bid to recapture Afghan territory lost to the Sikhs. He was driven back, which encouraged the Shah of Iran to invade western Afghanistan, seemingly intent on repeating his ancestor's march of Delhi – and supposedly with the connivance of Russia. Had Auckland thrown his weight behind

Dost Mohammad all might have been well but, on the advice of Colvin and Macnaghten, he chose to promote the restoration of Dost Mohammad's rival, the ousted ruler Shah Shuja, to the throne of Kabul.

These events caused great excitement in Nepal, leading to rumours of the impending downfall of John Company. The Durbar again began to despatch secret messengers and envoys, not only to Kabul but to numerous Indian states whose rulers might be inclined to join forces against British rule. 'Twenty-three of these missions were intercepted during the years 1838–39–40 en route towards various points, but especially Lahore,' wrote Hodgson some years later in a curious document listing his political services that purported to be the work of an anonymous 'Friend'.

The purpose of these secret communications was quite plain: 'To get rid of the British Envoy at the capital [i.e. Kathmandu], and thus to obtain free scope for intrigues with our allies, preparatory to conjoint hostile movements against us; the Sikhs, Sindians and Mahrattas being the allies chiefly desiderated ... If these could be won by treacherous defection from us, the heart of our territories could be struck at by a march at Patna and the Ganges, with terrible effect.'[16]

In the event, it was Nepal's own internecine power-struggles at court quite as much as the vigilance of the British border guards that prevented the Gorkhas from forming any such hostile alliances.

On 24 July 1837 news reached the British Residency that Raja Rajendra Bikram Shah's youngest son had died suddenly, supposedly killed by a poison intended for the child's mother, the Junior Queen Rani Samrajya Lakshmi Devi. At this time no less than four powerful clans were struggling to extend their power over the fifth, the Shah ruling family. Bhimsen Thapa's authority was slowly but surely being eroded, despite the support of his brother Ranbir Singh and his nephew Matabar Singh. The man who gained the most was Ranjang Pande, the youngest son of Damodar Pande – the man who more than three decades earlier had been overthrown and executed by order of Bhimsen Thapa.

However, the real power at court was the Senior Queen, Rani Samrajya Lakshmi Devi. At her behest Damodar Pande was brought in from the cold and his family's lands restored. It was then put about that Bhimsen Thapa was behind the supposed poisoning. Hodgson's view of the matter was reflected by a later political assistant and escort commander, Captain Thomas Smith, who put the blame for what ensued firmly of the shoulders of the Senior Queen and her desire for more power. 'Her disposition was restless in the extreme,' he wrote. 'She sighed for a share of the political authority of her husband ... The king, too weak to resist the accumulation of calumny, strongly and continually pressed, and feeling perhaps that he no longer needed the aid of his once valuable minister, caused Bhim Sing to be imprisoned upon all the charges, and in a very short time persecution reached its climax.'[17]

At the Senior Queen's urging, the king appointed Ranjang Pande as his Chief Minister, with inevitable consequences. Old Bhimsen Thapa, his brother and his nephew were imprisoned, brutally tortured and their lands confiscated.

At the Residency Brian Hodgson kept his head down, writing to his former boss and good friend Herbert Maddock, now Secretary of the Political and Foreign Department, to say that 'the sudden, noiseless and complete fall of General Bhim Sen demonstrate that ... the Raja will be his own master in future'.

But he was wrong. Fearing that the pathologically unstable Ranjang Pande would now seize power for himself, the other clan leaders united and forced the king to sack Ranjang Pande and restore Bhimsen to liberty. But the Pandes fought back and by January 1838 Ranjang was in a stronger position than before. The Thapa men fled for their lives – all except Bhimsen Thapa, who retreated to his ancestral home in Gorkha, broken both in body and spirit. In April he was seized and brought before the king in Durbar to face trial.

Terror now reigned in Kathmandu. Writing to Herbert Maddock in mid-April, Hodgson described the fearful atmosphere at court:

Many severities are inflicted and more apprehended ... The Senior Rani's irregular and violent ambition is said to find a ready tool in Ranjung ... She wants the Raja to resign in favour of her sons, Ranjung wants revenge on his numerous enemies, and the Raja, though he dreads with reason both the one and the other, yet gradually gives way to his imperious spouse, seduced by extravagant promises of the mighty things which Ranjang is to achieve against the Company, when once he has the complete direction of affairs.[18]

In his closing paragraph Hodgson called for the Governor-General to make his displeasure known by some show of force:

All persons of mark now look to the Company's Government, and earnestly hope that the Governor-General will ere long be led to address the Raja in such terms as may frighten him into justice at home and abroad, and redeem him from the coils of the Rani and [Ranjang] Pandi ... A rash and violent woman aiming at uncontrolled sway governs the Durbar, and all men of experience anticipate the worst that can happen unless renewed dread of the Company should speedily recall the Raja to safer counsels.

Before Calcutta could respond new charges were laid against Bhimsen Thapa. Most of the court physicians who had attended the supposedly poisoned child had already been pressed to death, but two who had survived were brought before the king to give evidence against Bhimsen. The first was a Brahman and could not be physically harmed, so he was declared an outcast and had his face burned to the point where his brains were exposed. His unfortunate assistant was a Newar, which made it permissible for him to be impaled and his heart torn from his chest.

As for Bhimsen Thapa, he was held in prison in chains but, in hearing that his wife was to be dragged through the streets naked, he grabbed a *kukri* from his jailors and cut his throat, dying of his wounds nine days later. 'His body,' wrote Thomas Smith, 'by order of the Rajah, was placed on the banks of the Bhagmatee and denied all favoured rites, a guard being placed over it by night and day, to watch that none approached it but jackals and vultures. His property [was] confiscated, and all his relations treated as outcastes. His favourite nephew Matabar Sing fled to the British territory, where he found shelter.'

According to a Nepalese source, Hodgson wept on being told of Bhimsen Thapa's death. In a message smuggled out from his prison cell, Bhimsen had begged him to intervene on his behalf but

Hodgson had felt himself unable to do so, as being bound by his Government's orders to remain above the fray.

In passing the news on to Herbert Maddock, Hodgson spoke of his admiration for his old enemy-cum-friend, describing him as a 'great and able statesman who for more than thirty years had ruled this kingdom with more than regal sway ... He was indeed a man born to exercise dominion over his fellows alike by the means of command and of persuasion. Nor am I aware of any native statesman of recent times, except Ranjit Singh, who is, all things considered, worthy to be compared to the late General Bhim Sen of Nepal.'[19]

These bloody events took place against the background of the early stages of the invasion of Afghanistan by Lord Auckland's much-vaunted Army of the Indus, as part of his declared intention to place Shah Shuja on the throne of Kabul in the place of Dost Mohommad. In July 1839 the stronghold of Ghazni was stormed, allowing the army to secure Kabul in the name of Shah Shuja.

In Calcutta Henry Thoby Prinsep was one of the few senior civil servants who believed this policy to be an act of folly and was prepared to say so, even though one of his closest friends, William Macnaghten, was its leading proponent. 'I stated this opinion,' he afterwards wrote in a private *Memoir*, albeit with the advantage of hindsight,

> both to Lord A. and to his Secretary, W. H. Macnaghten, with whom I was in weekly, even daily, correspondence, but they were already committed to the other course ... and the manner in which Lord A. fell into it was especially indicative of his character ... That was the act of Lord Auckland himself under the influence of the advisers who surrounded him, who were prepossessed in favour of Shah Shujah personally.[20]

In Nepal Hodgson had to accept that Lord Auckland was far too committed in Afghanistan to spare any troops should there be a further crisis in Nepal. It now became his chief responsibility to keep the Senior Queen on side, which he tried to do by dealing directly with her. 'I have been debating with her for three months,' he told Henry Thoby Prinsep in a private letter written in October

The Thundi Khel parade ground outside Kathmandu, scene of the
supposed army mutiny of June 1840, with Bhimsen Thapa's palace,
the Bagh Durbar, shown beside Bhimsen Thapa's nine-storey
watchtower. What was known as the Dhararara tower had just been
rebuilt after the earthquake of 1833, only to collapse again after the
earthquake of 1934. Viewed throughout Nepal as the symbol of the
country, it was utterly destroyed in the earthquake of 25 April 2015. BL
Lawrence Collection Add.Or.5240. © The British Library Board.

1839. 'She offered me a *kharita* [a silk bag in which formal letters
were enclosed] for the Governor-General full of all excellent dis-
course, rounded off with a tender of her troops to us to fight beyond
the Indus and elsewhere. She conceived – or rather, proposed and
wished – that this magnificent piece of humbug should procure her
a pardon for all ill-deeds and schemes of the last two years.'[21]

Hodgson refused to forward the *kharita* until various promised
reforms had been implemented: 'I have been on the verge of success
apparently twenty times during the debate, when the Durbar has
gone off again at a tangent. The points I have gained from the Durbar
are of some value, and if the greater politics of India go well for some
time to come, I may be able to keep the Durbar to the new course.'

But no sooner had this letter been despatched than news arrived
of the outbreak of hostilities between Britain and China at Canton,
in what became known as the First Opium War. This was now seized
on by the Durbar as a new opportunity to test the Company's resolve
and in April 1840 a small force of Gorkhas crossed the border due

south of Kathmandu to occupy a tract of British territory, declaring it to be back under Nepali rule.

Hodgson protested to the Durbar and demanded an immediate withdrawal. However, Lord Auckland's reaction was to instruct Hodgson to demand an explanation, in the first instance, with the warning that if the reply was unsatisfactory troops would then be sent to remove the intruders. The Durbar responded by assuring Hodgson that the supposed instigator of the encroachment would be punished and the trespassing troops withdrawn.

But then quite suddenly in mid-June a mutiny broke out among the troops in Kathmandu. At an early morning parade on the open ground known as Thundi Khel, on the eastern outskirts of Kathmandu, the six thousand troops present grounded their arms and refused to pick them up. Some of these soldiers then headed into the city and began to riot. A second contingent marched on the British Residency.

Hodgson was aware that something was in the air because at seven o'clock the previous evening he had been summoned to the Durbar together with Lieutenant Nicholetts. For three hours the Raja had engaged the two of them in trivial chit-chat. Then at ten o'clock, when Hodgson rose to go, the Raja begged him to stay a little while longer. The same thing happened at eleven o'clock and again at midnight. 'Soon after midnight,' wrote Hodgson some years later in a private note, 'at a sign from one of the Raja's attendants, His Highness asked me to go to the Queen's apartments. Her Highness [Rani Samrajya Lakshmi Devi, the Senior Queen] received me with scant civility, and presently grew angry and offensive.'

Suspecting that violence was planned, Hodgson tried to lighten the atmosphere by making a joke. The Senior Queen laughed, and this, apparently, gave the Raja the opportunity to bundle Hodgson and Nicholetts out of the room. 'It was daylight when I and the gentlemen left the palace,' Hodgson's account continues, 'and shortly afterwards came rumours of an uproar. It was reported to me that the troops of the capital were in a mutinous state, and were threatening mischief to the Residency, they having been told that the Resident had been all night insisting on a reduction of the Gorkha army by instructions of his Government.'

A large body of soldiers were then seen approaching the Residency. They stopped two hundred yards short of the gates and began to confer among themselves. Then a deputation came forward and explained to Hodgson that they had been ordered to kill him but were unwilling to 'perpetrate so cowardly an act as the destruction of the Resident' – and that 'if they were to do such a deed, they must have a *Lal-mohar* [document with the royal seal] to that effect'.

Hodgson had by now concluded that he had been set up and that the supposed mutiny was a ruse intended to cover an attempt on his life. His response was to despatch the Head *Munshi* of the Residency to the palace to inform the Raja that he had been forewarned of the purpose behind the mutiny, and that he had already sent two messengers by different routes to the Indian border carrying messages to this effect to be delivered to the Governor-General.

If, as Hodgson believed, this really was an attempt on his life, it backfired badly. The mutineers turned on one of the leading ministers and ransacked his house along with those of five other clan leaders. They then demanded that the Raja address them in person. According to Lieutenant Nicholetts, the man behind the plot was Ranjang Pande, who feigned sickness and stayed in his house.

Two days later the Raja did indeed address his assembled troops. According to reports brought back to the Residency, he explained that the reason he had ordered the pay cut was because he needed money to fight the British. He had been forced to be friends with the British only because of their great power, but if the troops agreed to take low pay for a year he would then be able to 'throw off the mask and indulge you in war'.

The troops had apparently responded with shouts of enthusiasm and at a second parade they gave the Raja their answer, their spokesmen declaring that there was no need for him to raise money:

> We want no money for making war; for war shall support itself.
> We will plunder Lucknow and Patna. But first we must get rid of
> the Resident who sees and foretells all ... Give the word and we
> will destroy the Resident and then war will follow of course ... Or
> if the English, as they say, are your friends and want peace, why
> do they keep possession of half your dominions? Let them restore

Kumaon and Sikkim. These are yours, demand them back, and if they refuse, drive out the Resident, and let us have war.[22]

Hodgson and his staff at the Residency were now in very real danger. The encroaching troops had failed to withdraw from British territory as had been promised, and the Durbar appeared intent on forcing the issue. On 1 September, acting on Lord Auckland's instructions, Hodgson delivered an ultimatum, giving the Durbar ten days to withdraw from British territory or face the military consequences.

Two weeks passed with no sign of the Nepalis giving way. Fearing the worst, Hodgson wrote a brief note to his parents in which he assured them all was well:

My dear Parents,
I steal a moment from official writing to tell you I am well & that you need entertain no fear for me tho war ensue with Nepal, as it probably will immediately. I have striven heartily & affectionately to save Nepal but she is in the hands of a sch [school] of mean scoundrels alike inaccessible to honesty or to wisdom – Oh that I had more health & strength to meet the crisis but He will support me upon whom is my main reliance even God Almighty. The [Calcutta] steamer is off on the 30th. I shall have to catch it.

Love to Fanny & Helena & believe me ever
Yours devotedly Afft. Son
B.H. Hodgson[23]

A second deadline was issued and again ignored, and then a third, although this time Hodgson was instructed to inform the Raja that an army brigade consisting of three infantry regiments, two squadrons of horse and a detail of artillery had now been ordered to proceed to Sugauli, on the Nepal border.

Only at this point did Raja Rajendra Bikram Shah crack. He overrode the Senior Queen and ordered the troop withdrawal. He also accepted Hodgson's terms which required him to make a public announcement, with Hodgson in attendance, stating that the British Resident had played no part in the reduction in the troops' pay. The

Raja was furthermore advised 'to listen to the friendly advice and warning of Mr Hodgson, ere it is too late' and that, if war between their two nations was to be avoided, he would do well to dismiss the Pande ministry and replace them with men less hostile to the HEICo.

The Raja did as he was told. Ranjang Pande was dismissed and replaced by Fateh Jung Chautaria, a bharadar considered by Hodgson to be favourably disposed towards the British. The crisis was over.

For his efforts Hodgson received the congratulations of the Government of India in a public despatch, and a private letter from Lord Auckland's Private Secretary conveying His Excellency's thanks 'for the marked ability, firmness and judgment with which you have met a long course of adverse and evasive negotiation on the part of the Nepalese Durbar'.[24]

Garbled versions of these events appeared in the press in England. 'My dearest mother,' reads part of a letter written by Brian Hodgson soon after this episode, 'Don't let the nonsense of the papers alarm you. 'Tis all stuff and ever has been. Before I was unarmed, as it were; whereas I have now a force close at hand consisting of five regiments of guns.'[25]

Perhaps it was just as well that old Mrs Hodgson was unaware that by 'close at hand' her son meant one hundred miles away.

The British Resident rides past the Balaju water-garden on the road
to Nawakot and Kakani. Brian Hodgson passed this way each time
he visited or returned from his summer house on Kakani ridge.
Detail from a watercolour by Raj Man Singh, previously assumed
to show Hodgson's successor, Henry Lawrence, but begun before
Hodgson's departure from Nepal in 1843. BL Lawrence Collection
Add.Or.5232. © The British Library Board (*see also Plate 33*).

10

'Events are working wonderfully in my favour': British Resident, 1840–43

The occupation of Kabul by Lord Auckland's Army of the Indus and the surrender of Dost Muhammad Khan appeared to put an end to talk of revolt on the Indian sub-continent. On 2 January 1841 Brian Hodgson had the great satisfaction of seeing no less than ninety-five bharadaris put their names to a formal engagement by which they agreed to recognise the desirability of 'firm and steady friendship' between the two governments, and that, to this end, the British Resident was 'ever and always to be treated in an honourable and friendly manner'.

So thoroughly obliging did this ministry become over the course of the next twelve months that it came to be spoken of within Nepal as the 'British ministry'. Hodgson's policy of firm but active diplomacy appeared at last to be paying off. Even so, he asked for the Dinapore brigade to remain where it was on the Nepal frontier for the time being.

For eight months during this period of relative calm in Nepal, Hodgson had what must surely have been the welcome company of a fellow ornithologist, Captain Samuel Tickell, a friend of his late brother William who had then become the latter's brother-in-law following William's marriage to his sister Mary. Tickell had spent the previous decade in various military postings on Bengal's southern borders and, like Hodgson, had began to develop an interest in ornithology, his first published paper, 'On the birds of Bhorabum and Dholbum' appearing in the *Journal of the Asiatic Society of Bengal* in 1833.

Tickell had probably been sent to Kathmandu to strengthen the Resident's military escort in the wake of the border crisis. During his time there he completed an ethnographic paper on the tribal people with whom he had previously been in contact in what is now Jharkhand State in central India. However, Tickell's real talent lay in his skills as an amateur artist and he had already started to assemble a portfolio of ornithological and natural history paintings that would eventually amount to fourteen volumes, afterwards presented to the Zoological Society of London.

These paintings were intended to form the basis for a major work on the natural history of India, which on the face of it made him Hodgson's rival. However, it appears that in 1840 the two saw each other as fellow enthusiasts and collaborators rather than rivals. It seems reasonable to assume that something of Tickell's painterly skills and techniques rubbed off on Hodgson's local artists, particularly in the placing of specimens in natural settings and in the addition of veneers, which now became regular features of the most finished of Hodgson's mammal and ornithological watercolours.

It was Samuel Tickell who recreated the ratification of the Treaty of Sugauli (*see Plate 1*). The addition of a basket of fruit, vegetables and a fish shown in that painting's left foreground – traditional offerings in Nepal made at the time of a farewell or departure on a journey – suggest that this painting may have been sketched at Makwanpur at the time of Tickell's departure from Nepal early in 1841, with the military details added later.[1]

That the continued machinations of the Senior Queen were now beginning to exasperate Hodgson is revealed in a short note he sent to his old friend, Dr Wallich, in England attached to some ornithological papers and drawings to be delivered to the Royal Asiatic Society in mid-March 1841. 'I am still squabbling here,' he wrote, 'having to do with a furious famina [?] the very quintessence of all that is detestable in womankind or indomitable obstinacy in evil.'[2] But by the end of that same month the Senior Queen had evidently had enough. She announced her intention of proceeding to Benares on pilgrimage and set off with her household entourage towards the Indian border.

She got as far as the town of Hetauda, at the edge of the Tarai, where the foothills end and the plains begin. Here she was joined by

A watercolour by Samuel Tickell showing the Red-tailed
Minla (*Minla ignotincta*), one of 78 bird species discovered by
Brian Hodgson in Nepal and Tibet. NHM Hodgson Album
055724. © The Trustees of the Natural History Museum.

A pair of Eurasian Nutcrackers (*Nucifraga caryacatactes*), specimens
obtained by Hodgson's hunters from south-east Tibet. In showing
their subjects in their natural settings and in painting with
watercolour on graphite, Hodgson's *chitrakars* employed techniques
probably learned from Samuel Tickell. NHM Hodgson Collection
069563. © The Trustees of the Natural History Museum.

her husband, Raja Rajendra, and their son, Surendra, the eleven-year-old heir apparent. Hodgson lost no time in despatching an emissary to remind the royal party that neither passports nor permissions to enter British territory had been obtained, and after a two week stalemate the royal party returned to Kathmandu.

But now notices began to appear on the city walls accusing the Chief Minister, Fateh Jung Chautaria, of conspiring with the British and calling for the return of Ranjang Pande. It was observed that on all ceremonial occasions the heir-apparent, Surendra, was given precedence over his father the king. According to the Resident's contacts, this was all being engineered by the Senior Queen, who had now given up on her husband and was grooming her son to take his place.

This unfortunate boy had inherited a psychopathic streak that was said to run in the royal family and he had been allowed in indulge his sadistic tastes:

> This young prince, who appeared to have a most ungovernable temper, as well as a most inhuman disposition, amused his leisure hours by acts of the grossest cruelty performed not only on animals, but upon men, who were tortured and mutilated in his presence upon the slightest and often most unjust grounds, for no other object than to gratify his brutal passions. The Rajah, instead of exercising any restraint upon these excesses of his son, constantly tried to evade all responsibility for his own acts under cover of pretended coercion on the part of the prince, of whose violence he professed to be afraid.[3]

An undated letter from Brian Hodgson to his father can be assigned to this period, written during a lull between storms. 'I have had another negotiation, another struggle, another victory,' he states. 'Yet all is unsettled, and my ambition is bounded just now to keeping things any how together until the return of the season of action in November.' Hodgson was concerned about the growing unrest in Afghanistan and how that would play in Kathmandu: 'All these untoward events are glad tidings to the insolent and restless faction of our Rani or Queen of Nepal, who is my great opponent, and the only effective one indeed, the Raja being but a poltroon who sits behind her petticoat.'

Hodgson closes his letter with a rare and all too brief reference to his children: 'My boy and girl are well and growing up fast. I must send them to school in the Western Hills ere long, unless you will take charge of them, but I may not put you to that trouble.'[4]

Unbeknown to Hodgson, his tribulations at the hands of the Senior Queen were nearly over. During her fortnight at Hetauda she had contracted the dreaded Tarai fever known to the Nepalis as the *ayul* and over the course of the summer of 1841 it became obvious that she was losing her grip on power. On 6 October Rani Samra-jya Lakshmi Devi finally expired and with her departure much of the opposition to the Chief Minister and to the British Resident fell away. Once again Hodgson found himself at the receiving end of a round of congratulations from Lord Auckland and his colleagues in the political service.

One of these colleagues was George Clerk, who had come through Haileybury and Fort William College with Hodgson and was at this time the Governor-General's envoy to Maharaja Ranjit Singh in Lahore. He wrote to tell Hodgson that in the course of attending Lord Auckland in Simla he had discovered that plans had been drawn up to declare war on Nepal. 'In the Governor-General's camp all were agog for war,' he afterwards wrote in a private note to Hodgson, 'and the Commander-in-Chief had his plans for the campaign ready cut and dry ... to crush Nepal at a blow'. That these plans were never put into execution was, in Hodgson's opinion, largely thanks to George Clerk and his advocacy of Hodgson's own arguments. Had they been followed through there could well have been a double disaster: 'If we had then gone to war with her [Nepal], the Cabul catastrophe must have come upon us ere we were free of her.'[5]

That disaster was now fast approaching, set in motion by William Macnaghten's fatal decision to order one of the two British brigades garrisoning Kabul to return to India, while at the same time cutting the subsidy he had been paying the Pathan tribes between Kabul and the Khyber Pass to keep the peace. Inevitably, the Pathans pinned down the withdrawing military brigade in the mountains, after which everything spiralled ever faster out of control. In November an Afghan mob attacked the British Residency in Kabul, overwhelming its escort and killing Alexander Burnes and his brother. The elderly general commanding the remaining British brigade was slow to react, and by the time the troops had been called to arms the city was in the hands of Dost Muhammad's Afghans.

What followed has been told many times over. Badly led and fatally unprepared, the Kabul brigade went to pieces. On 23 December William Macnaghten rode out to sign a treaty that he hoped would allow the brigade to withdraw to India, only to be cut down. Two weeks later, the brigade with all its dependants and camp followers – approaching seventeen thousand all told – was ordered to march out of Kabul and over the mountain to India. Just one survivor, Dr Brydon, reached the fort of Jalalabad, on 13 January 1842. It was the worst disaster in British military history and remained so until the fall of Singapore a century later.

News of the catastrophe reached Calcutta at the end of January. Overwhelmed by the magnitude of the calamity, the best that Lord Auckland could do was issue a statement declaring that the 'partial reverse' suffered in Afghanistan provided 'a new occasion for displaying the stability and vigour of the British power, and the admirable spirit and valour of the British Indian Army'. His period of rule as Governor-General was now drawing to a close and his successor, Lord Ellenborough, had already set out for India, so Auckland's thoughts were now focussed on how he might most speedily wash his hands of Afghanistan. His commander-in-chief appeared equally paralysed, so that it was largely thanks to the efforts of two of Brian Hodgson's Civilian colleagues – his friend George Clerk, newly appointed Agent to the Governor-General on the North-Western Frontier, and the more senior Thomas Robertson, Lieutenant-Governor of the North-Western Provinces in Agra – that troops were despatched to relieve Jalalabad and prevent that garrison also falling to the Afghans.

Almost the only good news received in Government House at this time of crisis was a despatch from Brian Hodgson sent to the Governor-General on 30 January enclosing an offer from the king of Nepal to make some of his troops available. It had Hodgson's full support because, in his opinion, it would give Nepal's unemployed soldiery some active service and so take the pressure off the present government.

Lord Auckland rejected the offer, while making known to Raja Rajendra Bikram Shah through Hodgson that he appreciated the gesture as 'proof of your amiable feeling and desire to promote the interests of the British Government', adding that 'if any future occasion should arise when they might co-operate with the British forces it would afford me the greatest satisfaction to see the Gorkha and the British soldier marching side by side as friends to the attack of a common enemy.'[6]

On Hodgson's advice, the British brigade based at Sugauli was now withdrawn – a gesture that went down extremely well with the Nepal Durbar. It also had the effect of freeing up more troops to be sent to the Punjab, earning Hodgson the heartfelt thanks of Thomas Roberston in Agra. 'If you can continue with the same success as heretofore to divert the Durbar from war,' he wrote on 24 February, 'you will indeed have accomplished a most important diversion in our favour.'[7]

On 28 February 1842 the Governor-General's seal of office passed from Lord Auckland to his successor, Lord Ellenborough. Broken in spirit and reputation though he was, Auckland had the grace to write a private letter to Brian Hodgson as his ship dropped its pilot at the mouth of the Hoogly:

> I write these few hasty lines to you, to take leave of you, and to wish you such good health as may enable you to complete your labours in Nepal, and afterwards to enjoy many years of comfort in England. It is most satisfactory to me on the eve of my departure from India, and when there is so much of gloom, and danger in one quarter of our political horizon, that the prospects in regard to Nepal are better and more promising than they have long been. Once more, I thank you for all you have done, and I wish you well.[8]

Lord Ellenborough was a dyed-in-the-wool Tory, the son of a former Lord Chief Justice and a political ally of the Duke of Wellington, on whose tailcoats he hoped to ride to become Foreign

Secretary. He was the very antithesis of his predecessor: sarcastic, humourless and incapable of trusting any opinions other than his own. Having opposed Lord Auckland's Afghan policy from the start, he arrived in India to find his worst predictions confirmed. His first response was to endorse the plans then being put into action to relieve the Jelalabad garrison and rescue the survivors, but then at the first sign of trouble to order the immediate withdrawal of the two relieving columns, only to countermand his order when a victory seemed certain – and all the while blaming his military commanders for disobeying his instructions.

It was soon obvious to all who came up against Lord Ellenborough that they were dealing with a devious character whose chief concern was his political advancement. His rough-shod conduct would bring about his recall to England before he had completed half his term – but he stayed in India long enough to destroy Brian Hodgson's career.

In Nepal, the Afghanistan disaster came midway between the collapse of the anti-British party at court after the death of the Senior Queen and its slow revival following the rise to power of the king's second wife. This lady, Rani Rajya Lakshmi Devi (not to be confused with the late Senior Queen, Rani Samrajya Lakshmi Devi), had hitherto been forced to play second fiddle but now began to promote herself as the protector of her step-son, the heir-apparent. However, Prince Surendra had also begun to make his presence felt, for all his tender years. He, too, began to build up his own party of supporters in opposition to both his father and his step-mother, and in alliance with the Pande faction. That this boy, not more than twelve or thirteen years old, was fully prepared to take on the king, his father, was demonstrated in a bizarre incident that took place in March of that year outside the gates of the British Residency.

This began with Raja Rajendra Bikram Shah learning that the press in India had reported the death of the Senior Queen as a poisoning. It put him in a rage and he sent for Hodgson to demand an explanation. Hodgson immediately set out for the palace but had got no further than the gates of the Residency when he saw the Raja and his son approaching. Hodgson explained that he would do what he could to find out who had been the author of the report, but

Brian Hodgson's nemesis, Edward Law, 1st Earl of Ellenborough, whose
two-year term of office as Governor-General of India was widely held to
have been a disaster. From an engraving drawn after his return from India.

Rajendra would have none of it. He turned on Hodgson in a fury,
demanding that the Governor-General surrender the miscreant up
to him: 'I will have him and flay him alive and rub him with salt
and lemon till he die. Further, tell the Governor-General that if this
infamous calumniator is not delivered up, there shall be war between
us.' At this point the heir-apparent joined in and began not only to
insult his father but to hit him, again and again.

Raja Rajendra subsequently had the grace to apologise to Hodgson
for his angry words, but it was a sign that the period of calm at court
was coming to an end.

Weeks later, on 23 April 1842, there occurred what became known
as the Kashinath incident, which had its origins in a rivalry between
an Indian trader from Benares named Kashinath and a second
Indian trader who took out a legal suit against him in Nepal. A lower
court found against Kashinath and fined him, only for the case to
be dismissed by the highest court in the land, the *Kot-Linga*. But
then an appeal was made to the lower court and the case reopened,

whereupon Kashinath, who was unwell and had been given shelter in the Residency grounds, appealed to the Resident. Hodgson immediately wrote a note of protest to the Raja, calling on him to annul the suit.

Again the Raja took umbrage. Early on the morning of 23 April Hodgson received an urgent note from a friendly minister warning him that the Raja intended to seize the Benares merchant. He barely had time to send a warning to his new assistant and escort commander Lieutenant Thomas Smith before the Raja, the crown prince and their retinues arrived at the gates of the Residency, complete with a regiment of soldiers with muskets loaded.

'With little preface, the Raja said to me he had come to demand and to insist on the surrender of the merchant,' was how Hodgson began his account of the events that followed. 'Notwithstanding the Raja's vehemence of demand, I steadfastly but courteously continued to refuse compliance.' At Hodgson's request, Kashinath came forward to make his obeisance to the Raja, whereupon the Raja lost all self-control:

> His Highness at length rushed at the poor merchant and attempted to bear him off. I threw my arm around the merchant and said sternly to the Raja, 'You take both of us or neither.' This was more than the Raja could screw up his resolution to do, although his hot-headed son urged him to do it with abuse and even blows. Seizing the moment, I made an appeal to the Raja's better feeling (I had known him from boyhood), and thus at length I cast the balance against the mischief-makers. But it was not until a full hour of imminent risk had elapsed, during which the friendly chiefs, as they passed and repassed me in the surging crowds, dropped in my ear the words, 'Be patient and firm; all depends on you.'[9]

But that was not quite the end of it. Some days later the Raja and heir-apparent again reappeared at the Residency gates, the son having apparently declared that since his father was too feeble to act against the Resident, he would do it himself. What Hodgson omitted to say in his report – presumably for reasons of propriety – was that the rites of mourning for the death of the Senior Queen had required these two royal figures to abstain for a set period from either riding horses or travelling in horse-drawn carriages, while their high status also forbade them to walk. It was left to Lieutenant Smith to provide the embarrassing detail on what then transpired:

> It had been raining heavily in the morning and at twelve o'clock we were informed that the Rajah and his son were outside the Residency gates. We went out to meet them and there found the Rajah and his son mounted on two very decrepit old chiefs. The heir apparent requested the Rajah at once to give us the order to pack up and take our departure for the plains. The Rajah refused, whereupon the heir apparent abused him most grossly, and urging his old chief close up to the Rajah, assaulted him. A fight ensued, and after scratching and pulling each other's hair for some time, the son got hold of his father, pulled him over, and down they went, chiefs and all, into a very dirty puddle. The two 'nags' extricating themselves, hobbled away as fast as they could, as did the other followers from fear. Up got the now two dirty kings, and after some little delay, fresh nags were obtained, and the Rajah and his son were taken away.[10]

Hodgson reported these bizarre events to Herbert Maddock, adding that they were part and parcel of the heir-apparent's attempts to drive a wedge between himself and the pro-British ministry. If no remonstrance was made, he argued, it would damage the British reputation in the eyes of their allies in Nepal 'our interests would be sadly weakened by the desertion of all our powerful friends'.

Maddock was at this time part of the entourage accompanying Lord Ellenborough on a tour of the North-Western Provinces. He now found himself, as Secretary of the Foreign and Political Department, in the most invidious position of serving as Lord Ellenborough's mouthpiece in all his dealings with Brian Hodgson. In this capacity he wrote write back to Hodgson informing him that in Lord Ellenborough's view he had badly mishandled the situation. Firstly, he had misled him by previously giving him the impression that relations between the two governments were 'of the most amicable and courteous character' and, secondly, Hodgson had acted irresponsibly in standing up to the king of Nepal in the matter of the Indian merchant: 'His Lordship cannot believe that you would act in a manner so entirely contrary to the known views and wishes of your Government as to attempt to extend the privileges of British subjects or your own authority beyond the just limits which laws of nations and a solemn Treaty assign to them; still less that you would evince a want of personal consideration for a friendly and independent sovereign.'

Hodgson was instructed to convey a translation of Lord Ellenborough's letter directly to Raja Rajendra together with the Governor-General's expressions of 'much disappointment and regret' over the events. He was also to report at once to the Governor-General for a personal conference, and to this end was to join the Governor-General's camp 'as soon as the season will permit you to do so'.

Hodgson was at a complete loss to how best to respond. Knowing nothing of Lord Ellenborough's character, he took the view that to forward a translation of the Governor-General's letter of reprimand in its existing form would be seriously impolitic and would undo all his good work in building up a pro-British ministry at the Durbar. He therefore took it upon himself *not* to deliver Lord Ellenborough's letter to the king – and to ignore his instructions to report to him in person in Simla.

Instead, he wrote his own note to Raja Rajendra, stating that the Governor-General wished to give the king an opportunity to apologise for the events of 23 April and that his Government would consider his claim of jurisdiction over British subjects charged with offences. At the same time he asked his assistant, Lieutenant Smith, to go to meet the Governor-General in his place, on the grounds that his own state of health did not allow him to make the journey across the plains in the full heat of summer. He also wrote an impassioned letter to Maddock explaining what he had done and why:

> For God's sake, do not distrust your old tried Resident, whose every act heretofore you have applauded ... For God's sake, don't trust the Rajah, whose very act heretofore you have denounced ... Remember that what has been achieved here with so much

applause of the Governor-General in Council has been achieved
by and through the Ministers, and against the Rajah, and that to
show the least distrust of the former, so that the latter may per-
ceive it, may be the death warrant or signal of disgrace of one or
more of those whose good faith to us has been as conspicuous as
the bad faith of the Rajah.[11]

This was a monumental blunder on Hodgson's part. But he was
confident that Ellenborough would come round to his way of thinking, as can be seen by a letter he wrote to his mother in which he
expressed his hopes that the new Governor-General would not be 'so
mad as to run blindfold upon his only course contrary to such testimony as the long tried sufficiency of my politics here. He seems preju-
diced – as are all of them at first – Lord A [Auckland] was sadly so yet
I reduced him to reason without public inconvenience having been
felt – so I shall this new broom if I have health & patience for it.'[12]
But the new broom was very different from the old one. Lord
Ellenborough's reply was received by Hodgson in early June and it
was damning: 'The step you have taken is not only in direct disobe-
dience of the instructions you received, but it may tend to produce
serious embarrassment to the Government, by compelling it to adopt
an extreme course with respect to the Raja of Nepal at a time when
it is certainly not desirable to create a division of the British forces.'
Hodgson was ordered to lose no time in carrying out Ellenborough's original instruction to deliver his letter in translation to the
Raja. He was also to cease his overt support for the Chautaria ministry. 'To the British Government it is a matter of indifference who are
the ministers of Nepal,' Hodgson was told. 'The Government loses a
portion of its power when it departs from its dignity and places itself
in a state of subordinate cooperation with the ministers of Nepal.'[13]
Even at this late stage Hodgson could have played the game, and
done as he had done once before in making profuse apologies to Lord
Bentinck for misunderstanding what he required of him. But Hodgson
was still convinced that the Governor-General would see sense. Instead
of bending the knee, he wrote a lengthy defence of his actions, setting
out the circumstances that had led to the creation of the Chautaria
ministry and why the future stability of relations between Britain and

Nepal depended on the survival of this faction as its 'sole pillar'. More unwisely still, he closed his letter with a light-hearted simile, declaring that he hoped the Governor-General would excuse his disregard for his orders on the grounds that he, Hodgson, had successfully played the game of temporising for three years and that even a master of that game was apt to make mistakes from time to time.

That letter sealed Hodgon's fate. On 21 June Herbert Maddock wrote to inform him that the Governor-General had directed that he be dismissed from his post: 'You will be relieved in your situation of Resident at the court of Nepal at the earliest period at which the season and the exigencies of the public service may permit such relief to take place.'[14]

In a brief and understandably despondent letter to his father written immediately after being informed of his dismissal, Hodgson appeared to accept his fate. 'My dearest Father,' he writes,

> You may look confidently to see me sooner than I had expected for the Gov. General & I are entirely at issue – so that I can do no more good here – and at the same time my health indispensably requires return to Europe – I shall shortly apply for Furlough on sick leave & for eventual tour of Pension as it may fall to my turn & I shall probably sail, please God, in January next, taking most likely the tour of the Cape, for a long sea voyage is said to be the thing I most need – I am cruelly pulled down by an enduring disease & enduring physickening[?] – grey, bald, wrinkled & yellow as imagination can paint, but in heart & mind a youth still & devoted to you & to my dear Mother & Sisters.
> God bless you
> BHH[15]

Lord Ellenborough had very quickly realised – or, more probably, had been made to realise by Maddock – that he had acted out of order. Twenty-four hours after writing the letter of dismissal Maddock was instructed to write Hodgson a second and now private letter assuring him that the Governor-General held him in high regard and suggesting that his earlier letter should remain off the record. 'My dear Hodgson,' it began,

Lord Ellenborough has been speaking today about you, express-
ing in the kindest tone his sense of your merits, services, and abili-
ties; saying that he hoped an opportunity of employing you to
your liking in some other field, and suggesting that the letter of
yesterday be kept a profound secret, [that] you should act on the
former summons [to come to the Governor-General's camp] and
consider yourself as only waiting for a favourable season to obey it
and to come and pay your respects to his Lordship, and explain to
him the state of affairs in Nepal.[16]

But Hodgson's dander was up, and his reply was blunt and to the
point: 'I answered, July 10th, that I cared not whether Lord Ellenborough cancelled his despatch of June 21st (ejecting me) or not, but
expected if that despatch were recorded, my answer to it should be
so likewise.'

In the event, Ellenborough's letter of dismissal was never logged.
However, Hodgson still had an important ally on the Supreme
Council in the person of his old patron and friend Henry Thoby
Prinsep. It is not known if Hodgson wrote to him in person but
Prinsep certainly got to know of the dismissal letter and made a
formal protest to Lord Ellenborough. Hodgson's fellow Politicals
also got to hear of it and they were equally troubled. It had always
been understood that as the Governor-General's agents in the field
they were expected to use their own discretion and best judgment
based on their knowledge of local conditions, and they expected this
to be taken into account when things went awry.

Among the letters of support received by Hodgson was one from
Thomas Robertson, Lieutenant-Governor of the North-Western
Provinces. He too had suffered from Lord Ellenborough's attacks
and was highly critical of his behaviour. 'He has contrived at starting
to make men careless of his praise and heedless of his censure,' he
wrote, 'His prepossessions against our service are intense, and lead
him into much that is unfair and foolish.' However, Robertson was
also sure that the Governor-General now understood how misplaced
his criticisms of Hodgson had been: 'I am satisfied that he now sees
that he was on the verge of falling into the most tremendous blunder
of provoking a war with Nepal, and will be glad enough to find that

nothing more is said of the despatch intimating his displeasure at your course of policy, although his stubborn pride will not admit of his acknowledging any mistake.'[17]

But Hodgson was given only a temporary reprieve. Ellenborough was now set on removing him from his post, regardless of Hodgson's explanations. Three weeks after rescinding his letter of dismissal he wrote to the HEICo's Court of Directors in London to inform them that Hodgson was inextricably linked with an 'erroneous system' that bound him to a particular faction at court and that he would soon be resigning on the grounds of ill-health: 'I have reason to think that the Gentleman's health will make it expedient for him to resign his office as soon as he can return to the plains. I should have otherwise have deemed it my duty to place on record all the grounds upon which I disapprove of his recent conduct and to act according to my view of what the public interest requires by relieving him from the charge of his present official duty at Cathmandoo.'[18]

Lord Ellenborough's plan, it seems, was to meet Hodgson and there persuade him to step down on the grounds of ill-health, thus saving the faces of both parties. We know from Hodgson's letters home that he had on several occasions written of following the course that Edward Gardner and others in the Bengal Civil Service had followed towards the end of their careers, which was to take official sick-leave and go home, and then hand in their resignation as their period of sick-leave drew to a close. To qualify for a full pension he had to serve for twenty-five years' service, which in his case meant staying on till April 1843, but there was nothing to stop him completing that remaining period on sick leave.

Hodgson would afterwards claim that he did not take this course because he felt that he had a duty to stay on in Nepal for as long as the Afghan crisis and the threat of war with Nepal remained. This is not a convincing explanation for his behaviour, which amounted to his fighting tooth and nail to stay on in Nepal for as long as he could.

By the end of June 1842 Hodgson had secured an official apology from Raja Rajendra and an agreement that the Indian merchant Kashinath would be allowed to leave Nepal unhindered. He had also abandoned his open support for the Chautaria ministry, while at the same time arguing in a series of lengthy and convoluted letters to the Governor-General that this process of disengagement had to be done slowly and spread over months rather than weeks, it being 'most desirable that the change from our existing policy towards Nepal to another should, if possible, be quiet and gradual, and be deferred until our affairs are adjust with Afghanistan and China.'

His efforts appeared to mollify Lord Ellenborough, to the extent that he wrote Hodgson a friendly letter in his own hand, describing him as a 'most zealous and able servant of the Government'. But he also made it quite clear that Hodgson still had to go: 'If a change of system should be adopted in treating with the Nepal Government, you are so mixed up with a party there that you would be unable to act efficiently in carrying out such a new system. It would succeed better in other, even if much less able, hands.'[19]

Part of Lord Ellenborough's more relaxed attitude can be attributed to the successes of what had now become known as the 'Army of Retribution' in Afghanistan. In July Jelalabad was relieved, in August the fortress of Ghazni recaptured, in September Kabul reoccupied and in October the city's bazaar burnt to the ground before the avenging army withdrew entirely from Afghanistan. It was a pyrrhic victory but it freed the HEICo's troops and it effectively extinguished the last hopes of the war party in Nepal.

Indeed, so warm did the tone of Lord Ellenborough's communications now become that Hodgson lulled himself into an entirely false sense of security about his future. And, as so often in the past, his opinions shifted from one extreme to another. 'I have already told you of my fracas with the Governor-General. It is over and I have triumphed'. This was how Hodgson begins a letter written to his father in early September that reveals how deluded he had allowed himself to become:

The impetuous and dashing but very able chief [Lord Ellenborough] has owned his error in rushing blindly *in medias res nostras*, and has left all to my judgement and discretion. This is deemed by many a far greater achievement than my past one of facing the restless and faithless Gorkhas, and I have great satisfaction in reflecting that by throwing myself into the breach made by Lord E's impetuosity I prevented much injury to the public interests ...

Lord E is a dasher & an able one, so that I hope he will sweep away only the cobwebs & spare the essentials of our affairs – I like such a man – his contempt for forms & formalities – and his strong energetic will ... I have some strain of these attributes myself & Lord E with the quick divination, candour & decision of genius speedily found it out & acted on the discovery. Thus when our debate was at the hottest it ceased as suddenly as it had commenced.[20]

Throughout the autumn of 1842 Hodgson continued his slow disengagement from the Durbar and the Chautaria ministry, having made it plain to all concerned that his support was no longer to be counted on. To reinforce the point he even withdrew himself from the Residency to his summer house at Kakani, returning to Kathmandu only when it became too cold to be bearable. Then in early November he was informed that his visit to Calcutta was no longer necessary – and that he was to be replaced sooner rather than later. He gave vent to his frustration in an angry letter to his parents written in early December in which he insisted that for the sake of his reputation he had to stay on in Nepal for at least another year:

The G. G. [Governor-General] has recanted both officially and privately his senseless and heartless assault on me of May and June; but I should be wanting of myself were I to afford opportunity to so crafty and cold-blooded a man to make out hereafter a fair or even plausible defence of his conduct and happy to turn the tables on me altogether. You know what a ticklish game diplomacy is, and that amid the fleeting, dubious phenomena of politics, nothing is easier than to give the semblance of arguments and facts that may suit the turn to gull the gentle public. I will not suffer such perversion to find room to operate, nor will I let another agent at the eleventh hour come in to reap the harvest of my labours for years past. To prevent this and to set and keep myself right as to the past and the future I must stay another year in India.[21]

Also included in this letter was one of Hodgson's rare references – or, perhaps more accurately, rare *surviving* references – to his children and what might be done with them once he had left Nepal: 'As to my dear boy and girl I cannot [bear] to part with them or to disown them, and therefore I suppose I must have a separate tent to pitch for myself on your shores, though in the neighbourhood of yours. Consider that point, as I will, further.' Hodgson's plan, then, was to return to England with Henry and Sarah and settle them and himself near his parents – but not yet.

Hodgson sat tight in Kathmandu through the Cold Weather months of 1842–43, still convinced that Lord Ellenborough would change his mind – which he did, to the extent of agreeing that he could stay on in Kathmandu until the end of the Hot Weather, at which point he was to leave Nepal as soon as it was safe to do so.

In early April 1843 he received a remarkably frank letter from Herbert Maddock that was partly an apology for his supine behaviour but also a guarded warning. Maddock had just been promoted to a seat on the Supreme Council which meant that he had been relieved of the disagreeable duty of acting as Lord Ellenborough's political mouthpiece and could speak his mind. 'I cannot pretend to account for the actions or policy of my late master Lord Ellenborough,' he wrote:

> His own way he will have as long as he rules over this country, and no other human being will be responsible for the acts of his government, for he will allow no one to share the responsibilities in any degree with him. Political Officers are the objects of his special aversion, and they can only do as they are bid, and that is the only way they can avoid his displeasure. However, I cannot bring myself to believe that his reign over us will be of much longer duration, for all the Ministers except the Duke of Wellington, are said to be perfectly disgusted with his arrogance and alarmed at his insanity.[22]

Brian Hodgson should have taken note. But within days of receiving Maddock's letter he was writing to the Governor-General asking for another extension – another full year – so that he could complete his work. This was because 'the superior opportunities for research here opened by the general and glorious pacification of India under your auspices, afford such strong reasons for remaining another year in Nepal that I am persuaded your Lordship will not exact my retirement'.[23]

This failed to wash with Lord Ellenborough. 'Sir,' he replied in his own hand:

> I have already twice, against my own better judgement, acquiesced in your remaining there: first, when I consented that the public letter of animadversion upon your conduct should not be placed upon the public records, it being then distinctly understood by me that you would retire during the last cold weather; secondly, when I was further induced to consent to your remaining till the ensuring cold weather. I do not think it desirable that you should remain beyond that period, and I shall then appoint your successor. If you desire to remain on service in India, I shall endeavour to find some other fit situation for you, but you ought to leave Nepal.[24]

Perfectly civil though this letter was, it contained an outright falsehood. Ellenborough had never written a 'public letter of animadversion' but a letter of dismissal that he himself had removed from the public record with the request that it remain secret. It seems to have made Hodgson all the more determined to stay on and so vindicate his policies.

Hodgson's withdrawal of support for the Chautaria ministry had had the effect of strengthening the position of the Junior Queen and weakening that of Raja Rajendra and his son, Prince Dipendra, culminating in the ousting of almost the entire Pande faction – accompanied by a new round of executions, imprisonment and exile. The Junior Queen had then invited the Thapas to return from exile, which they did under the leadership of Matabar Singh Thapa, the nephew of Hodgson's old foe Bhimsen Thapa.

Now it was the ousted Prince Surendra as well as representatives of the king, his father, who came knocking at Hodgson's door. And so again he wrote pleading for an extension, this time arguing that three senior bharadaris had come to see him on behalf of the king, begging him to postpone his departure due to the unsettled state of the country.

'You will not mix yourself up with any intrigues in the ruling family of Nepal,' Hodgson was reminded. Nevertheless, throughout the summer of 1843 Hodgson continued to badger the Governor-General with various arguments as to why he should stay on, culminating in what to Lord Ellenborough looked very much like a deliberate attempt to involve Raja Rajendra. It came in the form of an official red-sealed *kharita* from the king declaring Hodgson to be no less than the saviour of Nepal and requesting that he be allowed to extend his term of office. 'I have been perpetually reflecting on Mr Hodgson's perfect knowledge of the institutions and manners of my kingdom,' reads part of King Rajendra's letter – as translated by Hodgson –

and of the hill language, and likewise upon his long and zealous, kind and patient labours in the late troubled times, whereby the designs of evil men inimical to both governments were foiled, and peace and friendship with your State preserved. The more I think on these valuable qualifications and labours of Mr Hodgson, the more I am pained at his departure. It is therefore my earnest hope and request, for the benefit of my kingdom, that Mr Hodgson may be persuaded by your Lordship to remain a little while longer with me.[25]

The king's appeal did indeed bear all the hallmarks of the Resident and it was the final straw for Ellenborough. He refused to accept the *kharita* and in mid-August ordered that all Hodgson's letters be placed on the public record. This was followed by an announcement in the *Calcutta Gazette* of the appointment of Major Henry Lawrence to the post of British minister to the court of Nepal, with immediate effect – and without the customary reference to the previous incumbent.

But there has to be some better explanation for Brian Hodgson's increasingly desperate attempts to stay on in defiance of Lord Ellenborough's orders. The replacement of the Pandes by the Thapas had calmed rather than unsettled the country, there was no longer any war party to speak of and Hodgson himself was now free to retire to England with a very handsome pension of a thousand pounds a year. Of course, it could be argued that his pride was hurt and that he wished to leave Nepal with an unblemished record and no stain on his character. But there may also have been more personal reasons.

When Hodgson finally left Kathmandu he took with him his two children, Henry and Sarah, but left behind Mehr-ul-Nissa – and, possibly, a new-born second daughter. There have been persistent reports over the years in Kathmandu that Hodgson's *begum* Mehr-un-Nissa gave birth to a third child, a daughter, born at about the time of Hodgson's departure from Kathmandu on 5 December 1843.

There has never been any convincing evidence to support this claim. However, there are two drawings done by one of Hodgson's *chitrakar* painters that deserve to be more carefully scrutinised than they have been in the past.

The first is a painting from the Lawrence Collection now in the British Library. This collection was donated to the India Office Library by a descendent of Sir Henry Lawrence, the political officer who took over from Brian Hodgson as British Resident in December 1843.

Major Lawrence – as he then was – had been expecting to take over from Hodgson's friend George Clerk as the British Resident in Lahore. He was not pleased to learn that the Governor-General had appointed him to Kathmandu instead. However, he took up the offer at the urging of his doughty wife Honoria, who had already borne him a girl, Honoria Letitia, and a boy, Alexander. Honoria Lawrence and their two children joined Henry Lawrence in Kathmandu in January 1844, more than a month after he had taken over from Hodgson. A year later, on 24 January 1845, their second son, Henry, was born – the first European child to be born in Kathmandu. Henry Lawrence, it should be said, was five years younger than Hodgson. He had a thin face and a fair to reddish moustache and beard, not bushy but distinctive enough.

The Lawrences did not stay long in Kathmandu, leaving the Nepal Valley in December 1845. Henry Lawrence served thereafter with great distinction in the Punjab, achieving imperial immortality with his death at the famous siege of the British Residency at Lucknow in 1857.

The British Library's Lawrence Collection includes some forty drawings executed in Nepal by one or more Nepali artists, including

(Above) A finished watercolour of the British Residency from the
Lawrence Collection in the British Library showing what has always
been assumed to be the Lawrence family. BL Lawrence Collection
Add.Or.5223. © The British Library Board (*see also Plate 34*).
(Below) A pen-and-ink outline sketch of the same scene. One of twelve
such preliminary sketches now part of the Hodgson Collection at the Royal
Asiatic Society. RAS Hodgson Collection 022.058. © Royal Asiatic Society.

Hodgson's premier *chitrakar* Raj Man Singh. The assumption has always been that these were drawn for the Lawrences during their two years in Nepal. Of particular interest is a finished watercolour of the British Residency as seen from the main gate, with various human figures and animals in the foreground. Standings on the driveway on the left are a group of six people: a man in a dark blue jacket, as worn by British Politicals in India at the time, with a boy and a girl beside him; in front of them, two women wrapped in shawls, one of them holding a babe-in-arms. On the roof of the building behind them a second man in a blue jacket peers southwards through a telescope. The painting is inscribed on the front in pencil by an unknown hand 'Probably the Residency but not as in 1908'.

This watercolour was always been assumed to show the Lawrence family: that is to say, at the back, Henry Lawrence with seven-year-old Letitia and six-year-old Alexander; at the front Mrs Honoria Lawrence, with her new born son Henry in the arms of an *ayah* or native nurse.

However, among the many collections of drawings presented by Brian Hodgson to various institutions after his return to England is a portfolio of architectural drawings given to the Royal Asiatic Society. The best of these are one of two sets of fifty finished drawings of Nepalese religious architecture by Raj Man Singh (the other set went to the *Institut de France* in January 1858). Also included in that collection is a much less impressive set of twelve pen-and-ink drawings which came wrapped in a paper folder inscribed in ink in Hodgson's handwriting 'Twelve rough sketches of architectural series'. These are, indeed, rough, being pen-and-ink outlines drawn with the aid of a *camera lucida*, from which finished drawings in pencil were then made.

When these twelve pen-and-ink sketches from the Royal Asiatic Society collection are set side by side with twelve of the watercolours from the Lawrence Collection it immediately becomes obvious that they are linked: the first are the preliminary outline sketches for the finished watercolours. Both sets of drawings had a common origin but at some point they got separated. Hodgson's letters tell us that in the confusion of what he called his 'sudden ejection from Nepal' in December 1843 his papers and drawings were left 'utterly confused and mangled' and 'dissipated and dislocated'. The only possible inference is that in that confusion Hodgson took the set of twelve outline drawings with him, along with much else, but left behind what became known as the Lawrence watercolours.

One of these twelve outline pen-and-ink drawings is inscribed in ink in Brian Hodgson's distinctive handwriting 'British Embassy Mansion at Kathmandu'. Its shows a family group standing on the drive in front of the Residency. The handwriting of the caption shows that it was drawn for Hodgson and was seen by him, so this sketch must have been made *before* he left Kathmandu in December 1843. In that case we can safely conclude that the family group outlined in ink are Brian Hodgson and his family. In December 1843 Hodgson's boy Henry would have been about ten and his daughter Sarah about nine.

But then when we look at one of the finished watercolours in the Lawrence Collection we see precisely the same scene, identical in almost every respect other than the addition of colour and fine detail (*see pages 235 & 238 and Plate 34*). The family group in the pen-and-ink outline sketch is placed in exactly the same position as the family group in the finished watercolour – as is everything and everyone else. The one is patently based on the other, albeit one is an outline sketch and the other a finished painting.

What are we to make of this – and, in particular, the presence of a babe-in-arms in both pictures?

The observant reader, in examining the two groups, will also have noted that in the original pen-and-ink sketch the woman on the left in the foreground has her head covered in a shawl or *sari* in the local style, whereas in the finished watercolour she is shown wearing a European-style bonnet. It may well be that the finished painting does indeed show Mrs Honoria Lawrence and her new-born son Henry in the arms of an *ayah* – but if so it must have been modified or redrawn by the artist to reflect the changed circumstances.

That does not alter the fact that Brian Hodgson came away from Nepal in December 1843 with a pen-and-ink outline drawing that shows him with three children, so proving the existence of a second, new-born daughter – and with it the reason for Hodgson's increasingly desperate attempts to stay on.

The Hodgson family or the Lawrences? On the left, a detail of the original
pen-and-ink outline sketch from the Hodgson Collection, the Royal
Asiatic Society; on the right, the same detail of the finished watercolour
from the Lawrence Collection, the British Library. Does this prove the
truth of the stories about the new-born daughter that Brian Hodgson
left behind in Kathmandu along with his *begum* Mehr-un-Nissa?

When Henry Lawrence arrived in Kathmandu in early December he brought with him the news that the only position in Government service that the Governor-General was prepared to offer
Brian Hodgson was that of Assistant Sub-Commissioner in Simla.
Hodgson saw this for what it was – a deliberate snub intended to
force his resignation – and he immediately did just that. This petty
insult added greatly to Hodgson's sense of injustice. He was not the
kind of man to forgive or forget and this humiliation and the way
it was heaped on him by Lord Ellenborough left him a bitter and
unhappy man.

On 5 December the outgoing and the incoming British Residents
were together received in formal audience by Raja Rajendra Bikram
Shah in Durbar. The Raja burst into tears and spoke of Hodgson as
the saviour of Nepal whose sole exertions had prevented their two
nations from going to war. He then plucked a jewel from his turban
and handed it to Major Lawrence, begging Lawrence to allow him to
present it to Hodgson. He explained that this was a family heirloom

which he now wished to pass on to Hodgson's family, even though he knew that it was against the rules for British officials to accept gifts of any value. It was politely but firmly refused.

Of Hodgson's leave-taking from the country that had been his home for the better part of twenty-three years – and from the woman who had been his companion for the last seven and who had borne him two, if not three, children – very little is known beyond a few unreliable scraps of oral tradition. It may be that Hodgson left his new-born daughter behind because she was too young to travel, but it is clear that Hodgson had no plans to take her mother with him. However, if he followed long-standing Anglo-Indian custom, he would certainly have made provisions for her – and therefore for their third child.

After Hodgson's departure with their two older children Begum Mehr-un-Nissa is said to have returned to live with her parents in a house in what is now called *Musamagalli* or Muslim Lane, right in the heart of Kathmandu. Since this is far removed from the area north-west of the British Residency compound where her parents' community of *dhobi* washermen settled, it may well be that this house was bought for her by Hodgson.

There are conflicting accounts over whether Mehr-un-Nissa died before or after her eldest daughter Sarah's death in 1851 or, indeed, her son Henry's death in 1856. She is believed to have been buried in Kathmandu's Muslim cemetery in an area now known as *Begumka Immambara*, or the Shrine of the Begum – most likely named after a refugee Begum of Lucknow rather than Begum Mehr-un-Nissa. By one dubious account, her one surviving daughter grew up and married and has living descendents in Kathmandu. What all the oral histories seem to agree on is that Mehr-un-Nissa never got over the loss of her two children. Her death most probably occurred before 1853, the year in which Brian Hodgson married an Englishwoman.

At the same time, there can be no doubt that Brian Hodgson left Kathmandu with Henry and Sarah in great disarray and in great distress.

Brianstone, Brian Hodgson's bungalow in Jalapahar Estate, Darjeeling, a
four-bedroom bungalow said to be one of the oldest surviving buildings
in Darjeeling, now the Rectory of St Paul's School. NHM Hodgson
Collection 037016. © The Trustees of the Natural History Museum.

11

'T'was a happy lot while it lasted, so that I could not feel its chains till I attempted to break them': Pensioner, Europe, Darjeeling and England, 1843–1894

On the evening of Tuesday 6 February an extraordinary meeting was held at the Asiatic Society of Bengal in Calcutta. It was customary for the members of that learned body to meet on the first Wednesday of every month, but on this occasion there was a pressing reason for calling the meeting a day earlier: its subject was due, that very evening, to board the *Earl of Hardwicke*, bound for England. In the chair was William Bird, President of the Supreme Council and the most senior official in India after the Governor-General, Lord Ellenborough, who had declined the honour, having made no secret of his disdain for the Asiatic Society and its deliberations.

As Bird pointed out in his opening remarks, this was the first opportunity that Brian Hodgson had had to attend one of the Society's meetings – and also the last: 'Mr Hodgson sails tomorrow, and I am sure that there is not a Member here present who would not have regretted the loss of the only opportunity we shall ever have of seeing him in this place, and of testifying, as far as we are able, how highly we are sensible of the credit which his labours and researches have reflected on the Society.'

Nothing was said of the circumstances surrounding Hodgson's sudden arrival in Calcutta and his equally swift departure on the morrow – circumstances that would have been known to every person present. Instead, Bird concentrated on Hodgson's non-official achievements: 'Of their variety and extent, you may yourselves be able to form some judgement, when you hear that Mr Hodgson's contributions to the *Transactions* and *Journal* of this Society alone, according to a paper which I hold in my hand, amount to eighty-nine distinct papers.' Mr Hodgson had 'found time to enrich our knowledge of Zoology by new observations on known animals, and a series of discoveries of novel ones'. Yet, in Bird's opinion, his most valuable contribution had been his work 'on the literature and religion of the Boodhists, a work the most complete extant upon a subject till lately but little understood, and of the highest importance to the Philologist and the Historian'.

Bird closed his speech by proposing that 'as a testimony of the high sense entertained by this Society of Mr Hodgson's scientific and literary labours, and also as a mark of personal regard, he be requested to sit for some first-rate artist for his bust, to be placed in the public Meeting Room'. The motion was seconded and carried by general acclaim.

But time had run out on Brian Hodgson and he was unable either to reply to Mr Bird or to sit for his bust, which had to be done after his arrival in England. However, he still had the satisfaction of boarding the *Earl of Hardwicke* with the plaudits of his fellow Orientalists ringing in his ears, among them the eminent Bengali (and father of the future nationalist and Nobel Laureate Rabindranath Tagore) Dwakarnath Tagore, who had supported him in his vernacular campaign and now wrote to urge him to continue his good work:

> Your absence will be a great loss, for who can so well conduct an enterprise as the man who conceives and plans it. You must do what you can when away from India and you must keep my zeal alive by frequent letters. I will keep you informed respecting what is doing, and tell you both the best and the worst. I wish there were more of my own countrymen willing to assist in operations for the enlightenment and education of the people at large. The number at present is few but we must do our best.[1]

Brian Hodgson was only forty-three when he was prised out of his Himalayan eyrie and into retirement. It was his tragedy that he was to live for another fifty-one years.

On his arrival in England in the spring of 1844 Hodgson was astonished and gratified to find himself treated as something of a hero. Both in Parliament and in India House the tide had turned against Lord Ellenborough. Lord Macaulay had begun the process a year earlier by delivering another of his thundering orations in the House of Commons when seconding a motion calling on the HEICo's Court of Directors to recall Ellenborough as unfit to govern on account of his abuse of power. Although the vote went against him the wheels had been set in motion, and when Hodgson made his duty call on the Chairman of the HEICo he was greeted with open arms and the news that a despatch had just been sent ordering Lord Ellenborough to return to England. The Court of Directors had had enough of his arrogance in his dealings with them and had concluded that India was no longer safe in his hands.

Hodgson was asked to present his case to the Court of Directors. He certainly went so far as to draw up just such a statement but he never submitted it – a failure he came to regret in later years. Given the change of mood at India House, he would certainly have been welcomed back into the Bengal Civil Service. However, he must have also known that his chances of being allowed to resume his post in Nepal were nil and this may well have been the deciding factor. At the British Residency Major Henry Lawrence had reverted to Edward Gardner's old policy of non-intervention and that seemed to be working well enough.

After a grand dinner held in his honour in London, at which his health had been drunk 'amid the acclamations of some two hundred gentlemen, including 'the Minister for India', Hodgson joined his parents, who were now living in Canterbury. He now had a very handsome pension of a thousand pounds a year and talked of buying a small country estate in England where he might live with his parents and his two older children. However, he very soon moved on to visit his favourite sister Fanny, now the Baroness Nahuys and long settled in Arnhem in Holland, where her husband was the local governor.

But Fanny, of course, now had her own family, in which there was no comfortable room for a much loved but much older brother. Hodgson stayed with the Nahuyses throughout the summer of 1844 but with each passing month he grew increasingly depressed. To what extent this misery was due to feelings of remorse over the way he had abandoned his wife and newborn daughter and how much to the public humiliation he had suffered at the hands of Lord Ellenborough, it is impossible to judge. There is plenty of evidence to show how keenly Hodgson felt the blow to his pride and reputation but little to show on the other account. This could have been because Hodgson kept these things to himself or because his second wife – who worked closely with Hodgson's biographer after his death – did all she could to tidy up his image. We must also take into account Hodgson's growing sense of dislocation.

Hodgson soon began to talk of returning to India and the Himalayas. 'This will never do,' he wrote to his father in October 1844. 'I had far better return to India than continue thus a source of pain to those I love best, as well as myself. Accordingly, I have nearly decided to return, and the sooner, I think, the better.' He would resume his studies of nature while maintaining the 'requisite intercourse with the scientific bodies of Europe'.

His sense of no longer belonging, so familiar to old colonials who returned home after twenty or thirty years away to find themselves strangers in their own land, also played its part in shaping Hodgson's decision to go back to India. In a second letter to his father, sent from Holland a month later, he explained in poignant terms brimming with self-pity how much of an outsider he now felt:

> Surely no man who ever went to India had the fortune to become so alienated entirely from European ways from the first to the last. T'was the chance of the service and was a happy lot while it lasted, so that I could not feel its chains till I attempted to break them. I cannot resume them wholly, but I may in good part, and may find comfort and credit too in this partial resumption ... I may be happy or rather content in India I think, and if not, I can come back, whereas to stay moping here would be the worst of all, worse cannot be.[2]

Hodgson had deposited all that he had bought back by way of papers, drawings and zoological specimens with his parents in

Canterbury. He now handed over Henry and Sarah to the care of his sister and her husband and returned to England to make arrangement for the specimens to be examined by representatives of the British Museum and the College of Surgeons, so that they might take their pick for their own collections. 'I want to be rid of the skins and bones,' he explained, 'and, for the rest, shall be glad to keep my materials by me to be worked up, and added to, abroad.'

Now committed to returning to India, Hodgson spent the next five months trying to bring some order to his papers, thrown into a great muddle by his abrupt departure from Kathmandu: 'I must away to resume and complete my researches where alone they can be satisfactorily completed,' he explained in a letter to Fanny written in Canterbury just before Christmas 1844. 'My hurried departure amid overpowering vexations caused all my papers and other materials to be dissipated and dislocated, and I can collect the fragments in India alone. It will cost me a couple of years. Even if I fail I may be quieted by the reflection that failure came not till every effort had been made to avert it. If I succeed I shall come back comforted and strengthened to encounter the new life in Europe.'

This letter was quoted only in part by Hodgson's biographer. If it contained any reference to the future care of Henry and Sarah, now aged ten and nine, Hunter chose to omit it.

Brian Hodgson sailed for India in June 1845, travelling on board the *Alfred* by way of Cork, where he posted a number of poignant letters of farewell. To Fanny he poured out his feelings and his gratitude for all that she had done for him, and would continue to do: 'Words cannot tell what I owe you. In my dark hour you were my guardian angel, and in subsequent hours your sweet words and looks gave me to taste the only pleasure I have known for years. Whilst I breathe I shall cherish the memory of your tenderness. What a sweet and holy thing is true affection! There is nothing else worth living for, and would to God I could dedicate the remainder of my life to winning it and replaying it in a home of my own.' He now left his 'dear children' in her care. She was to cherish them and teach them 'to love me ever as "Aunt Fanny" loves me!'

To his father, Hodgson wrote to explain why he felt he had to go back to India:

I am still, as I have been for a year past, consumed with restlessness, and I too much dread lest, if I stayed, I should pass from despondent listless to petulant irritability which must and would certainly render me not only useless to you but vexatious. I am going forth therefore, alone and sad, to wander and I can but promise you to return so soon as I can hope to be free of the morbid fret and anxiety that are preying upon me. Travel may benefit me, and so I may commune with my own soul on the high seas and when I reach India, may possibly be enabled to resume and complete my researches ... Nay, if I find but peace of mind, I will return, though my researches remain incomplete.[3]

Hodgson reached Calcutta in November 1845. There to welcome him were two old friends: his former boss, Herbert Maddock, now Deputy-Governor of Bengal and knighted for his pains; and his former assistant, Dr Archie Campbell. After a decade as superintendent of the fast-growing hill station of Darjeeling, Campbell was now the leading figure of the station, comfortably settled with a wife and growing family at Beechwood, a large house on the ridge running south from Darjeeling Hill. Darjeeling itself was now starting to provide the same service as a summer retreat to the Government of Bengal as Simla was to the Central Government, and to this end Herbert Maddock had bought for himself a summerhouse there, a simple county bungalow with a thatch roof built on the ridge half a mile south of Dr Campbell's Beechwood.

It was Herbert Maddock who made it plain to Hodgson that there was no question of him being returned to Nepal in either an official or a private capacity. 'It seems my influence is considered to be still too great not to derange the political spheres were I to come within the region of their attraction,' Hodgson explained in a letter to Fanny sent in mid-December. 'What a nuisance it is sometimes to be of too much consequence! But I comfort myself for the loss of not getting to Nepal immediately that my voluntary self-denial in not going now is founded in pure love of that country and its people.'

Hodgson's arrival in Calcutta coincided with the start of the first round of the Anglo-Sikh Wars – the fiercest fought of all the military campaigns waged by John Company's armies – and he was surprised to find himself lodged at Government House, temporarily occupied by Herbert Maddock as he deputised for the new Governor-General, Lieutenant General Sir Henry Hardinge. Other than being Lord Ellenborough's brother-in-law, Hardinge had nothing in common with his predecessor. He was first and last a soldier and had not been at all discomfited to arrive in India to find two large armies squaring up to each other across the banks of the River Sutlej.

The Punjab had slid into near anarchy following the death of its long-time ruler Maharaja Ranjit Singh. Lord Ellenborough's response had been to establish a large military cantonment at Ferozepur just short of the River Sutlej and the Punjab border. This had rattled the Sikhs and in December 1845 a Sikh army crossed the Sutlej into British territory, whereupon Sir Henry Hardinge at once joined his commander-in-chief at the front. The first clash came at Mudki, a far bloodier battle followed at Ferozeshah five days later and then a more decisive engagement was fought and won at Subraon in February, leading to a peace treaty signed in Lahore in March 1846.

Early in 1846 Hodgson joined the Campbells in Darjeeling. He stayed with them at Beechwood for an undetermined period but then moved into the simple bungalow that Maddock had bought for his own use in the summer months and named Herbert Hill. A year later Maddock sold it to Hodgson, who renamed it Brianstone.

According to one of Hodgson's few European guests, Brianstone was sited 'in a narrow clearing of the majestic forest that then clothed the mountains of Sikkim on every side, and crept up to the very walls of the few houses of which the station consisted.' It looked directly out at the Himalayan ranges:

> Facing the north at an elevation of 7,500 feet, it commanded a view of the snowy Himalaya unrivalled for grandeur and extent. Immediately in front at about forty-seven miles distant, Kinchinjinga ... rears itself to 28,178 feet above sea level and 20,000 feet above Bryanstone [sic]. From its vast shoulders the perpetually snowed range I scrutinised east and west for about seventy miles, without the smallest break of the snowline. It is a wonderful panorama, startling in its effect when first revealed by the rising mists on a cloudless morning.[4]

This was the vista that greeted Brian Hodgson most mornings during the winter months of the twelve years that Brianstone served as his home – a view now enjoyed by the boarders of St. Paul's School, Darjeeling, the grounds of which are laid out around Brianstone, which serves as the home of the school's headmaster, the Rector, albeit entirely rebuilt and enlarged.

We know next to nothing about Hodgson's first years in Darjeeling. According to the visitor whose words are quoted above, Hodgson lived the life of a recluse and admitted no one to his house except his old friend Dr Campbell. But that ban applied only to Europeans. One of Hodgson's first actions after settling in must have been to send word to Kathmandu, which resulted in the return of some of the papers and drawings he had left behind. And with them came the first and most important of his *chitrakars*, Raj Man Singh – and others, too: 'He seldom had a staff of less than from ten to twenty persons (often many more), of various tongues and races, employed as translators, and collectors, artists, shooters, and stuffers.'

Bit by bit Hodgson reassembled the bits and pieces of his scattered researches and so resumed his studies. 'I write and read, and write and read,' he told his sister Fanny in a letter dated 5 December 1847:

My subjects are Ethnology and Zoology and Education – all ample fields and yet enough untrodden to render intelligent truthful labours permanently valuable. And such I trust will be mine. I will send you a copy of my work on Education, and also one of the several Essays on the Aborigines. But of Zoology you will not care to hear, though even that can be made rational and pleasant, and for my part, in the study of nature I find an extreme comfort and pleasure. The thing is so truthful and calm, and real, as I pursue it not in books but in actual subjects.

There is no record of Hodgson ever contacting his abandoned *bibi* in Kathmandu or his second daughter, but he did, at least, fret over his two older children left in the care of his sister and worry about what sort of future they faced. 'How inexpressibly comfortable it is for me to realise that my sweet Fan is the guardian of my poor brown children,' he wrote. 'They will have much to struggle against when their sensibilities become fully awake, in future contact with the white world! I often think of this painfully, being perpetually in the way of hearing what people say on the topic, always insulting and cruel!'[5]

Initially the main focus of Hodgson's resumed studies was on zoology, although now concentrated on mammals rather than birds. In 1846 and 1847 the *Journal of the Asiatic Society of Bengal* published Hodgson's papers on 'a new species of Tibetan antelope'; 'the Wild Sheep of Tibet'; 'a new form of the Hog kind or *Suidae*'; 'the Hispid hare of the Saul forest'; 'various genera of the Ruminants'; 'the Tibetan badger, *Taxida leucorus*'; 'a new species of Porcupine'; 'the *Charj* or *Otis Bengalensis*' (the Bengal bustard); 'the slatey-blue Magaderme' (false vampire bats); 'a new species of Plecotus' (long-eared bats); 'the tame sheep and goats of the sub-Himalayas and of Tibet'; 'the cat-toed Plantigrades of the sub-Himalayas'; 'the Wild-Ass and Wolf of Tibet'; and 'a new genus of *Suidae* [pigs] and a new species of *Taxidea* [badger]'.

These last two were among the twenty-two new species of Himalayan mammals whose discoveries are today credited to Hodgson. He had known of the existence of the diminutive Pygmy Hog, *Porcula salvania*, for many years but had been unable to obtain a specimen until one was killed and delivered to him in 1846. Similarly, the Tibetan badger, *Taxidia leucurus*, was 'a very fine specimen from the neighbourhood of Lassa', where it had been killed and 'well prepared without distortion' before being brought to Hodgson in Darjeeling, complete with skeleton.

The largest and probably the most unusual of the mammals discovered and named by Hodgson over this period also had its habitat some distance from Darjeeling. This was the Takin, a bovine creature only found in the eastern Himalayas, which had first come to his attention when Major Patterson sent him an incomplete skin from the Mishmi Hills. Hodgson subsequently obtained two more skins and the skull of a bull, enough to accurately describe this singular creature:

A large, massive and remarkable animal, denominated Takin ... Its nearest affinity is probably to the Gnoos; but it has various

TAXIDEA   *leucurus*   (Hodgson)

J. Black, Asiatic Lith: Press Cal:

(Above) The Tibetan badger, which Hodgson designated *Taxidia leucurus*. *Journal of the Asiatic Society of Bengal*, Vol. 16, 1847. (Below) The 'Pygmy Hog of Saul forest', which Hodgson named *Porcula salvania*, now called the *Sus salvanius*. *Journal of the Asiatic Society of Bengal*, Vol. 16, 1847.

Porcula Salvania, Pigmy Hog of Saul forest.

points of stronger connection with Musk Oxen ... An animal of high courage and great ferocity, so that it cannot be taken alive, and is killed by the natives with much trouble and some risk ... Strength and ferocity are inscribed in very legible characters on the form and aspect of the Takin, which is a much larger and bulkier animal than the lusty Caprine Antelope (*Thar*) of the Himalayas ... which it much resembles in colour as well as by its short Caprine tail, harsh adpressed hair, and vigorous make, suited to climbing these stupendous mountains ... The Takin is not much, if at all, inferior in size or bulk to the female Yak; and, as seen from the front especially, with its lunate horn displayed and its short tail concealed, it would be at once pronounced to belong to the Ox kind. [6]

All the plates illustrating these papers were lithographs based on the increasingly sophisticated drawings now being produced by Raj Man Singh and his fellow *chitrakars*.

However, as Hodgson settled into his new home a new *shoke* began to emerge, initially focussed on the various peoples inhabiting the eastern Himalayas at and about Sikkim and Darjeeling. This new interest was noted by an eminent visitor from Calcutta, Sir James Colvile, Advocate-General of Bengal, who came to Darjeeling in September 1847 to recover his health. Colvile was at that time President of the Asiatic Society of Bengal, which may explain why Hodgson not only admitted him into his house but allowed him to remain there for some weeks.

'I am living here in a Babel of tribes and nations,' Colvile wrote to a friend in England, 'and, to make them more interesting, I am living with an eminent ethnologist, who for more than twenty-five years has had, and profited by, peculiar opportunities of studying the varieties of men who inhabit the Sub-Himalaya. I have learned more about India from him in these few weeks than I have learned at Calcutta in nearly two years.' In this same letter Colvile referred to Hodgson's career being cut short by 'one of the most wanton acts of [Lord Ellenborough's] capricious tyranny', and how he had returned to the Himalayas to 'continue, but with crippled means, his scientific labours as a private gentleman'.[7]

Hodgson could be said to have began his ethnographic studies in Kathmandu in the course of compiling his report on the 'Military Tribes of Nepal' (1833), which began as a bid to find a solution to the endemic militarism of the Parbatiyas. In that first exercise Hodgson had identified significant features of the caste system as applied in Nepal and its ramifications in the form of sub-castes and inter-caste marriages and prohibitions. In much the same way, his paper on Nepal's legal system, 'Some accounts of the systems of law and police as recognised in the state of Nepal' (1834), had identified important divergences between Hindu law in India and as it was practised in Nepal, even though it had only came about as a result of ongoing disputes over British and Nepali jurisdiction. His work on the Newars had also broken new ground, even though it formed part of his explorations of Buddhism.

This renewed interest in the study of human groups may well have been awakened by the example of Dr Archie Campbell who, back in 1840, had three papers published in the *Journal of the Asiatic Society of Bengal,* all describing the languages and customs of local tribal groups living within the vicinity of Dajeeling: 'Note of the Mechis, together with a small vocabulary of the language'; 'Note on the Lepchas of Sikkim, with a vocabulary of the language'; and 'Note on the Limboos and other hill tribes hitherto undescribed'. Hodgson's response was to write 'A cursory notice of Nayakote', published in the same journal in 1841.

Nayakote – now Nuwakot – was a strategically important hill fort on the ancient trade route leading north from Kathmandu along the Trisuli River and on through the central Himayalan Range into Tibet. It was two days' march from Kathmandu and beyond his prescribed limits, so Hodgson must have had special permission to make what he called 'a hurried visit under disadvantageous circumstances'. Even so, he extracted an astonishing amount of information, such as how many varieties of rice were grown there and how they performed – the answer being twenty, all named, of which three could not be grown in the Nepal Valley.

Nuwakot fort was one of the Gorkhas' ancestral strongholds and after his takeover of the Nepal Valley Prithvi Narayan Shah had transported a number of skilled Newar craftsmen to Nawakot to build what became known as the *Saat Tale Darbar* or Seven Storey Palace, which became his winter residence. Hodgson's paper concentrated on what today would be called human geography, examining the many social groups settled in and around the little town, their occupations and their customs. It remains a model of its kind.

Five years on Brian Hodgson reapplied himself to this new branch of the social sciences. Then in November 1847 he re-entered the scholarly world with a bang, informing the three co-Secretaries of the Asiatic Society of Bengal (who shared the editorship of the Society's *Journal* between themselves) that he was preparing for the press 'a series of detailed memoirs on the Aborigines of the frontier in its Mountains and its Tarai'.

This was another of Hodgson's grandiose projects that never saw the light of completion, but it did result in more than a dozen ethnographic papers, initiated by a general outline, 'On the aborigines of the Sub-Himalayas', published in the *Journal of the Asiatic Society of Bengal* in January 1848 together with a 'Comparative vocabulary of the several languages and dialects of the eastern sub-Himalayas, from the Kali or Ghogra [Rivers], to the Dhanari [River]'.

Crude as these papers may appear today, they set out for the first time an overview of the main ethnic groups inhabiting Hodgson's defined area together with comparison of their languages, customs and identity, extending from the Bhutanese, Lepchas, Limbus, Kirantis, Suwars, Kocch, Bodos and Dhimals in the eastern Himalayas, to the Gurungs and Magars in western Nepal, the Newars and Murmis (Tamangs, *see Plate 32*) in central Nepal and the Bhotias south and north of the Central Himalayan Range.

These were believed by Hodgson to be indigenous, non-Hindu tribes, and their customs and languages – and the links between them – now became his main preoccupation, marred to some degree by Hodgson's unconcealed dislike of Nepal's ruling elite, the Khas, whom he mocked for their pretensions to racial purity: 'The Khas welcomed the Hindu immigrants into their mountains at an early period and became so intermixed with the Brahmanical and Kshatriyan tribes (the genuine Aryans) that all physical or lingual traces of their aboriginal lineage are now much weakened or obliterated. And as they have become, since the predominance of the Gorkali dynasty in Nepal, the predominant race in a Hindu kingdom, they are themselves very anxious that these few traces should remain unnoticed.'[8]

This was in marked contrast to Hodgson's sympathetic treatment of those who now found themselves at the bottom of the caste ladder, such as the Bodos and Dhimals, 'erratic cultivators of the wilds' who inhabited the jungles along the southern borders of Sikkim: 'The religion of the Bodos and Dhimals,' he declared, 'is distinguished by the absence of everything that is shoddy, ridiculous or incommodious. It lends no sanction to barbarous rites, nor does it hamper the commerce of life with tedious insane ceremonial observances.' These people had no hereditary priests, no liturgy, and no holy books: 'From all such crimes and mischiefs the religions of the Bodos and Dhimals is wholly free ... I have no hesitation in calling the religion of the amicable Bodos and Dhimals the religion of Nature, or rather, the early religion of man.'

The last of Hodgson's ethnographic papers, published in 1858 and 1859, were on the 'broken tribes' of the Kirantis or Kiratis. These were in part the descendents of a once powerful people who had ruled over a large part of the Indian plains as well as the Nepal Valley for generations before being overcome by the Mallas in the fourteenth century. They were now divided into some twenty tribal groups such as the Limbus, Sunuwars and Rais scattered through eastern Nepal. Hodgson considered them to be 'perhaps the most interesting of all the Himalayan races, not even excepting the Newars of Nepal proper, on account of their distinctly traceable antiquity as a nation and the peculiar structure of their language'. He was able to identify a common language base now divided into many local dialects and a distinctive animist culture that was 'very vague', with no names for any deities and no hereditary priesthood. However, they did 'believe heartily in the black arts' as practised by exponents called *krakra*, who were themselves opposed by others called *janicha* or *mangpa* – both exorcists and physicians who undid the damage done by the *krakra*. Here was a first account of the 'medicine-men' we today call shamans.

Hodgson's original Newar *chitrakar*, Raj Man Singh, was by now well established in Darjeeling and under Hodgson's direction he and one or more assistants turned their hands to depictions of the human form in various guises to illustrate Hodgson's papers on these various 'tribes'. The results, it must be said, were mixed, and only two were ever published: the profile and full face of a twenty-three-year-old Tibetan man, described as 'a good-humoured looking lad, fleshy and broad, but scarcely so tall or massive as the majority of his race' to illustrate a paper on 'Tibetan types of mankind', and a jungle-dwelling Chepang with a bow and arrow from Hodgson's paper 'On the Chepang and Kusunda tribes of Nepal'.

Few of these ethnographic drawings have survived, although very recently an album of just such drawings has come to light in the Ethnographic Library of the British Museum, where they appear to have lain unnoticed in a box since they were placed there by Augustus W. Franks in 1873! Originally there appear to have been sixty sheets, now reduced to thirty-nine, some crudely drawn but the best of them neatly executed and finished as watercolours – and enough to show a close correspondence between them and the subjects of Hodgson's published papers.

Some of these drawings can also be linked to watercolours in the collection of Dr Henry Oldfield now in the British Library. Oldfield came to Kathmandu as Residency Surgeon seven years after Hodgson's departure and occupied that post for thirteen years. He was a first-class watercolourist whose landscape paintings constitute a hugely valuable record of Nepal in the 1850s and early 1860s, but a number of drawings of 'native types' attributed to Oldfield have affinities with Hodgson's tribal drawings, which suggests that at least one of the *chitrakars* who joined Hodgson in Darjeeling went back to Kathmandu after his departure and there continued to ply his trade under Oldfield.

It was entirely typical of Hodgson that having started work on the ethnography of the Himalayan peoples he decided to expand his project to include all the so-called aboriginal peoples of the Indian sub-continent. As soon as his first two papers had appeared in print he sent copies to British officials all over India, inviting them to join with him 'as a means of enabling us to make a general comparison of all the Aborigines from Cape Comorin to the snows'. It was a grand plan and, of course, it came to nothing.

In April 1848 Hodgson received a visit from a young botanist named Joseph Hooker, son of the then Director of the Kew Gardens Sir William Hooker, and it is from this lively source that we have probably the most rounded portrait of the by now palpably eccentric retired Bengal civil servant in the last phase of his working life.

When first taken to meet him Hooker found Hodgson in his garden 'talking Tibetan to a Chinese-looking man, whom he was

(Above) A pencil drawing of a Limbu shaman with feathered head-
dress, drum and bells, described in Hodgson's hand as 'Impersonation of
goddess Bajra' and dated Dec. 1847. This may be the earliest drawing of a
Himalayan shaman. (Below) A watercolour showing Chepang tribesmen in
five characteristic poses. The central figure was reproduced as a lithograph
in Hodgson's paper on the Chepang and Kusunda tribes published in
the *Journal of the Asiatic Society of Bengal* in 1848. BM Ethnographic
Library, Hodgson Album. © The Trustees of the British Museum.

questioning about the geography of Central Asia'. He appeared 'sickly-looking', and 'ill & nervous to such a degree that he fancies the Darjeeling doctors want to kill him, & he will have no other medical attendant than myself, or Dr Campbell.'[9] But as Hooker got to know Hodgson better he found him to be a 'particularly gentlemanly and agreeable person ... with a grand forehead and delicate, finely-cut features. When arrayed in his furs and wearing the Scotch bonnet and eagle-feather with which it is his pleasure to adorn himself, he would make a striking picture.'[10] Hodgson could also be 'wickedly sarcastic', with much of that sarcasm being directed at that 'knave and coxcomb' Lord Ellenborough.

Despite the seventeen-year difference in their ages the two got on so well together that in June Hooker was invited to move into Brianstone, where he spent the next ten months as Hodgson's guest, even though days would pass without him even so much as catching sight of his host: 'Ever since his arrival in Darjiling he had lived the life of a hermit ... suffering from the effects of fevers contracted in Nepal and from incurable sleeplessness. He often told me that he did not know what sleep was, so active was his mind and so brief were the snatches of repose ... He slept in one of the supplementary apartments ... and not infrequently passed days and even weeks there, during which I never saw him except to give some simple remedies for his distressing ailment.'

Yet when they did meet Hooker gained an astonishing amount of information on every subject from his host, and when he afterwards published his *Himalayan Journals* he was generous in his praise for this self-taught savant:

> To be welcomed to the Himalaya by such a person and to be allowed the most unreserved intercourse, and the advantage of all his information and library, exercised a material influence on the progress I made in my studies, and on my travels. When I add that many of the subjects treated of in these volumes were discussed between us, it will be evident that it is impossible for me to divest much of this information thus insensibly obtained of the appearance of being the fruits of my own research.

Encapsulated in that paragraph was Brian Hodgson's true worth – not as a scholar in his own right but as collector, enabler and pioneer: the man on the spot who by his labours clears the path for better qualified men and women to follow. Neither Hodgson's great work on the aboriginal tribes of the Himalayas nor the physical geography of the Himalayas that he subsequent began to work on came to anything, but his preliminary papers on both subjects survive and are still read and valued, for all their infelicities and false trails.

At the start of the Cold Weather of 1848 Joseph Hooker was given permission to extend his plant hunting from Sikkim into eastern Nepal, 'over ground never before or since then traversed by any European, and to visit the jealously guarded passes of the Nepalese-Tibet frontier'. This was entirely thanks to Brian Hodgson, who had continued to keep in touch with events in Nepal.

During Hodgson's absence in England a major shift of power had taken place at the Nepal Durbar. Bhimsen Thapa's nephew, Matabar Singh Thapa, had returned from exile just before Brian Hodgson left Kathmandu. He had then began to build up his own power base within the army and by the spring of 1845 was poised to become the de facto ruler of Nepal, like his uncle before him.

But in May 1845 Matabar Singh was invited to the palace and murdered there in the presence of the king. It soon became known that the first shot was fired by Matabar Singh's own nephew, a young army officer named Jung Bahadur Kunwar, supposedly acting under duress. As a reward for this betrayal Jung Bahadur was given a post in a ministry dominated by the queen's supposed lover, Gagan Singh.

Sixteen months later, on the evening of 14 September 1846, Gagan Singh was shot dead by persons unknown in his own home. That same night, acting in alliance with the queen, Jung Bahadur's troops rounded up every bharadar and senior official and herded them into the courtyard of the palace armoury, the Kot. Fearing the worst, Raja Rajendra fled the scene and turned up at the British Residency at 2 a.m. in the morning, only to be turned away on the orders of Captain Ottley, the Acting Resident.

Shooting broke out and the infamous Kot Massacre followed, after which Jang Bahadur was proclaimed Prime Minister by the Junior Queen, who had persuaded herself that he would support her in promoting her son's claims to the throne. But Jung Bahadur had his own agenda. Claiming that the queen had initiated a plot against him, he killed a number of her followers and replaced them with his own supporters, stripped the queen of her powers and ordered her banishment to Benares. By this time King Rajendra had had enough and chose to accompany her into exile – only to have a change of heart and make a bid to reclaim his throne. He was arrested, dethroned and imprisoned in one of his own palaces, where he remained until his death.

On 12 May 1847 Surendra Bikram Shah came of age and at last got his wish to be anointed king – only to discover that this was in name only. He too became a virtual prisoner in his own palace. With the security of himself and his clan secured Prime Minister Jung Bahadar Rana – as he now styled himself – lost no time in re-establishing good relations with the British, both in India and in Britain. In 1849, with characteristic disregard for the taboos of the day, he decided to visit England – a thoroughly enlightening event that convinced him that England's industrial strength was so great that Nepal had no option but to remain an ally, albeit, an ally at arm's length.

Hodgson had known Jung Bahadur briefly when the latter was still a junior member of the Thapa clan and afterwards claimed that he had recognised in him the qualities that had distinguished his great-uncle Bhimsen Thapa. But, like his compatriots in Calcutta, Hodgson was also deeply suspicious of Jung Bahadur Rana as a man with blood on his hands who was not to be trusted.

We may reasonably assume that throughout his early years in Darjeeling the welfare of his two children in Europe continued to trouble Hodgson. He was certainly made aware that Sarah's health was fragile and that she pined for her mother. 'Oh that I was at her side to nurse her, cheer her or take her to the soft clime of Italy or her native India,' Hodgson wrote in a telling letter to his sister Fanny, undated but probably written in 1851. 'Her attachment to her mother spoke angel-tongued for her goodness of heart and warmth and depth of feeling. Oh that I had written oftener and more fondly to her. But I feared to excite a tenderness that I was not destined to repay ... I could not bring her to India and in you she had a more than Mother whom its seemed best for her to learn to love.'

Sarah Hodgson died of tuberculosis on 12 September of that same year. Her loss seems to have shocked Hodgson into having second thoughts about his treatment of his son, who was also in poor health. This resulted in Henry sailing for India towards the end of 1852. As a young man of mixed race Henry was barred from following his father's footsteps into the Indian Civil Service or taking a commission in the Indian Army, but there were opportunities in business and so it was decided that he should become a *zamindar* and manage an estate as a tenant of the Government in Bengal.

However, Henry arrived in Calcutta early in 1853 only to find his father so seriously unwell that he was on the point of boarding a ship for England. There was time only for the briefest of reunions before father and son went their separate ways. Hodgson had arranged for Henry to spend some time under the care of the Principal of the Sanskrit College in Benares but, just like his father, Henry was unable to bear the heat and was soon despatched to the care of Dr Campbell in Darjeeling

Brian Hodgson arrived in England with his health much improved, so much so that he proposed marriage to a Miss Anne Scott, whom he married at the British Embassy in the Hague. Five weeks later the two of them were on their way back to India and Darjeeling.

Hodgson's biographer assures us that for two years Brian Hodgson, his wife Anne and his son Henry shared a happy family life at Brianstone. For Henry's twentieth birthday on 15 October 1855 his step-mother put together an album listing his father's achievements together with copies of the letters of the scholars, scientists and other great men with whom he had corresponded.[11] But that was to be Henry's last birthday. What was said to be a liver condition returned and he died at Brianstone on 18 April 1856.

It may have been no more than a coincidence but not long after Henry's death Hodgson received some form of communication from Nepal: a request from its Prime Minister and de facto ruler, Jung Bahadur Rana, and a very flattering one that that. Would Hodgson take charge of the education of his future son-in-law, Gajraj Singh Thapa, widely seen as the Prime Minister's heir apparent, and to treat him as his own son? Hodgson was happy to put his scruples to one side, and so the young man came to live with the Hodgsons at Brianstone, where he remained for about a year.

News of a sepoy mutiny at Meerut and the mutineers' subsequent seizure of Delhi reached Darjeeling in late May 1857. Every mail thereafter brought news of fresh disasters as soldiers of the Bengal Army turned on their officers in one station after another. Within a matter of weeks it seemed all but inevitable that British rule in Bengal and its Upper Provinces was about to be violently brought to an end.

It was at this critical juncture that Brian Hodgson's reputation as an honest friend of Nepal brought him right back into the centre of things. Jung Bahadur Rana had immediately recalled Gajraj Singh Thapa to Kathmandu, but, as it turned out, only to use him as a conduit. Immediately after the fall of Delhi he wrote to the Governor-General, Lord Canning, placing the whole of the military resources of his country at his disposal. On the same day he sent a message to Hodgson through Gajraj Singh warning him of the massacres in Delhi. He told him of his offer to the Governor-General and asked him to join him in Calcutta at the earliest opportunity.

In the meantime Lord Canning had taken the advice of his officials. The majority regarded Jung Bahadur Rana's offer of troops as a double-edged sword that could easily be directed against them if the situation continued to deteriorate. So he prevaricated, initially declining the offer and then agreeing to take a token force to be used only in border security. Then in late June came the news of the surrender of the large military garrison at Cawnpore, followed by the double massacres of the men and then all their women and children. Delhi remained in the hands of the mutineers and the small British force camped outside the city appeared to be incapable of retaking it.

Jung Bahadur Rana could easily have taken offence at this sign of distrust and thrown in his lot with the rebels. Instead, he again contacted Hodgson through Gajraj Singh, urging him to use his good offices with Lord Canning and adding that if the British Government required his assistance he would himself go immediately to Lucknow, where Henry Lawrence was besieged in the Residency and holding out against enormous odds. He assured Hodgson that his troops would fight like lions and again he suggested that they should meet up in Calcutta.

Hodgson had initially held back, but now he invited himself and his wife to stay with his friend, Sir John Colville, then the Chief Justice of Bengal. 'I could not but be sensible that I had been out of the coach for years,' Hodgson wrote afterwards of what turned out to be a very timely visit to Calcutta that began in late October 1857, 'Moreover that I was liable to be ignored as an avowed friend of the Nepalese, who were then looked upon with much suspicion and dislike.' That such prejudice existed was confirmed when Anne Hodgson first met Lord Canning's wife, Charlotte Canning, who said to her point blank: 'You praise these Gorkhas like your husband, but I can assure you they are looked on here as being little better than the rebels.'

Thanks to the good offices of Sir John Colville, Hodgson was received by the Governor-General in early November and allowed to make his case:

> I used to go and dine with him [Lord Canning], accompanied sometimes by the Chief Justice, and sometimes not, but always in a strictly private way, and after dinner he would stroll off to the billiard table, and there talk to me by the hour on various subjects, but mostly those connected with the mutiny, Nepal and the Jung, the latter's confidence in me being no secret to his Lordship.[12]

These private chats gave Hodgson the opportunity to stress how securely Jung Bahadur Rana was established as the de facto ruler of Nepal and, in particular, the degree to which he had been influenced by his visit to England: 'A man of the Jang's talents could not have noted in vain the risks his country had run in times past from collision with a Power which again and again he had seen rise superior to every difficulty.' However, the trump card, as Hodgson saw it, was that Lord Canning was in a position to offer the Nepalis what they most desired – and which would most surely guarantee their continuing alliance: 'I pointed out to Lord Canning that Nepal most eagerly coveted the restoration of the Western Tarai. Recent events had placed it at our disposal; and the prospect of the grant of it to Nepal, while it might form a tie on the Jang, would offer to us the means of most conveniently rewarding the Durbar for faithful service.'

Lord Canning was persuaded, and in early December 1857 a Nepali army that eventually grew to seventeen thousand men, under the personal command of Prime Minister Jung Bahadur Rana, engaged the rebels in Oude as an ally of the HEICo. The addition of this force had a major impact on the course of the great rebellion, not least because it allowed Canning's military commanders to make better use of the troops they already had. It boosted the morale of the three regiments of so-called Gurkha troops who were already fighting with the Bengal Army and it gave impetus to the formation of a fourth and then a fifth Gurkha regiment – which in time grew to fifteen regiments, and continues to this day as a small but much admired element of Britain's armed forces.

Anne Scott was already in poor health when she reached Calcutta and she continued straight on to England. And although Brian Hodgson returned to Darjeeling it was only to settle his affairs and arrange for the transportation to England of his papers and collections. He had received news that his father was fading fast and had expressed a wish to see him once more before he died. 'I must cast away my long cherished ambition of writing that History of Nepal for which I have been collecting materials during half my life,' he wrote to his wife in late December 1857. 'I shall hardly have a month in Darjiling, and must then hurry down to Calcutta to prepare for my voyage.'[13]

On the final leg of his voyage home Hodgson disembarked in France and travelled to Paris, where he made over to the Académie des Inscriptions et Belles-Lettres the best of his Buddhist iconographic and architectural drawings along with a third tranche of Sanskrit manuscripts. This donation, he explained, was in memory of his friend Eugène Burnouf, who had died in 1852.

On 1 November 1858, shortly after Hodgson arrived in England, John Company, alias *Jan Kampani Bahadur*, the unique amalgam of trading company cum ruling power that Hodgson had served so loyally from 1819 to 1843, was formally wound up and British crown rule proclaimed in its stead.

Brian Houghton Hodgson's remaining thirty-six years have no part in this story except as a brief epilogue.

Four further papers – three ethnographic and one zoological, on a new species of Himalayan mole – appeared in the pages of the *Journal of the Asiatic Society of Bengal* in 1859, but they were no more than leftovers of his researches in Darjeeling. Fittingly enough, his last paper, published in the *Journal of the Asiatic Society* in 1861, was a short article entitled 'Notice on Buddhist symbols'. But this, too, was little more than tidying up: an accompanying note to a donation of some drawings of Buddhist iconography which, as he explained, were but a small part 'of my immense collection of drawings taken from the temples, statues, and pictures of Buddhism of Nepal' – adding, rather poignantly, that 'of the result I have no distinct recollection at this distance in time, but I believe that more pressing objects intervened to shut out from my view and memory of [sic] this project'.

Other than this failing memory it is hard to explain why Hodgson was unable to complete any of his projected major works. In his classic *Birds of India*, published in 1862, Dr Jerdon credited Hodgson with his discoveries and praised him for his 'deep research and great acumen'. Those discoveries and their attendant papers were indeed phenomenal. Hodgson is credited with the first descriptions of almost eighty new bird species in Nepal as well as over twenty mammals and seven reptiles and amphibians. But the fact is that better qualified ornithologists and zoologists using more accurately drawn illustrations soon eclipsed Hodgson and his *chitrakars*. Yet this does not explain why Hodgson failed to complete his other projects, where no obvious barriers stood in the way; for example, his projected 'History of Nepal' where he had no rivals in the field – or, at least, not before the arrival in Nepal of Dr Daniel Wright, who became Residency Surgeon in 1863, and who in 1877 published his 'History of Nepal, with an introductory sketch of the country and people', using a number of illustrations based on drawings by 'a native of Nepal' that are far too close to some of Hodgson's *chitrakar* drawings to be coincidences.

But long before 1877 Brian Hodgson had given up. By 1864 he had divested himself of virtually every part of his vast collection of manuscripts, papers and drawings; the bulk of it going to the India Office Library and the British Museum, bodies which in turn subdivided the material and passed it on to the most appropriate institutions, so that today the greater part of his papers are in the British Library and most of his natural history drawings and notes in the Natural History Museum.

Hodgson was at that time settled into a house in Dursely in Gloucester with his ailing wife and his equally ailing mother and parents-in-law. After Anne Hodgson died in 1867 he moved to The Grange at Alderley in the Cotswold Hills, also in Gloucester. In 1868 Hodgson's future biographer, William Hunter, visited him at The Grange in connection with his own work on a comparative dictionary and found the old man nursing many grievances, chiefly over the manner of his ejection from Nepal and the way his work had, as he saw it, been 'plagiarised and ignored in the same breath'. Hunter also noted that his host was still physically very active, rising early to ride but nevertheless 'grieves perpetually for his lost wife and children and clings mournfully to his son in law'.[14] However, Hodgson was far from living the life of a hermit. He received visitors, regularly travelled to London and wintered in the South of France and Italy. He even recovered from his grief sufficiently to marry again, this time to a vicar's daughter half his age: Susan, who looked after him devotedly for the rest of his life.

Other than the *Legion d'Honneur*, Hodgson received few honours, academic or political. The major exception was the Honorary Doctorate conferred on him by Oxford University, although even for this he had to wait until he was approaching seventy. The publication of his collected essays and papers in 1874, followed by two more volumes of collected works in 1880, gave him great satisfaction – offset by the publication in 1872 of a biography of his successor as Resident in Kathmandu, Sir Henry Lawrence. This caused him much distress as it supported Lord Ellenborough's line and criticised Hodgson for his political interference. He responded by producing his last known work: a none too subtle summary of his scholarly achievement and political services under eight headings, accompanied by a great many testimonials in the form of extracts from letters. This he published anonymously under the title of *Notes on the services of B. H. Hodgson, Esq, late British Minister at the Court in Nepal, collected by a friend.*

Hodgson sent out numerous copies of this self-published self-justification and although it fooled nobody it aroused a great deal of sympathy among those who had known his history and his worth. One of them was the great German linguist and professor of Oriental studies Max Müller, who had himself suffered a great injustice as an academic in his younger days, and who understood far better than most of his contemporaries what Hodgson had done for Buddhist studies and comparative linguistics.

The Autograph Book which Mrs Anne Hodgson had assembled for her ill-starred step-son for his birthday in 1853 had been brought back to England by his father, and after Brian Hodgson's death on 23 May 1894 it was presented to the Royal Asiatic Society by Susan, the second – or should that be the third? – Mrs Hodgson.

In it she had pasted some more letters from distinguished men, one of the last of which was from Max Müller. It contained sentiments which, surely, must have warmed Brian Hodgson's failing heart. It also provides an apt conclusion:

> I thought you had turned *Sanyasin* [ascetic in the final phase of life] and gone into the forest, having nobly finished your work as *Grihastha* [householder in the second phase of life], but you seem to be as young as ever, while your juniors have grown into white haired old men. Thanks for your pamphlet, which shall be private. I send you my last, which may interest you in showing how the germs which you sowed half a century ago are beginning to bear fruit. Karma = work done, which is, after all, the real satisfaction of life – everything else is like the foam on the sea – so the Buddhists say.[15]

Colour Plate List

Plate 17 Zoological Society of London, Mammals f.284.
© Zoological Society of London.

Plate 18 Zoological Society of London, Mammals F183.
© Zoological Society of London.

Plate 19 Zoological Society of London, Mammals f.12.
© Zoological Society of London.

Plate 20 Zoological Society of London, Mammals f.98.
© Zoological Society of London.

Plate 21 Zoological Society of London, Mammals f.69.
© Zoological Society of London.

Plate 22 Zoological Society of London, Mammals f.142.
© Zoological Society of London.

Plate 23 Zoological Society of London, Birds Vol.3, f.3.
© Zoological Society of London.

Plate 24 Zoological Society of London, Birds Vol.6, f. 56.
© Zoological Society of London.

Plate 25 Zoological Society of London, Birds Vol.3, f.70.
© Zoological Society of London.

Plate 26 Zoological Society of London, Birds Vol.5, f.135.
© Zoological Society of London.

Plate 27 Zoological Society of London, Birds Vol.2, p.82.
© Zoological Society of London.

Plate 28 Zoological Society of London, Birds Vol.4, p.131.
© Zoological Society of London.

Plate 29 British Library, Oldfield Collection Add.Or.3301.
© The British Library Board.

Plate 30 British Library, Lawrence Collection Add.Or.3229.
© The British Library Board.

Plate 31 British Museum, Ethnographic Library Asia 104–135.
© The Trustees of the British Museum.

Plate 32 British Museum, Ethnographic Library Asia 104–135.
© The Trustees of the British Museum.

Plate 33 British Library, Lawrence Collection Add.Or.5232.
© The British Library Board.

Plate 34 British Library, Lawrence Collection Add.Or.5223.
© The British Library Board.

Notes

1. **'Perpetual peace and friendship': Makwanpur, 4 March 1816**
   1. Sir Henry Thoby Prinsep, *History of the political and military transactions in India during the administration of the Marquess of Hastings, 1813–1823,* Vol. I, Appendix, 1825.
   2. Sir Charles Metcalfe, *Selections from the Papers of Lord Metcalfe,* Ed. Sir John Kaye, 1875.
   3. Dr Archibald Campbell, *Campbell's Sketches,* quoted in B. J. Hasrat, *History of Nepal as told by its own and contemporary historians,* 1970.
   4. Letter of 5 March 1816, *Papers respecting the Nepaul War: Papers regarding the administration of the Marquis of Hastings in India,* Vol. I, 1824.
   5. C. T. Daukes, *History of the Nepal Escort,* 1931.
   6. Daniel Wright Ed., *History of Nepal, translated from the Parbatiya by Munshi Shew Shunker Singh and Pandit Shri Gurunand,* 1877.

2. **'Qualified to discharge the duties of the public service':**
   Haileybury, Fort William College and Kumaon, 1816–20
   1. James Mill, usually quoted as from his *History of British India,* 1817, although the phrase is not found there.
   2. Lord Wellesley, *Notes with respect to the foundation of a College at Fort William,* 10 July 1800.
   3. *Minutes and Report of the Committee of Haileybury College,* 16 October 1804.
   4. David Waterhouse has shown in his essay 'Brian Hodgson – a biographical sketch' that Hodgson's biography and all subsequent accounts of his life were wrong in giving his date

of birth as 1 February 1800. Both Hodgson in a biographical note and his second wife in a family history gave the later date. Hodgson was granted a special licence to enter Haileybury underage in February 1816. This may have led to his adding a year to his age.

5. Calculating the modern values of monetary sums from two centuries ago is a nightmare because the relative value of a sum of money varies enormously over time depending on whether it is a commodity or an income, the latter being many times greater than the former. See L. H. Officer and S. H. Williamson, 'Five ways to compute the relative value of a UK pound amount, 1270 to present, *Measuring Worth*, 2013. But see also the more simplistic National Archives Currency Converter, which gives significantly lower figures.

6. James Mill, 'On Government in India', *Edinburgh Review*, Vol. 16, Issue 31, January 1810.

7. East India College Certificate, 5 Dec. 1817. Mrs Hodgson's Autograph Volume, Hodgson Papers, Royal Asiatic Society.

8. Notes in the Hodgson MS, Bodleian Library, Oxford, partially quoted in W. W. Hunter, *Life of Brian Houghton Hodgson*, 1896.

9. The D'Oylys could trace their Norman ancestry back to the eighth century. Sir Charles's father, the sixth baronet, had in his time been one of the most notorious nabobs of the day, having entered the HEICo's service specifically to replenish the family coffers, returning from Bengal in 1785 with enough loot to buy himself the traditional country estate and seat in Parliament – but apparently insufficient to satisfy 'a most expensive wife and hangers on of her family'. She had all but bankrupted him, which meant that at the age of fifty he had been forced to return to Calcutta, where Lord Wellesley found him a well-paid sinecure and where he died in January 1818. His title then passed to his son Charles, who had followed his father into Company service in 1798 and spent a decade as Collector of Dacca (now Dhaka in Bangladesh) before moving to Calcutta to take up the post of Collector of Customs.

10. R. Montgomery Martin, *The British Colonies: British Divisions in Asia*, Div.XI, 1855.

11. Elizabeth and her sister had been orphaned at an early age and taken into the care of their uncle, the laird of Raasay Island, off Skye, whose passion for Gaelic music he passed on to the two girls along with the ability to play the piano and the harp and – rather surprisingly – the unladylike pibroch. In 1813 the Ross sisters were despatched into the care of their distant aunt in India, together with their wedding trousseaus, for the express purpose of finding husbands. They duly obliged, Elizabeth marrying Sir Charles D'Oyly on 8 April 1815.

12. William Hickey's memoirs were first published in censored form in four volumes between 1913 and 1825, Ed. Alfred Spencer. *The Memoirs of William Hickey*, 1913–25.

13. Hodgson to his sister Fanny in letters dated 7 May 1830 and 22 October 1833, quoted by his biographer W. W. Hunter, their present locations unknown.

14. William Carey had come to Bengal in the guise of an indigo planter to convert heathen souls to Christ but had made little headway until he hit on the idea of printing his tracts in the vernacular languages. He learned Bengali and Sanskrit and in 1800 joined with two other missionaries to set up a printing press in the Danish trading colony of Serampore, located on the west bank of the Hoogly directly opposite Wellesley's weekend retreat at Barrackpore. He became increasingly Orientalised and after agreeing to a pact with Wellesley joined the staff of his College to supervise the teaching of Bengali and Sanskrit. By 1806 the three presses at Serampore were working round the clock to print not only missionary tracts in Bengali and six other vernacular languages, but also books for the College in those same languages, as well as Sanskrit classics such as the *Ramayana* and *Hitopedesha*, along with translations of the same into Bengali, for the Asiatic Society of Bengal. Carey is acknowledged to this day in West Bengal as 'the father of modern Bengali prose'.

15. William Carey, *Primitae Orientales*, 1804, cited in David Kopf, *British Orientalism and the Bengal Renaissance*, 1969.

16. 'Sketches of India', *Calcutta Journal*, Vol. I, Jan. 1822.

17. Report on Fort William College, *Asiatic Journal and Monthly Register*, Vo. IX, 1820.

18. Lord Hastings's speech was reported verbatim in the June issue of the Calcutta monthly *Asiatic Journal and Monthly Miscellany*, Vol. 9, 1819.

19. H. Montgomery Martin, *History of the British Colonies*, Vol. I, 1834, drawing on an early report by Hodgson's first mentor, William Traill, Commissioner of Kumaon.

20. Sir Henry Thoby Prinsep (junior), 'Three generations in India 1771–1914', three volumes of unpublished MSS including autobiographical material written by Henry Thoby Prinsep (senior) Eur. C 97, British Library.

21. Henry Thoby Prinsep, *History of the Political and Military Transactions in India during the Administration of the Marquess of Hastings, 1813–1823*, 1825.

22. The building survives as the Darah Shikoh Library on the campus of Ambedkar University close to the Kashmir Gate.

23. Maria, Lady Nugent, *A journal from the year 1811 till the year 1815, including a voyage to and residence in India,* 1839. A source drawn to my attention by William Dalrymple.

24. The term popularised by William Dalrymple, who has written sympathetically about them in *City of Djinns* and, of course, *White Mughals*.

25. G. W. Traill, 'Statistical Sketch of Kumaon', *Asiatic Researches*, Vol. XVI, 1828.

26. Notes in the Hodgson MS, Bodleian Library, Oxford, partially quoted in W. W. Hunter, *Life of Brian Houghton Hodgson*, 1896.

3. 'Spying on the nakedness of the land': Assistant to the Resident, Kathmandu, 1820–24

1. Father Guiseppe, 'An account of the kingdom of Nepál', *Asiatic Researches*, Vol. II, 1790.

2. Col. William Kirkpatrick, *An Account of the Kingdom of Nepaul, being the Substance of Observations made during a Mission to that Country, in the Year 1793*, 1811.

3. Quoted in Hasrat Bikrama, *History of Nepal as Told by its Own and Contemporary Chronicles*, 1970.

4. Francis Buchanan changed his surname to Hamilton, and is now generally known as Buchanan-Hamilton to avoid confusion. For more on his fascinating Indian career see Charles Allen, *The Buddha and the Sahibs*, 2002; Mark Watson and Henry Noltie, 'The Nepalese, Burmese and Indian Natural History Archives of Dr Francis Buchanan (later Hamilton)'.

5. Francis Buchanan-Hamilton to William Roxburgh, 2 March 1810, NHM-BL f.63. Quoted in Watson and Noltie, above.

6. Quoted by Dr Ambrose Oldfield, *Sketches from Nepal*, Vol. I, 1880.

7. Quoted second-hand in Hasrat Bikrama, *History of Nepal as Told by its Own and Contemporary Chronicles*, 1970.

8. Quoted in Hasrat Bikrama, *History of Nepal as Told by its Own and Contemporary Chronicles*, 1970.

9. F. Henvey, 'Note on the position of Resident in Nepal', *Foreign and Secret Department*, 1877. Quoted by T. R. Manandhar, 'British Residents in the Court of Nepal during the 19th century', *Voice of History*, Vol. XX, No. 1, 2005.

10. John Malcolm, *Central India*, Vol. I, 1823.

11. These harsh words are not directly attributed to Gardner but were taken from the British Residency records of that period in Hasrat Bikrama, *History of Nepal as Told by its Own and Contemporary Chronicles*, 1970.

12. J. Mallet & M. R. Smith, quoting from an obituary, *The Linnean* newsletter, Vol. 12, No. 2, 1996.

13. My thanks to Dr Mark Watson for this botanical information, contained in his unpublished paper 'Edward Gardner – the lost botanist of Nepal'.

14. In fact, more than a year passed before Lord Hastings actually handed over power on 1 January 1823 to an acting Governor-General, John Adams, who held the post for seven months till the arrival of Lord Amherst in August 1823.

15. This note from William Bayley is quoted by Hodgson's biographer W. W. Hunter, *Life of Brian Houghton Hodgson*, 1896, but without reference as to its dating or source.

4. 'The strenuous idleness of woodcock shooting': Postmaster
   and Assistant to the Resident, Kathmandu, 1824–25

1. MSS Eur. C 97 'Three generations in India 1771–1914', British
   Library.
2. Captain James Kershaw, *Views in the Birman Empire*, 1831.
3. Quoted by W. W. Hunter, *Life of Brian Houghton Hodgson*,
   1896, its present location unknown.
4. B. H. Hodgson, 'On some of the *Scolopacidae* of Nepal',
   Gleanings in Science, Vol. III, 1831.
5. 'Remarks on the procreation of the Rhinosceros', *The Quarterly
   Oriental Magazine, Review and Register*, Vol. III, No. VII, June
   1825.
6. B. H. Hodgson to Nathaniel Wallich, dated 15 May 1824,
   Wallich Letters, Library of the Calcutta Botanic Garden, with
   thanks to Dr Martin Krieger of the University of Kiel for
   making copies of this and subsequent letters available to me.
7. *The Quarterly Oriental Magazine, Review and Register*, Vol. I,
   March and June 1824.
8. *The Quarterly Oriental Magazine, Review and Register*, Vol. II,
   September and December 1824.
9. *The Quarterly Oriental Magazine, Review and Register*, Vol. III,
   No. V, March 1825.
10. Dr Clarke Abel had had the misfortune of being declared
    bankrupt just as he had begun to make a name for himself in
    England as a naturalist, at which point that great promoter of
    the natural sciences, Sir Joseph Banks, had found him a post
    as surgeon to Lord Amherst's embassy to China. The mission
    was a political disaster, made worse for Dr Abel when all the
    plants and seeds he had collected in China were lost after their
    ship struck a coral reef and sank. However, Lord Amherst
    retained him as his surgeon when he replaced Lord Hastings as
    Governor-General in India and Dr Abel had prospered under
    his patronage.
11. B. H. Hodgson to Dr Wallich in a letter dated 17 December
    1825, now in the Wallich Papers of the Calcutta Botanic
    Garden.

12. Dr Abel also arranged for abridged versions of both Hodgson's papers to be published in England in the unlikely pages of *The Philosophical Magazine and Journal*, Vol. 68, September 1826.

13. *The Quarterly Oriental Magazine, Review and Register*, Vol. III, No. V, March 1825. The Nepali word for the wild dog is *wan, so* 'wah' was probably Dr Abel's misreading.

14. B. H. Hodgson to Dr Wallich in a letter dated 28 September 1825, now in the Wallich Papers of the Calcutta Botanic Garden.

15. B. H. Hodgson, 'Sketch of Buddhism, derived from Bauddha Scriptures of Nipál', *Journal of the Royal Asiatic Society*, Vol. 2, 1830.

16. B. H. Hodgson, 'Sketch of Buddhism', *Essays on the languages, literature and religion of Nepál and Tibet, together with further papers on the geography, ethnology and commerce of these countries*, 1874.

17. B. H. Hodgson to W. B. Bayley, 5 December 1824, present location unknown, quoted by W. W. Hunter, *Life of Brian Houghton Hodgson*, 1896.

18. Hodgson to his sister Fanny in a letter dated 1 December 1825, present location unknown, quoted by Hunter.

19. Hodgson to his sister Fanny in a letter dated 23 April 1829, present location unknown., quoted by Hunter.

20. As reported in *The Quarterly Oriental Magazine, Review and Register*, Vol. III. No. VII, June 1825

21. List of donations received, *Transactions of the Royal Asiatic Society*, Vol. I, 1827.

22. B. H. Hodgson, 'A disputation respecting caste by a Buddhist', *Essays on the languages, literature and religion of Nepál and Tibet, together with further papers on the geography, ethnology and commerce of these countries*, 1874.

5. 'My old Bauddha': Assistant to the Resident, 1825–28

1. *The Quarterly Oriental Magazine, Review and Register*, Vol. VI, No. VIII, December 1826.

2. B. H. Hodgson, 'Architectural illustrations of Buddhism', 1857, reprinted in D. Waterhouse, *The Origins of Himalayan studies*, 2004.

3. B. H. Hodgson, 'Sketch of Buddhism, derived from the Bauddha Scriptures of Nepal,' as later amended in *Essays on the languages, literature and religion of Nepál and Tibet, together with further papers on the geography, ethnology and commerce of these countries*, 1874.

4. Henry Ambrose Oldfield, *Sketches from Nipal, historical and descriptive*, Vol. I, 1880.

5. As reported in *The Quarterly Oriental Magazine, Review and Register*, Vol. VII, December 1825.

6. H. H. Wilson, 'Note on the literature of Thibet', *Gleanings in Science*, Vol. 3. August 1831. Hodgson also planned to send a set of the even larger *Stangyur*: 'a collection of a still more voluminous description than the preceding, and extending to 225 volumes ... divided into two great classes, the *Gyut* and *Do*, or mystical doctrines and miscellaneous aphorisms.' However, I can find no evidence of its receipt in Calcutta.

7. B. H. Hodgson, 'Sketch of Buddhism', *Essays on the languages, literature and religion of Nepál and Tibet, together with further papers on the geography, ethnology and commerce of these countries*, 1874.

8. BH Hodgson, 'Notices of the Languages, literature and religion of the Bauddhas of Nepal and Bhot,' *Asiatic Researches*, Vol. XVI, 1828.

9. Adi Shankara, eighth century Hindu reformer, travelled widely through India propagating the doctrine of Advaita Vedanta and establishing *mathas*, colleges as centres of his teaching, resulting in a major revival of Shaivism and popular Hinduism. Despite the claims of Buddhists in Nepal and Tibet, there is no solid evidence that he initiated pogroms against Buddhists, even through he attacked Buddhist monasticism.

10. B. H. Hodgson in a letter to Dr Wallich dated 17 October 1827, which he afterwards included in his introduction to his 'Sketches of Buddhism'.

11. Introductory letter to Dr Wallich, as quoted in B. H. Hodgson, 'Sketch of Buddhism, derived from the Bauddha Scriptures of Nepal,' *Transactions of the Royal Asiatic Society*, Vol. III, 1828.

12. BH Hodgson, 'Notices of the Languages, literature and religion of the Bauddhas of Nepal and Bhot,' *Asiatic Researches*, Vol. XVI, 1828.

13. *The Quarterly Oriental Magazine, Review and Register*, Vol. VII, No. VIII, March 1827.

14. 'Búddh Gayah, according to a Nipaulese Búddha who visited it', *The Quarterly Oriental Magazine, Review and Register*, Vol. VII, June 1827.

15. Hodgson's note 31, 'Sketch of Buddhism, derived from the Bauddha Scriptures of Nipal', *Transactions of the Royal Asiatic Society*, Vol. 2, 1830.

16. B. H. Hodgson, 'Sketch of Buddhism, derived from the Bauddha Scriptures of Nipal, *Transactions of the Royal Asiatic Society*, Vol. 2, 1830.

17. Letters of 30 December 1829 and 29 April 1830 quoted in Theodore Duka, *Life of Alexander Csoma de Körös*, 1885.

18. Eugène Burnouf to Hodgson, letter dated 28 August 1837, quoted by W. W. Hunter in his biography.

19. See David Gellner, 'Hodgson's blind alley? One the so-called four schools of Nepalese Buddhism', *Journal of International Association of Buddhist Studies*, 12 (1)-7–19, 1989.

6. 'Untutored eyes and ears, sedulously employed': Acting Resident, 1828–31

1. Sir Henry Thoby Prinsep, 'Three generations in India 1771–1914', Vol. II, MSS Eur. C 97, British Library.

2. Lord William Bendinck to Charles Grant, 21 December 1832, quoted in P. Spear, 'Lord William Bendinck', *Journal of Indian History*, Vol. XIX, 1940.

3. Hodgson to his sister Fanny in a letter dated 23 April 1829, quoted by his biographer W. W. Hunter, its present location unknown.

4. Hodgson to his sister Fanny in a letter dated 7 May 1830, quoted by his biographer W. W. Hunter, its present location unknown.

5. B. H.Hodgson, *Notes on the Services of B. H. Hodgson, Esq., late British Minister at the court of Nepal*, undated. Although nominally 'Collected by a friend', this was undoubtedly written by Hodgson himself in the late 1860s.

6. My thanks to Dr Mark Watson, David Lowther and Ann Sylph for this information, contained in their unpublished paper 'Hodgson's Tibetan Mastiffs: survival at sea, twice presented to the London Zoo, and tragic demise'.

7. B. H. Hodgson, 'On the *Chiru* or Antilope *Hodgsonii*', *Gleanings in Science*, Nov. 1830.

8. B. H. Hodgson, 'Some account of a new species of Felis', *Gleanings in Science*, March 1831.

7. **'The truth is that these are saving times': Assistant Resident again, 1831–33**

1. Letter extracts as quoted in Whelpton 'The political role of Brian Hodgson', in *The origins of Himalayan studies*, Ed. D. Waterhouse.

2. Hodgson to his sister Fanny in a letter dated 7 May 1830, quoted by his biographer W. W. Hunter, its present location unknown.

3. Brian Hodgson, abstract from *Recorded and Unrecorded Notes*, in *Nepal Residency Papers,* Vol. I British Library.

4. Hodgson's Report to Government, dated October 1832, was afterwards read before the Asiatic Society of Bengal in January 1833 and subsequently published as 'Origin and classification of the military tribes of Nepal', *Journal of the Asiatic Society of Bengal*, Vol. II, 1833.

5. Hodgson to H. T. Prinsep, 30 March 1830, Foreign and Political Correspondence, quoted by K. L. Pradhan, *Brian Hodgson and the Kathmandu Residency*, 2001.

6. B. H. Hodgson, *Paper II, Selections from the Records of the Government of Bengal*, Vol. XXVII, dated 1831.

7. B. H. Hodgson, 'The wild goat and the wild sheep of Nepal', *Asiatic Researches*, Vol. XVIII, 1833.

8. T. Jerdon, Catalogue of the Birds of the Indian Peninsula, 1839.

9. B. H. Hodgson, Classical terminology of natural history', *Journal of the Asiatic Society of Bengal,* Vol. 10, 1841. My thanks to Aasheesh Pittie for this information, carried in his article 'A dictionary of scientific birds' names originating from the Indian region', *Buceros*, Vol. 9, No. 2, 2004.

10. Hodgson to Macnaghten. See notes 55 and 71 in Pradhan Thapa Politics in Nepal YD. 2011.a.8851.

11. B. H. Hodgson, 'Some account of the law and police as recognised in the state of Nepal', *Asiatic Researches*, Vol. XVII, 1832.

12. Lord Bentinck to B. H. Hodgson, See Ch. VI. Note 57 Pradhan Thapa Politics in Nepal YD. 2011.a.8851.

13. Macnaghten had graduated from Fort William College two years before Hodgson with the greatest number of awards ever made to a single scholar, amounting to 7000 rupees in prize money. Born in Calcutta as the son of a high court judge, Macnaghten was fluent in Persian, Arabic, Hindustani, Bengali, Tamil, Telegu, Kanarese, Marathi and Sanskrit. The witty and waspish Miss Emily Eden was later to damn him for a protocol-obsessed pedant who 'speaks Persian rather more fluently than English; Arabic better than Persian; but, for familiar conversation, rather prefers Sanscrit'. In the first of his *Flashman* adventures the novelist George Macdonald Fraser portrayed Macnaghten as an arrogant megalomaniac, and modern historians have tended to take the same line. To his contemporaries, however, Macnaghten was a good man undone by ambition – and a foolish Governor-General.

14. Hodgson to his sister Fanny in a letter dated 22 October 1833, quoted by his biographer W. W. Hunter, its present location unknown.

15. A century later Bhatgaon was again the worst hit town in the Nepal Valley in the even more severe Nepal-Bihar earthquake of 1934.

8. 'Reason over barbarism': British Resident, 1833–1835

1. General Committee for Public Instruction Correspondence XII, folios 585–664.
2. Charles Trevelyan to Lord William Bentinck, 18 March 1833, Bengal Papers 2013, quoted in J. F. Hilliker, *Charles Trevelyan as an educational reformer in India 1827–1838*, 1974.
3. Charles Trevelyan, *A series of papers on the application of the Roman alphabet to all the Oriental languages*, 1834.
4. The Bengali scholar and entrepreneur Ram Komal Sen was the first Indian to be closely involved with the Asiatic Society both as its 'native secretary' and print manager. Like many of his peers, he sought to take full advantage of Western learning but was also fearful of the price to be paid in terms of the loss of his own culture. When his two-volume *Dictionary of the English and Bengali Languages* appeared in print in 1834 he hedged his bets, dedicating the work to Lord Bentinck with the remark that the book was intended to 'diffuse the literature of the west among the natives of India', while at the same time demanding that Bengali would be recognised as 'a most excellent language, equal in strength to any other'.
5. Thomas Macaulay to his sister Margaret, 7 Dec. 1834, quoted in G. M. Trevelyan, *The life and letters of Lord Macaulay*. Vol. I, 1876.
6. Thomas Macaulay to a friend, 15 Dec. 1834, Macaulay Papers, Trinity College, Cambridge, quoted in John Rosselli, *Lord William Bentinck*, 1974.
7. Charles Trevelyan, *On the education of the people of India*, 1838.
8. William H. Macnaghten, *Minute* of 14 March, 1835, quoted in David Kopf, *British Orientalism and the Bengal Renaissance*, 1969.
9. 'Three generations in India 1771–1914', three volumes of unpublished MSS including autobiographical material written by Henry Thoby Prinsep (the elder). Eur. C 97, British Library.
10. James Prinsep, *Journal of the Asiatic Society of Bengal*, April 1835, Vol. 4, 1835.
11. James Prinsep, *Journal of the Asiatic Society of Bengal*, July 1835, Vol. 4, 1835.

12. H. T. Prinsep to Hodgson in a letter dated 6 August 1835. Royal Asiatic Society, Hodgson Collection Autograph Book.

13. B. H. Hodgson to James Prinsep, 29 April 1835, letter 169, MSS Eur. C351, British Library.

14. A third edition including three more letters was published in 1848.

15. Wilson in a letter to L. Wilkinson, 26 October 1838, quoted in Hunter, *Life of Brian Houghton Hodgson*.

16. *Third Report of Education in Bengal*, 1838, quoted in Hunter, *Life of Brian Houghton Hodgson*.

9. 'Nepal has real and rational charms for me': British Resident, 1835–40

1. Hodgson to his sister Fanny in a letter dated 1 August 1835, quoted by his biographer W. W. Hunter, its present location unknown.

2. Brian Hodgson, *Recorded and Unrecorded Notes: Nepal Residency Papers*, quoted in Hasrat, *History of Nepal*.

3. B. H. Hodgson to Frances Hodgson, 10 December 1834, Hodgson MSS Vol. 16, Hodgson Papers, Bodleian Library.

4. B. H. Hodgson to Frances Hodgson, 1 August 1835, quoted in Hunter, *Life of Brian Houghton Hodgson*.

5. B. H. Hodgson to Frances Hodgson, 1 August 1835, quoted in Hunter, *Life of Brian Houghton Hodgson*.

6. For example, John Keay, *India discovered*, 1982; Charles Allen, *The Buddha and the Sahibs*, 2002; *Ashoka: the search for India's lost emperor*, 2012.

7. Hodgson to James Prinsep, March 1835, afterwards published by Prinsep in the *Journal of the Asiatic Society of Bengal*, April 1835, Vol. IV, 1835.

8. Hodgson's reference to Amritanandaas 'the most learned Buddhist then, or now, living in this country' in his paper 'Quotations from original Sanscrit authorities in proof and illustration of Mr Hodgson's sketch of Buddhism', published in the *Journal of the Asiatic Society of Bengal* in January 1836, has been taken to mean that he was then unaware of Amrita Nanda's death. However, as the editor James Prinsep explained

in his introduction, this paper was a reprint of the original article, hence Hodgson's uncorrected remark suggesting the pandit was still alive.

9. B. H. Hodgson to E. Burnouf, 1 May 1837, Hodgson Collection, British Library, quoted in Ann Datta and Carol Inskipp, 'Zoology ... amuses me much', Ed. D. Waterhouse, *The origins of Himalayan studies*.

10. James Prinsep to B. H. Hodgson, 1838, Hodgson Collection, Royal Asiatic Society, quoted in Ann Datta and Carol Inskipp, 'Zoology ... amuses me much', Ed. D. Waterhouse, *The origins of Himalayan studies*.

11. B. H. Hodgson to James Prinsep, 3 April 1836, Prinsep Papers, Royal Asiatic Society.

12. B. H. Hodgson to Sir Alexander Johnston, 20 June 1835, Johnston Papers, Royal Asiatic Society.

13. B. H. Hodgson to James Prinsep, 1836, Prinsep Letters, British Library, quoted in Ann Datta and Carol Inskipp, 'Zoology ... amuses me much', Ed. D. Waterhouse, *The origins of Himalayan studies*.

14. B. H. Hodgson to his father, July 1837, quoted in Hunter, *Life of Brian Houghton Hodgson*.

15. E. Blyth to H. Strickland, 1845, quoted in Ann Datta and Carol Inskipp, 'Zoology ... amuses me much', Ed. D. Waterhouse, *The origins of Himalayan studies*.

16. B. H. Hodgson, *Notes on the Services of B. H. Hodgson, Es., late British Minister at the Court of Nepal, collected by a friend*, undated, British Library, Hodgson Collection

17. Thomas Smith, *Narrative of Five Years' Residence at Nepaul*, 1846.

18. B. H. Hodgson to H. Maddock, 14 April 1839, apparently quoted in full in Hunter, *Life of Brian Houghton Hodgson*.

19. B. H. Hodgson to H. Maddock, 30 July 1839, quoted in Hunter, *Life of Brian Houghton Hodgson*.

20. H. T. Prinsep, MS *Three generations in India*, Vol. II, British Library.

21. B. H. Hodgson to H. T. Prinsep, 18 October 1839, quoted in Hunter, *Life of Brian Houghton Hodgson*.

22. Dr Henry Oldfield, *Sketches from Nipal*, Vol. I, 1880.

23. B. H. Hodgson to his parents, 14 Sep. 1840, Hodgson MSS Vol. 16, Hodgson Papers, Bodleian Library, Oxford.

24. Henry Torrens to B. H. Hodgson, 26 October 1840, Foreign and Secret Consultations, British Library.

25. B. H. Hodgson to his mother, 26 Nov. 1840, Hodgson MSS Vol. 16, Hodgson Papers, Bodleian Library, Oxford.

10. 'Events are working wonderfully in my favour': British Resident, 1840–43

1. Tickell's painting is signed and dated 'SRT 1849'. It is now is the collection of a direct male descendant of Jung Bahadur Rana which suggests that this idealised representation of the ratification of the Treaty of Sugauli was drawn by Tickell specifically for Jung Bahadur Rana. In 1849 Jung Bahadur and his brother Dhir Shumsher set out on the first stage of their journey to England, so the supposition has to be that Tickell met Jung Bahadur and his brother at Makwanpur and escorted them on the next stage of their journey from to Patna.

2. B. H. Hodgson to Dr Nathaniel Wallich, 16 March 1841, Wallich Papers, Calcutta Botanic Garden.

3. Dr Henry Oldfield, *Sketches from Nipal*, Vol. I, 1880.

4. B. H. Hodgson to his father, undated, quoted in Hunter, *Life of Brian Houghton Hodgson*.

5. Sir George Clerk to B. H. Hodgson, 21 August 1872, extracts from which were quoted by Hodgson in a footnote together with further additions added in his own in ink to the printed copy now in the British Library, *Notes on the Services of B. H. Hodgson, Esq., late British Minister at the Court of Nepal, collected by a friend*, undated, British Library, Hodgson Collection.

6. Lord Auckland to Raja Rajendra Birkram Shah, 22 February 1842, quoted in Hunter, *Life of Brian Houghton Hodgson*.

7. Quoted in B. H. Hodgson, *Notes on the Services of B. H. Hodgson, Esq.*

8. Lord Auckland to B. H. Hodgson, Sand Heads, 7 March 1842. Quoted in B. H. Hodgson, *Notes on the Services of B.*

H. Hodgson, Esq., late British Minister at the Court of Nepal, collected by a friend.

9. Quoted without source in Hunter, *Life of Brian Houghton Hodgson.*

10. Thomas Smith, *Narrative of Five Years' Residence at Nepaul,* 1846.

11. B. H. Hodgson to Herbert Maddock, 16 May 1842, quoted in John Whelpton, 'The political role of Brian Hodgson', Ed. D. Waterhouse, *The origins of Himalayan studies,* 2004.

12. B. H. Hodgson to his mother, 30 May 1842, Hodgson MSS Vol. 16, Hodgson Papers, Bodleian Library.

13. Herbert Maddock to B. H. Hodgson, 5 June 1842, quoted in K. L. Pradhan, *Brian Hodgson at the Kathmandu Residency.*

14. Herbert Maddock to B. H. Hodgson, 18 June 1842, quoted in Hunter, *Life of Brian Houghton Hodgson.*

15. B. H. Hodgson to his father, 29 June 1840, Hodgson MSS Vol. 16, Hodgson Papers, Bodleian Library, Oxford.

16. Herbert Maddock to B. H. Hodgson, 22 June 1842, quoted in Hunter, *Life of Brian Houghton Hodgson.*

17. Thomas Robertson to B. H. Hodgson, 22 July 1842, quoted in Hunter, *Life of Brian Houghton Hodgson.*

18. Lord Ellenborough in a dispatch dated 8 July 1842, quoted in K. L. Pradhan, *Brian Hodgson at the Kathmandu Residency.*

19. Lord Ellenborough in a private letter from Allahabad dated 6 July 1842, quoted in Hunter, *Life of Brian Houghton Hodgson.*

20. B. H. Hodgson to his father, 5 September 1842, Hodgson MSS Vol. 16, Hodgson Papers, Bodleian Library, Oxford.

21. B. H. Hodgson to his father, 6 Dec. 1842, Hodgson MSS Vol. 16, Hodgson Papers, Bodleian Library, Oxford.

22. Herbert Maddock to B. H. Hodgson, Calcutta 4 April 1843, quoted in Hunter, *Life of Brian Houghton Hodgson.*

23. B. H. Hodgson to Lord Ellenborough, 22 May 1843, quoted in K. L. Pradhan, *Brian Hodgson at the Kathmandu Residency.*

24. Lord Ellenborough to B. H. Hodgson, 2 June 1843, quoted in K. L. Pradhan, *Brian Hodgson at the Kathmandu Residency.*

25. The original *kharita* and translation are contained in the Hodgson Autograph Book, a collection of letters complied by

the second Mrs Hodgson, afterwards presented by her to the Royal Asiatic Society.

11. 'T'was a happy lot while it lasted, so that I could not feel its chains till I attempted to break them.': Pensioner, Europe, Darjeeling and England, 1843–1894

1. Dwakarnath Tagore to B. H. Hodgson. 12 Nov. 1843, Hodgson Autograph Book, Royal Asiatic Library.
2. B. H. Hoddson to his father, Arnheim 15 Nov. 1844, Hodgson MSS Vol. 16, Hodgson Papers, Bodleian Library, Oxford.
3. B. H. Hodgson to his sister, Cork 29 June 1845, and to his father, Cork 1 July 1845, , Hodgson MSS Vol. 16, Hodgson Papers, Bodleian Library, Oxford.
4. Sir Joseph Hooker, *Himalayan Journals*, 1854.
5. B. H. Hodgson to his sister Fanny, undated but 1847, Hodgson MSS Vol. 16, Hodgson Papers, Bodleian Library, Oxford, quoted in 'A biographical sketch', Ed. D. Waterhouse, *The origins of Himalayan studies*, 2004.
6. B. H. Hodgson, 'On the Tibetan badger, *Taxidia leucurus*', *Journal of the Royal Asiatic Society*, Vol. 16, 1847.
7. Sir James Colvile to Monkton Milnes, 11 October 1847, quoted in Hunter, *Life of Brian Houghton Hodgson*.
8. B. H. Hodgson, 'Ethnography and geography of the sub-Himalaya – extract from a letter from B. H. Hodgson, Esq., to Captain Cunningham, Tibet Commission', *Journal of the Royal Asiatic Society*, Vol. 17, Part 1, 1848.
9. Joseph Hooker in a letter to his fiancé, quoted by David Arnold, 'Hodgson, Hooker and the Himalayan Frontier 1848–1850', Ed. D. Waterhouse, *The origins of Himalayan studies*.
10. Joseph Hooker to a friend, L. Huxley, *Life and letters of Sir Joseph Dalon Hooker*, Vol. I, 1918, quoted by David Arnold, 'Hodgson, Hooker and the Himalayan Frontier 1848–1850', Ed. D. Waterhouse, *The origins of Himalayan studies*, 2004.
11. The album is now preserved among the Hodgson Papers at the Royal Asiatic Society.
12. These several quotations are taken from a letter written to W. H. Hunter on 14 March 1866 after included in B. H. Hodgson's

privately printed *Notes on the services of B. H. Hodgson, Esq.,
late British Minister at the Court of Nepal, collected by a friend.*

13. B. H.Hodgson in a letter quoted in Hunter, *Life of Brian
Houghton Hodgson.*

14. William Hunter, in a letter to his wife, October 1868, F. S.
Skrine, *Life of Sir William Wilson Hunter,* 1901, quoted in
'Brian Hodgson – a biographical sketch', Ed. D. Waterhouse,
The origins of the Himalayan studies, 2004.

15. Max Muller to Brian Hodgson in a letter dated 6 July 1883.
Royal Asiatic Society, Hodgson Collection, Autograph Book.

Acknowledgements

My prime sources were, of course, Brian Hodgson's own works and those who have written about him and them, most notably David Waterhouse and the contributors to his *Origins of Himalayan Studies: Brian Houghton Hodgson in Nepal and Darjeeling 1829–1858*. In particular: John Whelpton, Jerry Losty, Ann Datta and Carol Inskipp.

A great many other individuals, both in their professional and private capacities, have made my researches that much easier in all sorts of ways.

In Nepal: His Excellency Dr Suresh Chalise, ambassador for Nepal in the UK; Kanak Dixit of *Himal Southasian*; Lok Bhakta and Kabita Rana; Lisa and Tenzing Choegyal; Bidur Dongol of Vajra Bookshop; Hem Sagar Baral, ornithologist extraordinaire; the Sanskritist Ramesh Dhungel. At the British Embassy in Kathmandu, His Excellency Andy Sparkes, British Ambassador, and his PA, Kapindra Neupane.

In the United Kingdom: former British ambassadors to Nepal, Barney Smith and Andrew Hall; at the Royal Asiatic Society, the Director, Alison Ohta, the retiring librarian Kathy Lazenbatt, her successor, Ed Weech, and the assistant librarian, Alice Heans; at the British Library, Dr Catherine Eagleton, Head of Asian and African Studies, Dr Jerry Losty, former Keeper of Prints and Drawings, John Falconer, Lead Curator Visual Arts and Curator of Photographs, Burkhard Quessel, Curator of Tibetan Collections, Xiao Wei Bond, Curator of European Manuscripts, Malina Roy, Curator Visual Art Collections; at the British Museum, Richard Blurton, Curator of South Asia Collections, and James Hamill, AOA Department; at the School of Oriental and African Studies, Professor Mike Hutt, Director of the South Asia Institute; at the Zoological Society of

London, Librarians Ann Sylph and Michael Palmer, and Jane Loveless; at the Natural History Museum, Judith Magee, Special Collections Manager, and Revinder Chahal; at the Linnean Society, Dr Gina Douglas, Hon. Archivist; at the Balfour and Newton Libraries, Librarian Jane Acred; at Haileybury College, the Master and Toby Parker, Hon. Archivist, and Russell Matcham; at the Britain-Nepal Society, Lt.-Col. Jerry Birch and Roger Potter. Among unaffiliated individuals, the late Raleigh Trevelyan, Michael Palin, Dr Adrian Thomas, Diana Wooldridge, and my brother Col. Mike Allen.

In Germany, Dr Martin Krieger at the University of Kiel, Germany. In India, G. M. Kapur, Director Bengal INTACH, and Shyamal Lakshminarayan.

My special thanks to Dr Mark Watson, of the Royal Edinburgh Botanic Garden, for many suggestions and revelations, and to Professor David Gellner of the School of Anthropology and Museum Ethnography, Oxford, for volunteering to read my manuscript and for his many valuable corrections and observations – although I should stress that the remaining errors and opinions are my responsibility alone.

The completion of this book would not have been possible without the award of a generous work in progress grant from the Society of Authors, for which I am most grateful. Finally, my thanks to Barbara Schwepcke and her team at Haus Publishing, with my particular thanks to Harry Hall, Emma Henderson and Victor Rohm. As always, my last words are for Lizzie and my family, with heartfelt thanks for their patience and constancy.